THREE MORMON CLASSICS

LEAVES FROM MY JOURNAL

MY FIRST MISSION

JACOB HAMBLIN

9.95

COLLECTOR'S EDITION SERIES

THE GOSPEL KINGDOM
Writings and Discourses of John Taylor
Arranged by G. Homer Durham

EVIDENCES AND RECONCILIATIONS
John A. Widtsoe
Arranged by G. Homer Durham

LEHI IN THE DESERT
and
THE WORLD OF THE JAREDITES
Hugh Nibley

THREE MORMON CLASSICS
Compiled by Preston Nibley

THREE MORMON CLASSICS

LEAVES FROM MY JOURNAL

Wilford Woodruff

MY FIRST MISSION

George Q. Cannon

JACOB HAMBLIN

James A. Little

Compiled by

PRESTON NIBLEY

COLLECTOR'S EDITION

BOOKCRAFT
Salt Lake City, Utah

ISBN 0-88494-049-7

First Collector's Edition Printing, 1988

Printed in the United States of America

FOREWORD

This book, THREE MORMON CLASSICS, brings again before the public three remarkable little volumes which have been out of print for many years.

In 1879, George Q. Cannon published, at Salt Lake City, the first book of his Faith Promoting Series. This was a small volume written by himself, entitled MY FIRST MISSION. It contained an account of the author's mission to the Hawaiian Islands in 1850, when he was twenty-three years of age; his desire to learn the native language; the manner in which it came to him and his great success in proselyting after he was able to make his message known.

George Q. Cannon had little opportunity to attend school in his youth, due to his life on the frontier, yet, through his diligence, he acquired a mastery of the English language and a style which mark him as an outstanding writer. There is no narrative in our Church literature which excels George Q. Cannon's account of his first mission to the Hawaiian Islands.

In 1881, the third volume of the Faith Promoting Series was issued from the press, entitled LEAVES FROM MY JOURNAL, by Wilford Woodruff. Again there was given to the Church and the world a great narrative of successful missionary work. In clear, lucid style President Woodruff related some of his remarkable experiences in preaching the gospel in the early days of the Church.

President Wilford Woodruff was a humble, sincere man. In his missionary labors he did not seek to promote himself; he sought only to do the will of his Heavenly Father, and bring the light of the gospel to those who dwelt in darkness. Through his humility and diligence he attained great success in his proselyting work. He was, perhaps, the most outstanding missionary that the Church has produced in the one hundred fourteen years of its existence.

Again in 1881, under the direction of George Q. Cannon, the fifth volume of the Faith Promoting Series was published, under the title JACOB HAMBLIN, by James A. Little. The manuscript for this volume originated in Kanab, Utah, where, for a number of years, Jacob Hamblin and James A. Little resided. Jacob Hamblin had lived an interesting life in his missionary labors among the Indians of southern Utah and northern Arizona, and James A. Little, a man of considerable literary ability, took advantage of his opportunity to record the history of the famous scout and missionary while he was yet alive. As a result, we have one of the best, if not the best, account of missionary work among the Indians of the southwest, in all our Church literature.

In arranging these three books for publication, we have placed them in chronological order. The events related by President Woodruff in LEAVES FROM MY JOURNAL come first; MY FIRST MISSION, second; and JACOB HAMBLIN, third.

It is our hope that readers of today will find interest and enjoyment in perusing the accounts of the experiences of three great missionaries, Wilford Woodruff, George Q. Cannon and Jacob Hamblin.

The Compiler.

PUBLISHER'S PREFACE
TO THE COLLECTOR'S EDITION

Leaves from My Journal, My First Mission, and *Jacob Hamblin* were originally published over a century ago with a specific hope in the publisher's mind—to offer Latter-day Saint readers literature that was not only interesting and enjoyable but also inherently faith promoting. The spirit that pervades this writing is the same which burned in the hearts of the subjects of these three famous narratives—Wilford Woodruff, George Q. Cannon, and Jacob Hamblin.

Although these three men all became known as outstanding missionaries, they gained those reputations in significantly different fields of labor and by means of quite diverse proselyting methods. Wilford Woodruff was unrelenting in calling upon his faith in God to work the miracle of conversion. As Preston Nibley noted in the foreword to this volume, he became, "perhaps, the most outstanding missionary that the Church has produced" in modern times. George Q. Cannon rose from difficult straits to become one of the truly great men of the early Church in this dispensation. His four-year mission in the Hawaiian Islands was marked by a determination born of the Spirit to do the Lord's will, despite his own undeserved feelings of inadequacy. Jacob Hamblin spent virtually a lifetime of service among the Indians of the American Southwest. His personal creed of speaking honestly and fearlessly to avoid problems and win friends—rather than using force to obtain his desires—became his legacy to Indian and white man alike.

Despite these differences, all three men were one in this regard—each had a steadfast devotion to preaching the everlasting gospel and its saving precepts to the children of God. Each survived trials and difficulties that could have cost his life; however, each placed his life in the hands of the almighty Lord in whom he believed, and each was preserved in his life's labor.

It is thus with pride that Bookcraft seeks with this memorable Collector's Edition printing to kindle again among LDS readers the legacy of these men and their works. In so doing, we hope to preserve and reaffirm the publisher's original quest of offering quality writing that will lift the soul, promote faith, and nourish the spirit of commitment to build the kingdom of God.

CONTENTS

LEAVES FROM MY JOURNAL

By WILFORD WOODRUFF

WILFORD WOODRUFF

WILFORD WOODRUFF

was born at Farmington, Connecticut, on March 1,
1807. In December, 1833, he was baptized and became a member of the L.D.S. Church at Richland,
New York. The following year he went to Missouri and then began his missionary labors in the
Southern States and Fox Islands, which continued
for four years. On April 26, 1839, he was ordained
an Apostle at Far West, Missouri. The following
year he went to England, where he labored with
great diligence for nearly two years. He returned
to Nauvoo in the fall of 1841. In 1844 he was in
the east when the Prophet Joseph Smith was killed.
In 1846 he again went to England to preside over
the European mission. He was with the pioneer
company which came to Salt Lake valley in July
1847. After a short mission to the east he moved
to the valley in 1850, and thereafter made his per-
manent home in Salt Lake City. He was interested
in everything that developed the Church and State.
In 1877 he was made president of the St. George
Temple. In 1887, at the death of President John
Taylor, he became the active head of the Church
in his capacity as president of the Twelve. In 1889
the First Presidency was organized with Wilford
Woodruff as President of the Church. He presided
for nine years in this capacity, until his death on
September 2, 1898. He was honored, respected and
loved by all who knew him.

CHAPTER I

FOR the benefit of the young Latter-day Saints, for whom the Faith-Promoting Series is especially designed, I will relate some incidents from my experience. I will commence by giving a short account of some events of my childhood and youth.

I spent the first years of my life under the influence of what history has called the "Blue Laws" of Connecticut.

No man, boy or child of any age was permitted to play or do any work from sunset Saturday night until Sunday night. After sunset on Sunday evening, men might work, and boys might jump, shout and play as much as they pleased.

Our parents were very strict with us on Saturday night, and all day Sunday we had to sit very still and say over the Presbyterian catechism and some passages in the Bible.

The people of Connecticut in those days thought it wicked to believe in any religion, or belong to any church, except the Presbyterian. They did not believe in having any prophets, apostles, or revelations, as they had in the days of Jesus, and as we now have in the Church of Jesus Christ of Latter-day Saints.

There was an aged man in Connecticut, however, by the name of Robert Mason, who did not believe like the rest of the people. He believed it was necessary to have prophets, apostles, dreams, visions and revelations in the church of Christ, the same as they had who lived in ancient days; and he believed the Lord would raise up a people and a church, in the last days, with prophets, apostles, and all the gifts, powers and blessings, which it ever contained in any age of the world.

The people called this man, the Old Prophet Mason.

He frequently came to my father's house when I was a boy, and taught me and my brothers those principles; and I believed him.

This prophet prayed a great deal, and he had dreams and visions and the Lord showed him many things, by visions, which were to come to pass in the last days.

I will here relate one vision, which he related to me. The last time I ever saw him, he said: "I was laboring in my field at mid-day when I was enwrapped in a vision. I was placed in the midst of a vast forest of fruit trees: I was very hungry, and walked a long way through the orchard, searching for fruit to eat; but I could not find any in the whole orchard, and I wept because I could find no fruit. While I stood gazing at the orchard, and wondering why there was no fruit, the trees began to fall to the ground upon every side of me, until there was not one tree standing in the whole orchard; and while I was marveling at the scene, I saw young sprouts start up from the roots of the trees which had fallen, and they opened into young, thrifty trees before my eyes. They budded, blossomed, and bore fruit until the trees were loaded with the finest fruit I ever beheld, and I rejoiced to see so much fine fruit. I stepped up to a tree and picked my hands full of fruit, and marveled at its beauty, and as I was about to taste of it the vision closed, and I found myself in the field in the same place I was at the commencement of the vision.

"I then knelt upon the ground, and prayed unto the Lord, and asked Him, in the name of Jesus Christ, to show me the meaning of the vision. The Lord said unto me: 'This is the interpretation of the vision: the great trees of the forest repesented the generation of men in which you live. There is no church of Christ, or kingdom of God upon the earth in your generation. There is no fruit of the church of Christ upon the earth. There is no man ordained of God to administer in any of the ordinances of the gospel of salvation upon the earth in this day and generation. But, in the next generation, I the Lord will set up my kingdom and my church upon the earth, and the fruits of the kingdom and church of Christ, such as have followed the prophets, apostles and saints in every dispensation, shall again be found in all their fullness upon the earth. You will live to see the day, and handle the fruit; but will never partake of it in the flesh.' "

When the old prophet had finished relating the vision and interpretation, he said to me, calling me by my Christian name: "I shall never partake of this fruit in the flesh; but you will, and you will become a conspicuous actor in that kingdom." He then turned and left me. These were the last words he ever spoke to me upon the earth.

This was a very striking circumstance, as I had spent many hours and days, during twenty years, with this old Father Mason, and he had never named this vision to me before. But at the beginning of this last conversation he told me that he felt impelled by the Spirit of the Lord to relate it to me.

He had the vision about the year 1800, and he related it to me in 1830—the same spring that the Church was organized.

This vision, with his other teachings to me, made a great impression upon my mind, and I prayed a great deal to the Lord to lead me by His Spirit, and prepare me for His church when it did come.

In 1832, I left Connecticut, and traveled with my eldest brother to Oswego County, New York; and in the winter of 1833, I saw, for the first time in my life, an Elder of the Church of Jesus Christ of Latter-day Saints. He preached in a schoolhouse near where I lived. I attended the meeting, and the Spirit of the Lord bore record to me that what I heard was true. I invited the Elder to my house, and next day I, with my eldest brother, went down into the water and was baptized. We were the first two baptized in Oswego County, New York.

When I was baptized I thought of what the old prophet had said to me.

In the spring of 1834, I went to Kirtland, saw the Prophet Joseph Smith, and went with him, and with more than two hundred others in Zion's Camp, up to Missouri. When I arrived, at my journey's end, I took the first opportunity and wrote a long letter to Father Mason, and told him I had found the church of Christ that he had told me about. I told him about its organization and the coming forth of the Book of Mormon; that the Church had Prophets, Apostles, and all the gifts and blessings in it, and that the true fruit of the kingdom and church of Christ were manifest among the Saints as the Lord had shown him in the vision. He received my letter and read it over many times, and handled it as he had handled the fruit in the vision; but he was very aged, and soon died. He did not live to see any Elder to administer the ordinances of the gospel unto him.

The first opportunity I had, after the doctrine of baptism for the dead was revealed, I went forth and was baptized for him. He was a good man and a true prophet, for his prophecies have been fulfilled.

[8]

CHAPTER II

I ARRIVED at Kirtland on the 25th of April, 1834, and for the first time saw the Prophet Joseph Smith. He invited me to his house. I spent about a week with him, and became acquainted with him and his family, also with many of the Elders and Saints living in Kirtland, quite a number of whom were preparing to go up to Zion.

On Sunday, the 27th of April, I attended a meeting in a schoolhouse in Kirtland, and for the first time heard Elders Sidney Rigdon, Orson Hyde, Orson Pratt and others speak and bear testimony to the work of God, and much of the Spirit of God was poured out upon the Saints.

It was the 26th of April, 1834, that I was first introduced to Elders Brigham Young and Heber C. Kimball. When I met Brother Brigham, he had his hands full of butcher knives; he gave me one, and told me to go and put a good handle on it, which I did. I also had a good sword, which Brother Joseph wanted, and I gave it to him. He carried it all the way in Zion's Camp to Missouri, and when he returned home he gave it back to me.

When I was called to go on a mission to the South I left the sword and knife with Lyman Wight. When he was taken prisoner at Far West, with Joseph and Hyrum, he had both the sword and the knife with him. All their weapons were taken from them, so were the arms of many of the Saints at Far West, under promise that they should be returned to them when they were prepared to leave the State. When the brethren went to get their arms, Father James Allred saw my sword, which Lyman Wight had laid down, and took it and left his own, and afterwards gave it to me and I still have it. I prize it because the

Prophet Joseph carried it in Zion's Camp. The knife I never regained.

The first day of May, 1834, was appointed for the Camp of Zion to start from Kirtland to go up to Missouri for the redemption of their brethren. Only a small portion of the Camp was ready. The Prophet told those who were ready, to go to New Portage and wait for the remainder. I left, in company with about twenty men, with the baggage wagons. At night we pitched our tents. I went to the top of the hill and looked down upon the camp of Israel. I knelt upon the ground and prayed. I rejoiced and praised the Lord that I had lived to see some of the tents of Israel pitched, and a company gathered by the commandment of God to go up and help redeem Zion.

We tarried at New Portage until the 6th, when we were joined by the Prophet and eighty-five more men. The day before they arrived, while passing through the village of Middlebury, the people tried to count them; but the Lord multiplied them in the eyes of the people, so that those who numbered them said there were four hundred of them.

On the 7th, Brother Joseph organized the camp, which consisted of about one hundred and thirty men. On the following day we continued our journey. We pitched our tents at night and had prayers night and morning. The Prophet told us every day what we should do.

We were nearly all young men, gathered from all parts of the country, and strangers to each other; but we got acquainted very soon, and had a happy time together.

It was a great school for us to be led by a Prophet of God a thousand miles, through cities, towns, villages, and through the wilderness.

When persons stood by to count us they could not tell how many we numbered; some said five hundred, others one thousand.

Many were astonished as we passed through their towns. One lady ran to her door, pushed her spectacles to the top of her head, raised her hands, and exclaimed: "What under heaven has broken loose?" She stood in that position the last I saw of her.

The published history of Zion's Camp gives an account of the bones of a man which we dug out of a mound. His name was Zelph. The Lord showed the Prophet the history of the man in a vision. The arrow, by which he was killed, was found among his bones. One of his thigh bones was broken by a stone slung in battle. The bone was put into my wagon, and I carried it to Clay County, Missouri, and buried it in the earth.

The Lord delivered Israel in the days of Moses by dividing the Red Sea, so they went over dry shod. When their enemies tried to do the same, the water closed upon them and they were drowned. The Lord delivered Zion's Camp from their enemies on the 19th of June, 1834, by piling up the waters in Fishing River forty feet in one night, so our enemies could not cross. He also sent a great hail storm which broke them up and sent them seeking for shelter.

The camp of Zion arrived at Brother Burk's, in Clay County, Missouri, on the 24th of June, 1834, and we pitched our tents on the premises. He told some of the brethren of my company that he had a spare room that some of us might occupy if we would clean it. Our company accepted the offer, and, fearing some other company would get it first, left all other business and went to work, cleaning out the room, and immediately spread down our blankets, so as to hold a right to the room. It was but a short time afterwards that our brethren, who were attacked by cholera, were brought in and laid upon our beds. None of us ever used those blankets again, for they were buried with the dead. So we gained nothing but experience by being selfish, and we lost our bedding.

I will exhort all my young friends to not cherish selfishness; but if you have any, get rid of it as soon as possible. Be generous and noble-hearted, kind to your parents, brothers, sisters and play-mates. Never contend with them; but try to make peace whenever you can. Whenever you are blessed with any good thing, be willing to share it with others. By cultivating these principles while you are young, you will lay a foundation to do much good through your lives, and you will be beloved and respected of the Lord and all good men.

CHAPTER III

AFTER Joseph, the Prophet, had led Zion's Camp to Missouri, and we had passed through all the trials of that journey, and had buried a number of our brethren, as recorded in history, the Prophet called the Camp together, and organized the Church in Zion, and gave much good counsel to all.

He advised all the young men, who had no families, to stay in Missouri and not return to Kirtland. Not having any family, I stopped with Lyman Wight, as did Milton Holmes and Heman Hyde. We spent the summer together, laboring hard, cutting wheat, quarrying rock, making brick, or anything else we could find to do.

In the fall I had a desire to go and preach the gospel.

I knew the gospel which the Lord had revealed to Joseph Smith was true, and of such great value that I wanted to tell it to the people who had not heard it. It was so good and plain, it seemed to me I could make the people believe it.

I was but a Teacher, and it is not a Teacher's office to go abroad and preach. I dared not tell any of the authorities of the Church that I wanted to preach, lest they might think I was seeking for an office.

I went into the woods where no one could see me, and I prayed to the Lord to open my way so that I could go and preach the gospel. While I was praying the Spirit of the Lord came upon me, and told me my prayer was heard and that my request should be granted.

I felt very happy, and got up and walked out of the woods into the traveled road, and there I met a High Priest who had lived in the same house with me some six months.

He had not said a word to me about preaching the gospel; but now, as soon as I met him, he said, "The Lord has revealed to me that it is your privilege to be ordained, and to go and preach the gospel."

I told him I was willing to do whatever the Lord required of me. I did not tell him I had just asked the Lord to let me go and preach.

In a few days a council was called at Lyman Wight's, and I was ordained a Priest and sent on a mission into Arkansas and Tennessee, in company with an Elder. This mission was given us by Elder Edward Partridge, who was the first Bishop ordained in the Church.

The law of God to us in those days was to go without purse or scrip. Our journey lay through Jackson County, from which the Saints had just been driven, and it was dangerous for a "Mormon" to be found in that part of the State.

We put some Books of Mormon and some clothing into our valises, strapped them on our backs, and started on foot. We crossed the ferry into Jackson County, and went through it.

In some instances the Lord preserved us, as it were by miracle, from the mob.

We dared not go to houses and get food, so we picked and ate raw corn, and slept on the ground, and did any way we could until we got out of the county.

We dared not preach while in that county, and we did but little preaching in the State of Missouri. The first time I attempted to preach was on Sunday, in a tavern, in the early part of December, 1834. It was snowing at the time, and the room was full of people. As I commenced to speak the landlord opened the door, and the snow blew on the people; and when I inquired the object of having the door opened in a snowstorm, he informed me that he wanted some light on the subject. I found that it was the custom of the country.

How much good I did in that sermon I never knew, and probably never shall know until I meet that congregation in judgment.

In the southern portion of Missouri and the northern part of Arkansas, in 1834, there were but very few inhabitants.

We visited a place called Harmony Mission, on the Osage river, one of the most crooked rivers in the west. This mission was kept by a Presbyterian minister and his family.

We arrived there on Sunday night at sunset. We had walked all day with nothing to eat, and were very hungry and tired. Neither the minister nor his wife would give us anything to eat, nor let us stay over night, because we were "Mormons," and the only chance we had was to go twelve miles farther down the river, to an Osage Indian trading-post, kept by a Frenchman named Jereu. And this wicked priest, who would not give us a piece of bread, lied to us about the road, and sent us across the swamp, and we wallowed knee deep in mud and water till ten o'clock at night in trying to follow this crooked river. We then left the swamp, and put out into the prairie, to lie in the grass for the night.

When we came out of the swamp, we heard an Indian drumming on a tin pail and singing. It was very dark, but we traveled towards the noise, and when we drew near the Indian camp quite a number of large Indian dogs came out to meet us. They smelt us, but did not bark nor bite.

We were soon surrounded by Osage Indians, and kindly received by Mr. Jereu and his wife, who was an Indian. She gave us an excellent supper and a good bed, which we were thankful for after the fatigue of the day.

As I laid my head on the pillow I felt to thank God, from the bottom of my heart, for the exchange of the barbarous treatment of a civilized Presbyterian priest, for the humane, kind and generous treatment of the savage Osage Indians.

May God reward them both according to their deserts.

CHAPTER IV

WE AROSE in the morning, after a good night's rest. I was somewhat lame, from wading in the swamp the night before. We had a good breakfast. Mr. Jereu sent an Indian to see us across the river, and informed us that it was sixty miles to the nearest settlement of either white or red men.

We were too bashful to ask for anything to take with us to eat; so we crossed the river and started on our day's journey of sixty miles without a morsel of food of any kind. What for? To preach the gospel of Jesus Christ, to save this generation.

We started about sunrise and crossed a thirty-mile prairie, apparently as level as a house floor, without shrub or water. We arrived at timber about two o'clock in the afternoon. As we approached the timber a large black bear came out towards us. We were not afraid of him, for we were on the Lord's business, and had not mocked God's prophets as did the forty-two wicked children who said to Elisha, "Go up thou bald head," for which they were torn by bears.

When the bear got within eight rods of us he sat on his haunches and looked at us a moment, and then ran away; and we went on our way rejoicing. We had to travel in the night, which was cloudy and very dark, so we had great difficulty to keep the road. Soon a large drove of wolves gathered around, and followed us. They came very close, and at times it seemed as though they would eat us up.

We had materials for striking a light, and at ten o'clock, not knowing where we were, and the wolves becoming so bold, we thought it wisdom to make a fire; so we stopped and gathered a lot of oak limbs that lay on the ground, and lit them, and as our fire began to burn the wolves left us.

As we were about to lay down on the ground—for we had no blankets—we heard a dog bark.

My companion said it was a wolf; I said it was a dog; but soon we heard a cow bell. Then we each took a firebrand and went about a quarter of a mile, and found the house, which was sixty miles from where we started that morning.

It was an old log cabin, about twelve feet square, with no door, but an old blanket was hung up in the door-way. There was no furniture except one bedstead, upon which lay a woman, several children and several small dogs. A man lay on the bare floor with his feet to the fire-place, and all were asleep. I went in and spoke to the man, but did not wake him. I stepped to him, and laid my hand on his shoulder. The moment he felt the weight of my hand he jumped to his feet, and ran around the room as though he was frightened; but he was quieted when we informed him we were friends.

The cause of his fright was, he had shot a panther a few nights before, and he thought its mate had jumped upon him.

He asked us what we wanted; we told him we wished to stop with him all night, and would like something to eat. He informed us we might lay on the floor as he did, but that he had not a mouthful for us to eat, as he had to depend on his gun to get breakfast for his family in the morning. So we lay on the bare floor, and slept through a long, rainy night, which was pretty hard after walking sixty miles without anything to eat. That was the hardest day's work of my life.

The man's name was Williams. He was in the mob in Jackson County; and after the Saints were driven out, he, with many others, went south.

We got up in the morning and walked in the rain twelve miles to the house of a man named Bemon, who was also one of the mob from Jackson County. They were about sitting down to breakfast as we came in.

In those days it was the custom of the Missourians to ask you to eat even if they intended to cut your throat as soon as you got through; so he asked us to take breakfast, and we were very glad of the invitation.

He knew we were "Mormons," and as soon as we began to eat he began to swear about the "Mormons." He had a large platter of bacon and eggs, and plenty of bread on the table, and his swearing did not hinder our eating, for the harder he swore the harder we ate, until we got our stomachs full; then we arose from the table, took our hats, thanked him for our breakfast, and the last we heard of him he was still swearing.

I trust the Lord will reward him for our breakfast.

CHAPTER V

IN THE early days of the Church, it was a great treat to an Elder in his travels through the country to find a "Mormon"; it was so with us. We were hardly in Arkansas when we heard of a family named Akeman. They were in Jackson County in the persecutions. Some of the sons had been tied up there and whipped on their bare backs with hickory switches by the mob. We heard of their living on Petit Jean River, in the Arkansas Territory, and we went a long way to visit them.

There had recently been heavy rains, and a creek that we had to cross was swollen to a rapid stream of eight rods in width. There was no person living nearer than two miles from the crossing, and no boat. The people living at the last house on the road, some three miles from the crossing, said we would have to tarry till the water fell before we could cross. We did not stop, feeling to trust in God.

Just as we arrived at the rolling flood a negro, on a powerful horse, entered the stream on the opposite side and rode through it. On our making our wants known to him, he took us, one at a time, behind him and carried us safely over, and we went on our way rejoicing.

We arrived that night within five miles of Mr. Akeman's and were kindly entertained by a stranger. During the night I had the following dream:

I thought an angel came to us, and told us we were commanded of the Lord to follow a certain straight path, which was pointed out to us, let it lead us wherever it might. After we had walked in it awhile we came to the door of a house, which was in the line of a high wall running north and south, so that we could not go around. I opened the door and saw the room was filled with large serpents, and I shuddered at the sight. My companion said he would not go into the room for fear of the serpents. I told him I should try to go through the room though they killed me, for the Lord had commanded it. As I stepped into the room the serpents coiled themselves up, and raised their heads some two feet from the floor, to spring at me. There was one much larger than the rest in the center of the room, which raised its head nearly as high as mine and made a spring at me. At that instant I felt as though nothing but the power of God could save me, and I stood still. Just before the serpent reached me he dropped dead at my feet; all the rest dropped dead, swelled up, turned black, burst open, took fire and were consumed before my eyes, and we went through the room unharmed, and thanked God for our deliverance.

I awoke in the morning and pondered upon the dream. We took breakfast, and started on our journey on Sunday morning, to visit Mr. Akeman. I related to my companion my dream, and told him we should see something strange. We had great anticipations of meeting Mr. Akeman, supposing him to be a member of the Church. When we arrived at his house he received us very coldly, and we soon found that he had apostatized. He brought railing accusations against the Book of Mormon and the authorities of the Church.

Word was sent through all the settlements on the river for twenty miles that two "Mormon" preachers were in the place. A mob was soon raised, and warning sent to us to leave immediately or we would be tarred and feathered, ridden on a rail and hanged. I soon saw where the serpents were. My companion wanted to leave; I told him no, I would stay and see my dream fulfilled.

There was an old gentleman and lady, named Hubbel, who had read the Book of Mormon and believed. Father Hubbel came to see us, and invited us to make our home with him while we stayed in the place. We did so, and labored for him some three weeks with our axes, clearing land, while we were waiting to see the salvation of God.

I was commanded of the Lord by the Holy Ghost to go and warn Mr. Akeman to repent of his wickedness. I did so, and each time he railed against me, and the last time he ordered me out of his house. When I went out he followed me, and was very angry. When he came up to me, about eight rods from the house, he fell dead at my feet, turned black and swelled up, as I saw the serpents do in my dream.

His family, as well as ourselves, felt it was the judgment of God upon him. I preached his funeral sermon. Many of the mob died suddenly. We stayed about two weeks after Akeman's death and preached, baptized Mr. Hubbel and his wife, and then continued on our journey.

CHAPTER VI

WE CONCLUDED to go down the Arkansas river and cross into Tennessee. We could not get passage on the boat, because of the low water, so we went on the bank of the river and cut down a sound cottonwood tree, three feet through, and cut off a twelve-foot length from the butt end; and in two days we dug out a canoe. We made a pair of oars and a rudder, and on the 11th of March, 1835, we launched our canoe, and commenced our voyage down the Arkansas river, without provisions.

The first day we sailed twenty-five miles, and stopped at night with a poor family who lived on the bank of the river. These kind folks gave us supper and breakfast, and, in the morning, gave us a johnny-cake and piece of pork to take with us on our journey.

We traveled about fifty miles that day, and at night stopped in a village called Cadron, at an old tavern, which was deserted because it was believed to be haunted by evil spirits.

We made a fire in the tavern, roasted a piece of our pork, ate our supper, said our prayers, went into a chamber, lay down on the bare floor, and were soon asleep.

I dreamed I was at my father's house in a good feather bed, and I had a good night's rest. When I awoke the bed vanished, and I found myself on the bare floor and well rested, not having been troubled with evil spirits or anything else.

We thanked the Lord for his goodness to us, ate the remainder of our provisions and continued our journey down the river to Little Rock, the capital of Arkansas, which then consisted of only a few cabins.

After visiting the place, we crossed the river and tied up our canoe, which had carried us safely one hundred and fifty miles.

We then took the old military road, leading from Little Rock to Memphis, Tennessee. This road lay through swamps, and was covered with mud and water most of the way, for one hundred and seventy miles. We walked forty miles a day through mud and water knee deep.

On the 24th of March, after traveling some ten miles through mud, I was taken lame with a sharp pain in my knee. I sat down on a log.

My companion, who was anxious to get to his home in Kirtland, left me sitting in an alligator swamp. I did not see him again for two years. I knelt down in the mud and prayed, and the Lord healed me, and I went on my way rejoicing.

On the 27th of March, I arrived at Memphis, weary and hungry. I went to the best tavern in the place, kept by Mr. Josiah Jackson. I told him I was a stranger, and had no money. I asked him if he would keep me over night.

He inquired of me what my business was.

I told him I was a preacher of the gospel.

He laughed and said that I did not look much like a preacher.

I did not blame him, as all the preachers he had ever been acquainted with rode on fine horses or in fine carriages, clothed in broadcloth, and had large salaries, and would see this whole world sink to perdition before they would wade through one hundred and seventy miles of mud to save the people.

The landlord wanted a little fun, so he said he would keep me if I would preach. He wanted to see if I could preach.

I must confess that by this time I became a little mischievous, and pleaded with him not to set me preaching.

The more I plead to be excused, the more determined Mr. Jackson was that I should preach. He took my valise, and the landlady got me a good supper.

I sat down in a large hall to eat supper. Before I got through, the room began to be filled with some of the rich and fashionable of Memphis, dressed in their broadcloth and silk, while my appearance was such as you can imagine, after traveling through the mud as I had been.

When I had finished eating, the table was carried out of the room over the heads of the people. I was placed in the corner of the room, with a stand having a Bible, hymn book and candle on it, hemmed in by a dozen men, with the landlord in the center.

There were present some five hundred persons who had come together, not to hear a good sermon, but to have some fun.

Now boys, how would you like this position? On your first mission, without a companion or friend, and to be called upon to preach to such a congregation? With me it was one of the most pleasing hours of my life, although I felt as though I should like company.

I read a hymn, and asked them to sing. Not a soul would sing a word.

I told them I had not the gift of singing; but with the help of the Lord I would both pray and preach. I knelt down to pray and the men around me dropped on their knees. I prayed to the Lord to give me His spirit and to show me the hearts of the people. I promised the Lord in my prayer I would deliver to that congregation whatever He would give to me. I arose and spoke one hour and a half and it was one of the best sermons of my life.

The lives of the congregation were opened to the vision of my mind, and I told them of their wicked deeds and the reward they would obtain. The men who surrounded me dropped their heads. Three minutes after I closed I was the only person in the room.

Soon I was shown to a bed, in a room adjoining a large one in which were assembled many of the men whom I had been preaching to. I could hear their conversation.

One man said he would like to know how that "Mormon" boy knew of their past lives.

In a little while they got to disputing about some doctrinal point. One suggested calling me to decide the point. The landlord said "No; we have had enough for once."

In the morning I had a good breakfast. The landlord said if I came that way again to stop at his house, and stay as long as I might choose.

CHAPTER VII

AFTER leaving Memphis, I traveled through the country to Benton County and preached on the way as I had opportunity.

I stopped one night with an Esquire Hardman, an Episcopalian.

Most of the night was spent by the family in music and dancing.

In the morning, at the breakfast table, Mr. Hardman asked me if we believed in music and dancing.

I told him we did not really consider them essential to salvation.

He said he did and therefore should not join our Church.

On the 4th of April, 1835, I had the happy privilege of meeting Elder Warren Parrish at the house of Brother Frys. He had been preaching in that part of Tennessee, in company with David W. Patten, and had baptized a number and organized several small branches.

Brother Patten had returned home, and Brother Parrish was laboring alone. I joined him in the ministry, and we labored together three months and nineteen days, when he was called to Kirtland.

During the time we were together, we traveled through several counties in Tennessee for the distance of seven hundred and sixty miles, and preached the gospel daily as we had the opportunity. We baptized some twenty persons.

By the counsel of the Prophet Joseph Smith and Oliver Cowdery, Elder Parrish ordained me an Elder, and left me to take charge of the branches that had been raised up in that neighborhood.

As soon as I was left alone, I extended my circuit and labors. For a season I had large congregations; many seemed to believe, and I baptized a number.

On the 15th of August I had an appointment at the house of Brother Taylor, the step-father of Abraham O. Smoot.

I had to cross Bloody River, which I had to swim in consequence of heavy rains. While crossing, my horse became entangled in a tree top, and almost drowned; but I succeeded in getting him loose.

We swam to the shore separately. He reached the shore first, and waited until I came out. I got into the saddle, and went on my way in good spirits, and had a good meeting.

On the 20th of October I baptized three Campbellites, one of whom was a deacon. I then rode twelve miles to Mr. Greenwood's, who was eighty years old, and had been a soldier under General Washington. His wife, who was ninety-three years old, I found quite smart, and busy carding wool. I preached at their house, and baptized both of them.

On the following day I preached at the house of Benjamin L. Clapp and baptized seven Campbellites and one Baptist.

On the 16th of November I preached at Brother Camp's and baptized three. On the day following, it being Sunday, I preached again at Brother Clapp's and baptized five. At the close of the meeting I mounted my horse to ride to Clark's River, in company with Seth Utley, four other brethren and two sisters. The distance was twenty miles.

We came to a stream which was so swollen by rains, that we could not cross without swimming our horses. To swim would not be safe for the females, so we went up the stream to find a ford. In the attempt we were overtaken by a severe storm of wind and rain, and lost our way in the darkness, and wandered through creeks and mud. But the Lord does not forsake His Saints in any of their troubles. While we were in the woods suffering under the blast of the storm, groping like the blind for the wall, a bright light suddenly shone around us and revealed to us our dangerous situation on the edge of a gulf. The light continued with us until we found the road; we then went on our way rejoicing, though the darkness returned and the rain continued.

We reached Brother Henry Thomas' in safety about nine o'clock at night, having been five hours in the storm and forded streams many times. None of us felt to complain, but were thankful to God for His preserving care.

On the following day I preached in Damon Creek and organized a branch called the Damon Creek Branch, and ordained Daniel Thomas a Teacher.

On the 19th of December I again preached at the house of Brother Clapp, and baptized five persons: one was a Campbellite preacher.

On the following day I preached at the house of Brother Henry Thomas, when a mob of about fifty persons collected, headed by a Baptist preacher, who, after asking one question, advised the mob to not lay hands on any man on account of his principles.

The advice was good and well taken.

At the close of the meeting I baptized three persons, one seventy-eight years old.

This brings the year 1835 to a close—the first year of my mission, during which time I had traveled three thousand two hundred and forty-eight miles, held one hundred and seventy meetings, baptized forty-three persons—three of whom were Campbellite preachers—assisted Elder Parrish to baptize twenty more, confirmed thirty-five, organized three branches, ordained two Teachers and one Deacon, procured thirty subscribers for the *Messenger and Advocate,* one hundred and seventy-three signers to the petition to the governor of Missouri for redress of wrongs done the Saints in Jackson County, had three mobs rise against me—but was not harmed, wrote eighteen letters, received ten, and finally closed the labors of the year 1835 by eating johnny-cake, butter and honey at Brother A. O. Smoot's.

CHAPTER VIII

I SPENT the fore part of January, 1836, (the weather being very cold) at the house of A. O. Smoot, in Kentucky, studying Kirkham's English Grammar. I continued to travel and preach in Kentucky and Tennessee and baptized all that would believe my testimony.

On the 26th of February we held a conference at the house of Brother Lewis Clapp (father of B. L. Clapp). There were represented one hundred and three members in that mission. I ordained A. O. Smoot and Benjamin Boyston, Elders, and Daniel Thomas and Benjamin L. Clapp, Priests. I also ordained one Teacher and two Deacons.

After conference I took Brothers Smoot and Clapp with me to preach. The former traveled with me constantly till the 21st of April, when we had the privilege of meeting with Elder David W. Patten, who had come direct from Kirtland, and who had been ordained one of the Twelve Apostles.

It was a happy meeting. He gave us an account of the endowments at Kirtland, the glorious blessings received, the ministration of angels, the organization of the Twelve Apostles and Seventies, and informed me that I was appointed a member of the second quorum of Seventies. All of this was glorious news to me, and caused my heart to rejoice.

On the 27th of May we were joined by Elder Warren Parrish, direct from Kirtland. We had a happy time together.

On the 28th, we held a conference at Brother Seth Utley's, where were represented all the branches of the Church in the South.

I was ordained on the 31st of May a member of the second quorum of Seventies under the hands of David W. Patten and Warren Parrish.

At the close of the conference we separated for a short time. Elders Patten and Parrish labored in Tennessee, Brother Smoot and myself in Kentucky. On the 9th of June we all met at Damon Creek branch, where Brother Patten baptized two. One was Father Henry Thomas, who had been a revolutionary soldier under General Washington, and father of Daniel and Henry Thomas.

A warrant was issued, on the oath of a priest, against D. W. Patten, W. Parrish and myself. We were accused in the warrant of the great "crime" of testifying that Christ would come in this generation, and that we promised the Holy Ghost to those whom we baptized. Brothers Patten and Parrish were taken on the 19th of June. I being in another county, escaped being arrested. The brethren were put under two thousand dollars bond to appear at court. Albert Petty and Seth Utley were their bondsmen. They were tried on the 22nd of June. They pleaded their own cause. Although men came forward and testified they did receive the Holy Ghost after they were baptized, the brethren were condemned; but were finally released by paying the expense of the mob court.

There was one peculiar circumstance connected with this trial by a mob court, which was armed to the teeth. When the trial was through with, the people were not willing to permit more than one to speak. Warren Parrish had said but few words, and they were not willing to let David Patten speak. But he, feeling the injustice of the court, and being filled with the power of God, arose to his feet and delivered a speech of about twenty minutes, holding them spell-bound while he told them of their wickedness and the abominations that they were guilty of, also of the curse of God that awaited them, if they did not repent, for taking up two harmless, inoffensive men for preaching the gospel of Christ.

When he got through his speech the judge said, "You must be armed with secret weapons, or you would not talk in this fearless manner to an armed court."

Brother Patten replied: "I have weapons that you know not of, and they are given me of God, for He gives me all the power I have."

The judge seemed willing to get rid of them almost upon any terms, and offered to dismiss them if their friends would pay the costs, which the brethren present freely offered to do.

When the two were released, they mounted their horses and rode a mile to Seth Utley's; but as soon as they had left, the court became ashamed that they had been let go so easy and the whole mob mounted their horses to follow them to Utley's.

One of the Saints, seeing the state of affairs, went on before the mob to warn the brethren, so that they had time to ride into the woods near by.

They traveled along about three miles to Brother Albert Petty's, and went to bed. The night was dark, and they went to sleep.

But Brother Patten was warned in a dream to get up and flee, as the mob would soon be there. They both arose, saddled their animals, and rode into the adjoining county.

The house they had just left was soon surrounded by the mob, but the brethren had escaped through the mercy of God.

I was invited to hold a meeting at a Baptist meeting-house, on the 27th of June. On my arrival I met a large congregation; but, on commencing meeting, Parson Browning ordered the meeting to be closed. I told the people I had come ten miles to preach the gospel to them, and was willing to stand in a cart, on a pile of wood, on a fence, or any other place they would appoint, to have that privilege.

One man said he owned the fence and land in front of the meeting house, and we might use both, for he did not believe "Mormonism" would hurt either.

So the congregation crossed the road, took down the fence and made seats of it, and I preached to them one hour and a half. At the close Mr. Randolph Alexander bore testimony to the truth of what had been said. He invited me home with him, bought a Book of Mormon, and was baptized, and I organized a branch in that place.

On the 18th of July, Brother A. O. Smoot and I arrived at a ferry on the Tennessee River, and, as the ferryman was not at home, the woman kindly gave us permission to use the ferry-boat. We led our horses on board, and took the oars to cross the river. Brother Smoot had never used an oar, and I had not for some years, so we made awkward work of it. Soon he broke one oar, and I let another fall overboard, which left us only one broken oar to get to shore with. We narrowly escaped running into a steamboat. We struck shore half a mile below the landing place; tied up the boat, jumped on the bank with our horses, and went on our way with blistered hands, thankful to get off so well.

On Sunday, the 31st of July, A. O. Smoot and I preached at Mr. David Crider's, Weakly County, Tennessee. After the meeting Mr. Crider was baptized. A mob gathered and threatened us, and poisoned our horses so that the one I rode, belonging to Samuel West, died a few days after. This horse had carried me thousands of miles while preaching the gospel.

I continued to travel with Brothers Smoot, Patten and Parrish in Tennessee and Kentucky, and we baptized all who would receive our testimony.

On the second day of September we held a general conference at the Damon Creek Branch. Elder Thomas B. Marsh, President of the Twelve Apostles, presided. All the branches in Tennessee and Kentucky were represented.

Brothers Randolph Alexander, Benjamin L. Clapp and Johnson F. Lane were ordained Elders and Lindsay Bradey was ordained to the lesser Priesthood.

I assisted President Marsh to obtain fifteen hundred dollars from the Southern brethren, to enter land in Missouri for the Church. The brethren made me a present of fifty dollars, which I sent by President Marsh to enter forty acres of land for me. Elder Smoot and I were released from the Southern Mission with permission to go to Kirtland.

CHAPTER IX

HAVING returned from my Southern mission in the autumn of 1836, in company with Elders A. O. Smoot and Jesse Turpin, I spent the following winter in Kirtland. During this time I attended the school of Professor Haws, who taught Greek, Latin and English grammar. I confined my studies mostly to Latin and English grammar.

This winter and the following spring, in some respects, may be regarded as one of the most interesting periods of the history of the Church, when we consider the endowments and teachings given in the temple, and the great apostasy which followed.

I was married to Miss Phoebe Whitmore Carter, on the 13th of April, 1837, and received my patriarchal blessing under the hands of Father Joseph Smith, the Patriarch, two days after.

I felt impressed by the Spirit of God to take a mission to the Fox islands, situated east of the Maine shore, a country I knew nothing about. I made my feelings known to the Apostles, and they advised me to go.

Feeling that it was my duty to go upon this mission, I did not tarry at home one year after having married a wife, as the law of Moses would have allowed. On the contrary, I started just one month and one day after that important event, leaving my wife with Sister Hale, with whom she expected to stay for a season.

I left Kirtland in good spirits, in company with Elder Jonathan H. Hale, and walked twelve miles to Fairport, where we were joined by Elder Milton Holmes. There we went aboard the steamer *Sandusky,* and made our way to Buffalo, and proceeded thence to Syracuse, by way of the Erie Canal. We then walked to Richland, Oswego Co., N. Y., where I met my two brothers, whom I had not seen for several years.

After spending one night there, we continued our journey to Sackett's Harbor, and crossed Lake Ontario on the steamer *Oneida,* to Kingston, Upper Canada, and from there also by steamer along the canal to Jones' Falls, whence we walked to a place called Bastard, Leeds County.

Here we found a branch of the Church, presided over by John E. Page and James Blakesly. We accompanied them to their place of meeting, and attended a conference with them, at which three hundred members of the Church were represented.

Thirty-two persons presented themselves for ordination, whom I was requested to ordain, in company with Elder Wm. Draper. We ordained seven Elders, nine Priests, eleven Teachers and five Deacons.

We spoke to the people several times during this conference, and at its close we were called upon to administer to a woman who was possessed of the devil. At times she was dumb, and greatly afflicted with the evil spirits that dwelt in her. She believed in Jesus and in us as His servants, and wished us to administer to her. Four of us laid our hands upon her head and commanded the devil, in the name of Jesus Christ, to depart out of her. It was immediately done, and the woman arose with great joy, and gave thanks and praise unto God; for, according to her faith, she was made whole from that hour.

A child, also, that was sick, was healed by the laying on of hands, according to the word of God.

We walked thirty miles to visit another branch of the Saints at Leeds, where we met with John Gordon and John Snider. Here we held a meeting and bore our testimony to the people.

A Sister Carns here came to us and requested to have the ordinance for the healing of the sick performed for two of her children who were afflicted. One was a suckling child, which was lying at the point of death. I took it in my arms and presented it before the Elders, who laid their hands upon it, and it was made whole immediately, and I handed it back to the mother entirely healed.

We afterwards laid hands upon the other, when it was also healed. It was done by the power of God, in the name of Jesus Christ, and the parents praised God for His goodness.

After leaving the Saints in this place, we returned to

Kingston, and crossed Lake Ontario in company with Isaac Russell, John Goodson and John Snider.

Brother Russell seemed to be constantly troubled with evil spirits, which followed him when he subsequently went upon a mission to England, where Apostles Orson Hyde and Heber C. Kimball, when administering to him, had a severe contest with them, as Brother Kimball has related in his history.

Brothers Russell, Goodson and Snider continued with us to Schenectady, where they left us to proceed to New York, to join Elders Kimball and Hyde to go upon their mission to England.

After leaving these brethren we traveled by rail to Albany, and walked from there to Canaan, Conn., where we found a branch of the Church, including Jesse and Julian Moses and Francis K. Benedict.

We held a two-days' meeting with the Saints in Canaan, and I ordained Julian Moses and Francis K. Benedict Elders.

After holding several meetings in the town of Colebrook, and visiting my half sister, Eunice Woodruff, who was teaching school there, I proceeded to Avon, the place of my birth. There I visited many of my former neighbors and relatives, and the grave of my mother, Bulah Woodruff, who died June 11th, 1808, when twenty-six years of age. The following verse was upon her tombstone:

"A pleasing form, a generous heart,
 A good companion, just without art;
 Just in her dealings, faithful to her friend,
 Beloved through life, lamented in the end."

At the close of the day I walked six miles to Farmington, where my father, Aphek Woodruff, was living, and

I had the happy privilege of once more meeting with him and my stepmother, whom I had not seen for seven years. They greeted me with great kindness, and it was a happy meeting.

After visiting with my father a day or two, I returned to Avon, where most of my relatives lived, and held meetings with them, and on the 12th of June, 1837, I baptized my uncle, Ozem Woodruff, his wife Hannah, and his son John, and we rejoiced together, for this was in fulfillment of a dream I had in 1818, when I was eleven years of age.

On the 15th of July I had an appointment to preach at the house of my uncle, Adna Hart. While there I had the happy privilege of meeting with my wife, Phoebe W. Woodruff, who had come from Kirtland to meet me and accompany me to her father's home in Scarboro, Maine.

Those who had assembled to hear me preach were relatives, neighbors and former friends. After meeting we returned to Farmington to my father's home, where I spent the night with my father, step-mother, sister and wife. Elder Hale was also with us.

On the 19th of July, Elder Hale left us to go to his friends in New Rowley, Mass., and on the same evening I held a meeting in the Methodist meetinghouse in the town of Farmington. I had a large congregation of citizens, with whom I had been acquainted from my youth. My parents, wife and sister attended the meeting. The congregation seemed satisfied with the doctrines I taught, and they requested me to hold another meeting; but I felt anxious to continue my journey, and on the 20th of July I parted with my father, step-mother and sister, and took stage for Hartford with my wife.

On my arrival at Hartford, not having money to pay the fare of both of us, I paid my wife's fare to Rowley,

Mass., where there was a branch of the Church, presided over by Brother Nathaniel Holmes, father of Jonathan and Milton Holmes, and I journeyed on foot.

The first day I walked fifty-two miles, the second forty-eight, and the third day thirty-six miles, and arrived at Rowley at two o'clock, making 136 miles in a little over two and a half days.

I spent eight days at New Rowley, holding meetings and visiting the Saints, including the Holmes family, and left there on the 1st of August.

On the 8th of August, in company with my wife and Elder Hale, I visited my wife's father, Ezra Carter, and his family in Scarboro, Maine, it being the first time I had ever seen any of her relatives. We were very kindly received. My wife had been absent from her father's home about one year.

I spent eight days with Father Carter and household, and one day I went to sea with Fabian and Ezra Carter, my brothers-in-law, in a boat, to fish with hooks. We caught 250 cod, haddock and hake, and we saw four whales, two at a time, it being the first time in my life I had ever seen the kind of a fish which is said to have swallowed Jonah.

On the 18th of August, 1837, I parted with my wife and her father's household, leaving her with them, and, in company with Jonathan H. Hale, started upon the mission that I had in view when I left Kirtland.

We walked ten miles to Portland, and took passage on the steamboat *Bangor,* which carried us to Owl's Head, where we went on board of a sloop which landed us on North Fox Island at 2 o'clock, a. m., on the 20th.

CHAPTER X

THE town of Vinal Haven includes both North and South Fox Islands, in lat. 44° north, and long. 69° 10′ west. The population numbered, at the time of my visit, about 1,800. The inhabitants were intelligent and industrious, and hospitable to strangers. They got most of their wealth and living by fishing. The town fitted out over one hundred licensed sailing vessels, besides smaller craft.

North Fox Island is nine miles long by two miles in width and had a population of 800. They had a post office, one store, a Baptist church and meetinghouse, four schoolhouses, and a tide grist mill.

The land was rather poor, yet there were some good farms. The products were wheat, barley, oats, potatoes and grass. The principal timber was fir, spruce, hemlock and birch. Raspberries and gooseberries grew in great abundance, and some upland cranberries were raised. The principal stock of the island was sheep.

South Fox Island comes as near being without any definite form as any spot on earth I ever saw. It would be difficult for any person to describe it. It is about ten miles in length by five in width, and is one universal mass of rocks, formed into shelves, hills, and valleys, and cut up into necks and points to make room for the coves and harbors that run through and through the island.

The population was 1,000. The inhabitants got their living entirely by fishing. There is no chance for farming upon the island, and but a few garden patches, which are cultivated at great expense. Some few sheep are raised there.

Many of the inhabitants fish in the region of Newfoundland, and bring their fish home and cure them on flakes and prepare them for the market. They supply the market with great quantities of cod, mackerel and boxed herring.

Upon this island there were two stores, three tide saw mills, six school houses and a small branch of the Methodist church, presided over by a priest.

What timber there is upon this island, such as pine, fir, spruce, hemlock and birch, and the wortleberries, raspberries and gooseberries, mostly grows out of the cracks of the rocks.

Great quantities of fish, and in almost endless variety, inhabit the coves and harbors around the island. The whale, blackfish, shark, ground shark, pilot-fish, horse mackerel, sturgeon, salmon, halibut, cod, pollock, tom cod, hake, haddock, mackerel, shad bass, alewife, herring, pohagen, dolphin, whiting, frost-fish, flounder, smelt, skate, shrimp, skid, cusk, blueback, scollop, dogfish, muttonfish, lumpfish, squid, five-fingers, monkfish, horsefish, sunfish, swordfish, thresher, cat, scupog, tootog, eyefish, cunner, ling, also the eel, lobster, clam, muscle, periwinkle, porpoise, seal, etc., are found there.

Thus I have given a brief description of Vinal Haven. It was quite dark when we landed there without a farthing in money. We made our way over the rocks and through the cedars the best way we could, until we found a house, when we rapped at the door. A woman put her head out of the window, and asked who was there and what was wanted.

I told her we were two strangers and wanted a bed to lie down upon until morning.

She led us in and gave us a bed, and we slept until quite late, it being Sunday morning. When we came out and took breakfast it was nearly noon. I asked what she charged for our entertainment, and she replied that we were welcome.

I then asked her if there was any religion, or minister or church on the island.

She informed me there was a Baptist minister by the name of Newton, who had a congregation and a meeting house about five miles from there.

We thanked her for her kindness, walked to the meeting house and stepped inside the doorway. We stood there until a deacon came to the door, when I asked him to go and tell the minister in the pulpit that there were two servants of God at the door, who had a message to deliver to that people, and wished the privilege of delivering it.

He sent for us to come to the pulpit, so we walked through the congregation with our valises under our arms, and took a seat by the side of the minister, who was about to speak as we came to the door.

He arose, delivered his discourse to the people, occupying about half an hour. When he closed he asked me what was my wish.

I told him we wished to speak to the people at any hour that would suit his or their convenience; so he gave notice that there were two strangers present who would speak to the people at five o'clock that evening.

We were quite a source of wonderment to the people, who had no idea who we were.

Mr. Newton asked us to go home to tea with him, and we gladly accepted the invitation. When we arrived at his house I opened my valise and took out the Bible, Book of Mormon, and Doctrine and Covenants, laid them upon the table and took my seat.

Mr. Newton took up the books and looked at them, but said nothing. I then asked him if there were any school houses upon the island, and if so, whether they were free to preach in.

He answered that there were four, numbered respectively from one to four, and that they were free.

Mr. Newton and family accompanied us to the meeting-house, where we met a large congregation, none of whom knew who we were or anything about our profession, except the minister.

Elder Hale and I went to the stand, and I arose with peculiar feelings, and addressed the congregation for one hour, taking for my text Galatians 1:8-9.

This was the first time that I or any other Elder of the Church of Jesus Christ of Latter-day Saints had (to my knowledge) attempted to preach the fullness of the gospel and the Book of Mormon to the inhabitants of any island of the sea.

I had much liberty in speaking, and informed the people that the Lord had raised up a prophet and organized His Church as in the days of Christ and the ancient apostles, with prophets, apostles, and the gifts as anciently, and that He had brought forth the Book of Mormon.

At the close of my remarks Elder Hale bore testimony.

I gave liberty for any one to speak that might wish to. As no one responded, I announced that we would hold meetings the next four evenings in the schoolhouses, beginning at No. 1.

CHAPTER XI

DURING the first thirteen days of our sojourn upon the island we preached seventeen discourses, being invited by the people to tarry with them. I left a copy of the Doctrine and Covenants with Mr. Newton for his perusal.

He read it, and the Spirit of God bore testimony to him of its truth. He pondered over it for days, and he walked his room until midnight trying to decide whether to receive or reject it.

He and his family attended about a dozen of my first meetings, and then he made up his mind, contrary to the dictation of the Spirit of God to him, to reject the testimony, and come out against me. However, we commenced baptizing his flock.

The first two we baptized were a sea captain, by the name of Justin Eames, and his wife. Brother Jonathan H. Hale went down into the sea and baptized them on the 3rd of September, and these were the first baptisms performed by proper authority upon any of the islands of the sea (to my knowledge) in this dispensation.

Before we left Kirtland some of the leading apostates there had tried to discourage Brother Hale about going upon his mission, telling him he would never baptize anyone, and he had better remain at home. When Captain Eames offered himself for baptism, I told Brother Hale to go and baptize him, and prove these men false prophets, and he did so.

On the following Sabbath I baptized his brother, Ebenezer Eames, another sea captain, and a young lady.

Mr. Newton, the Baptist minister, now commenced a war against us, and sent to the South Island for a Mr. Douglass, a Methodist minister (with whom he had been at variance for years) to come over and help him put down "Mormonism."

Mr. Douglass came over, and they got as many people together as they could and held a conference. He railed against Joseph, the prophet, and the Book of Mormon, and, taking the Book in his hand, with out-stretched arm, declared that he feared none of the judgments of God that would come upon him for rejecting it as the word of God. (I never heard what his sentiments upon this subject were at the end of his term of fourteen years' imprisonment in the Thomaston penitentiary, for an outrage upon his daughter, the judgment of which was given upon the testimony of his wife and daughter.)

I was present and heard Mr. Douglass' speech upon this occasion, and took minutes of the same. When he closed I arose and informed the people that I would meet with them next Sunday in the meetinghouse, and answer Mr. Douglass, and wished him as well as the people to be present.

I informed the people that Mr. Douglass had made false statements against Joseph Smith and the Latter-day Saints, with whom he had no acquaintance, and he had misquoted much scripture, all of which I could correct.

We continued to baptize the people of the North Island until we had baptized every person who owned an interest in the Baptist meetinghouse. I then followed Mr. Douglass home to the South Island and preached the gospel to and baptized nearly all the members of his church.

The excitement became great upon both islands, and on Sunday, the 17th of September, I met a large assembly from both islands, and took the same subject that Mr. Douglass had dwelt upon in his remarks against the Book of Mormon and our principles.

I spoke two and a half hours and answered every objection against the Book of Mormon, Joseph Smith or our principles.

I had good attention, and the people seemed satisfied. At the close of the meeting Elder Hale administered the ordinance of baptism.

Mr. Newton, in order to save his cause, went to the mainland and brought over several ministers with him and held a protracted meeting. They hoped by this to stop the work of God, but all to no avail, for the whole people would attend our meeting and receive the word of God, and we continued to baptize.

We visited the dwellings of most of the inhabitants during our sojourn there.

Upon one occasion, while standing upon Mr. Carver's farm on the east end of the North Island, we counted fifty-five islands in that region, the majority of which were not inhabited. We also saw twenty ships under sail at the same time.

We had no lack for food while upon the island, for if we did not wish to trouble our friends for a dinner, we only had to borrow a spade or a hoe and a kettle and go to the beach and dig a peck of clams. These, when boiled, would make a delicious meal, which we often availed ourselves of.

One day Elder Hale and I ascended to the top of a high granite rock upon the South Island for prayer and supplication. We sat down under the shade of a pine tree which grew out of a fissure in a rock, and Elder Hale read the 16th chapter of Jeremiah, where mention is made of the hunters and fishers that God would send in the last days to gather Israel.

Of a truth, here we were upon an island of the sea, standing upon a rock where we could survey the gallant ships and also the islands, which were as full of rocks, ledges and caves as any part of the earth. And what had brought us here? To search out the blood of Ephraim, the honest and meek of the earth, and gather them from those islands, rocks, holes, and caves of the earth unto Zion.

We prayed and rejoiced together. The Spirit of God

rested upon us; we spoke of Christ and the ancient prophets and apostles in Jerusalem; of Nephi, Alma, Mormon
and Moroni in America; Joseph, Hyrum, Oliver and the
apostles in our own day, and we rejoiced that we were upon
the islands of the sea searching out the blood of Israel.

While being filled with these meditations and the Spirit
of God, we fell upon our knees and gave thanks to the God
of heaven, and felt to pray for all Israel.

After spending most of the day in praise and thanksgiving, we descended to the settlement and held a meeting
with the people.

On the 6th of September we called upon Captain Benjamin Coombs, and visited his flakes, where he had one
thousand quintals of codfish drying for the market. They
had mostly been caught in the region of Newfoundland.
While we were passing Carvey's Wharf our attention was
called to a large school of mackerel playing by the side of
the wharf. Several men were pitching them out with
hooks. We also flung in a hook and caught all we wanted,
then went on our way.

CHAPTER XII

WE CONTINUED to labor, preaching and baptizing, and organized a branch of the Church upon each
island, and, finally, on the second of October, we parted
from the Saints on the North Island to return to Scarboro for a short time.

We walked from Thomaston to Bath, a distance of
forty-six miles, in one day, and at the latter place attended
a Baptist convention. I also preached there to a large congregation in the evening, and the people gave good attention and wished to learn more about our doctrines.

On the following day we walked thirty-six miles to Portland, and the next day to Scarboro. Here I again met with my wife and her father's family.

The time had come for me to give the parting hand to Brother Jonathan H. Hale. We had traveled during the season over two thousand miles together, with our hearts and spirits well united.

He felt it his duty to return to his family in Kirtland, but duty called me to return to my field of labor upon the islands.

On the 9th of October I accompanied Brother Hale one mile upon his journey. We retired to a grove and knelt down and prayed together, and had a good time, and, after commending each other to God, we parted, he to return to Kirtland, and I to Fox Islands.

I spent fourteen days visiting the Saints and friends, and holding meetings among them, and on the 28th of October I took leave of Father Carter and family, and in company with my wife rode to Portland, and spent the night with my brother-in-law, Ezra Carter.

A severe storm arose, so we could not go to sea until November 1st, when we took steamer to Owl's Head, carriage to Thomaston and sloop to Fox Islands.

My second visit to these islands was made under very different circumstances to the first. On my first visit I was an entire stranger to the people, and they were strangers to the gospel, but upon my second I met many Saints who had received the gospel, and who hailed me, and my companion also, with glad hearts.

On Sunday, the 5th of November, I met with a large assembly of Saints and friends, and again commenced baptizing such as would receive my testimony.

After visiting the North Island and holding meetings with the Saints there, and baptizing two after meeting, I embarked on board a sloop, with Captain Coombs, for another island, called the Isle of Holt. We arrived at noon, and I preached to the people at night in their schoolhouse, and had an attentive audience. I spent the night with John Turner, Esq., who purchased a copy of the Book of Mormon.

On the following day we returned to Fox Islands, and as St. Paul once had to row hard to make the land in a storm, we had to row hard to make it in a calm.

After preaching on the North Island again, and baptizing two persons at the close of the meeting, I returned again to the mainland in company with Mrs. Woodruff and others, where I spent fifteen days, during which time I visited among the people, held twelve meetings and baptized several persons.

On the 13th of December I returned again to the North Island, where I held several meetings, and then crossed over to South Island.

On the 20th of December I spent an hour with Mr. Isaac Crockett in clearing away large blocks of ice from the water in a cove, in order to baptize him, which I did when the tide came in. I also baptized two more in the same place on the 26th, and again two others on the 27th.

On the 28th I held a meeting at a schoolhouse, when William Douglass, the Methodist minister, came and wanted me to work a miracle, that he might believe, and otherwise railed against me.

I told him what class of men asked for signs, and that he was a wicked and adulterous man, and predicted that the curse of God would rest upon him, and that his wickedness would be made manifest in the eyes of the people.

(While visiting these islands several years afterwards, I learned that the prediction had really been fulfilled, and that he was serving out a fourteen years' term of imprisonment for a beastly crime.)

Mrs. Woodruff crossed the thoroughfare in a boat and walked ten miles, the length of the island, to meet me, on the last day of the year. I held a meeting the same day in the schoolhouse, and at the close of the meeting baptized two persons in the sea, at full tide before a large assembly.

January 1st, 1838, found me standing upon one of the islands of the sea, a minister of the gospel of life and salvation unto the people, laboring alone, though blessed with the society of Mrs. Woodruff, my companion. I had been declaring the word of the Lord through the islands many days, the Spirit of God was working among the people, prejudice was giving way, and the power of God was manifest by signs following those who believed.

I spent this New Year's Day visiting the Saints and their neighbors, and met a congregation at Captain Charles Brown's, where I spoke to them for awhile; and at the close of my remarks led three persons down into the sea and baptized them. Two of these were sea captains, namely Charles Brown and Jesse Coombs, and the third was the wife of Captain Coombs. After confirming them, we spent the evening in preaching, singing and praying.

I held meetings almost daily with the Saints up to the 13th, when I crossed to the North Island. Here I found that the seed I had sown was bringing forth fruit. Six persons were ready for baptism.

But my mission upon these islands was not an exception to the general rule; success did not come without many obstacles presenting themselves. Those who rejected the word were frequently inspired by the evil one to make an attempt at persecution.

Some of those who felt to oppose me went down to the harbor and got a swivel and small arms, and planted them close by the schoolhouse, near the seashore, and while I was speaking, they commenced firing their cannon and guns. I continued speaking in great plainness, but my voice was mingled with the report of musketry.

I told the people my garments were clear of the blood of the inhabitants of that island, and asked if any wished to embrace the gospel. Two persons came forward and wished to be baptized, and I baptized them.

On the following day when I went down to the seaside to baptize a man, the rabble commenced firing guns again, as on the previous night. I afterwards learned that notices were posted up warning me to leave the town, but I thought it was better to obey God than man, and therefore did not go.

The next day I baptized three persons, and two days subsequently a couple of others.

I had ample evidence of the fact that lying spirits had gone out into the world, for three persons whom I had baptized had been visited by Mr. Douglass, who told them that I denied the Bible and could not be depended upon; and they yielded to his insinuations until the devil took possession of them and they were in a disaffected condition and sent for me.

When I met them they were in great affliction, but when I instructed them in regard to the principles of the gospel, and administered to them, they were delivered from the evil influence and rejoiced.

CHAPTER XIII

ON THE 15th of February I again crossed to the North Island, and after remaining there seven days visiting, we returned to Camden. Here I met Brother James Townsend, who had just arrived from Scarboro.

I ordained Brother Townsend to the office of an Elder, and we concluded to take a journey to Bangor, and offer the gospel to the inhabitants of that city.

We undertook the journey on foot in the dead of winter, when the snow was very deep, and the first day broke the road for seven miles to Scarsmont. The day following, it being Sunday, we held two meetings, preached the gospel to the people, and were kindly entertained.

On the evening of the next day we wallowed through snowdrifts for a mile, to meet an appointment to preach in a schoolhouse, and I got one of my ears frozen on the way; but notwithstanding the severity of the weather, we had quite a large and attentive audience. We also spent the next two days with the people there and held meetings.

On the evening of the 21st of February, as we came out of the schoolhouse, a light appeared in the northeastern horizon, and spread to the west and soon rolled over our heads. It had the appearance of fire, blood and smoke, and at times resembled contending armies. The heavens were illuminated for the space of half an hour. It seemed at times as though the veil was about to rend in twain and the elements were contending with each other.

We looked upon it as one of the signs in the heavens predicted by the prophets of old, as to appear in the last days. We were wading through deep snowdrifts most of the time while witnessing this remarkable scene.

The following day we walked fifteen miles through

deep snow to Belfast, and after being refused lodgings for the night by eight families, we were kindly entertained by Mr. Thomas Teppley.

There was an interesting incident connected with our stay at his house. After eating supper, it being late in the evening, Mr. Teppley placed a stand before me with a Bible upon it, asking me to read a chapter and have prayers with them, he being a religious man.

I opened the Bible mechanically, when, the 25th chapter of Matthew being the first to catch my eye, I read it, and, as I closed the book, Mr. Teppley turned to his wife and said, "Is not this a strange thing?" Then he explained to us that he had just read that chapter and closed the book when we rapped at the door, and he felt impressed to say, "Walk in, gentlemen,"

There is probably no other chapter in the whole book that would have the same influence in causing any one to feed a person who professed to be a servant of God, and asked for bread.

After becoming acquainted with his circumstances I thought it providential that we were led to his house, for although he was a professor of religion and a Methodist, he was in a state of despair, believing he had committed the unpardonable sin.

However, I told him what the unpardonable sin was, and that he had not committed it; but that it was a trick of the devil to make him think so, in order to torment him. He then acknowledged that he went down to the wharf a few evenings before, with the intention of drowning himself, but when he looked into the cold, dark water he desisted and returned home, and had said nothing previous to anyone about it.

I taught him the principles of the gospel, which proved a comfort to him.

We spent the following day in visiting the people of Belfast, and in the evening preached in a brick schoolhouse, provided by Mr. Teppley, and many wished to hear more from us.

We next visited Northport and Frankfort, holding meetings at both places, and on the 1st of March, 1838, we entered Bangor, which at that time had a population of ten thousand. This was my birthday, I being thirty-one years of age.

I visited some of the leading men of Bangor, and they granted me the use of the City Hall, where I preached to good audiences for two successive evenings. This was the first time a Latter-day Saint Elder had preached in that town. Many were anxious to learn more about our principles, but our visits through all the towns from Thomaston to Bangor were necessarily brief, owing to our appointments upon the islands. It was like casting bread upon the waters and trusting in God for the result.

On the 5th of March we sailed from Penobscot for the Isle of Holt, where I held a meeting on the following evening.

The next day I took passage on the mail boat for the North Island, where I again had the privilege of meeting with the Saints for prayer and praise before the Lord.

On my arrival I received a package of letters from friends abroad. One was from Kirtland and gave an account of the apostasy and tribulation which the Saints were passing through. Joseph the prophet and others, with their families, had gone to Far West, and the Saints were following them.

Brother Townsend returned home, and I was again left alone in the ministry.

On the afternoon of the 22nd of March, Brother Sterrett and I, accompanied by our wives, went several hundred yards from shore to a sand bar (it being low tide) to dig clams. The ground near the shore was very much lower than the bar we were on, and while we were all busy digging clams and talking "Mormonism," the dashing of the waves of the incoming tide against the shore suddenly made us conscious that we had fifty yards of water between us and the shore.

The surf waves also added to our difficulty, and, as we had no boat, our only alternative was to cross our four arms, thus forming a kind of arm-chair for our wives to sit upon, and carry them in turn to the shore, wading through two and a half feet of water.

By the time we got our wives and clams safely landed, the truth of the maxim was firmly impressed upon our minds, that "Time and tide wait for no man," not even for a preacher of the gospel.

CHAPTER XIV

ON THE 28th of March, I received a letter from Zion, requesting me to counsel the Saints I had baptized to sell their property and gather up to Zion.

About this time the Lord was manifesting Himself upon the islands in various ways, by dreams, visions, healings, signs and wonders. I will relate one peculiar circumstance of this kind that occurred.

Mr. Ebenezer Carver had been investigating our doctrines for quite a length of time, and, having a great desire to know the truth of our religion, he walked to the seashore, wishing that he might have some manifestation in proof of its truth.

The passage of scripture came to his mind that there would be no sign given "but the sign of the Prophet Jonas," and while this thought was in his mind a large fish arose to the top of the water, a distance from him in the sea, and suddenly sank out of sight. He much desired to see it again, and soon it arose to the top of the water, accompanied by another fish of about the same size, and one of them swam on the water in a straight line towards Mr. Carver as he stood on the shore. It came as near to him as the water would permit; and then stopped and gazed at him with a penetrating eye, as though it had a message for him. It then returned to its mate in the ocean and swam out of sight.

Mr. Carver retraced his steps homeward, meditating upon the scene and the wonderful condescension of the Lord.

It is proper to remark that this was at a season of the year when fish of that size are never known upon those shores or seas, and they are never, at any season, known to come ashore as in the case mentioned.

Mr. Carver was convinced that it was intended by the Lord as a sign to him.

Two days after the event, I visited Mr. Carver at his house, and found his wife confined to her bed with a fever, and she requested me to administer to her. I placed my hands upon her head, the power of God rested upon me, and I commanded her in the name of Jesus Christ to arise and walk.

She arose and was healed from that instant, and she walked down to the sea and I baptized her in the same place where the fish visited her husband. I confirmed her there, and she was filled with the Holy Ghost and returned to her home rejoicing.

I now called the people together and exhorted them to sell their property and prepare to accompany me to the land of Zion. I had labored hard for many days for the temporal and spiritual welfare of the inhabitants of those islands, and the Lord had blessed my labors and given me many souls as seals of my ministry, for which I felt to praise Him; and now I felt to labor quite as zealously to gather out those who had embraced the gospel, and lead them to Zion.

The worst difficulty which the Saints had to contend with in that day was from false brethren. Warren Parrish, who had been a prominent Elder in the Church, and had labored with me as a missionary, had apostatized and been cut off from the Church. Learning that I was building up branches of the Church upon the island, he and other apostates conspired to block up my way by writing lies to the people and stirring up a spirit of mobocracy upon the islands.

They succeeded in exerting a strong influence with the wicked, but I knew they could not hinder the work of God.

On the 6th of April I held a meeting at Brother Ebenezer Carver's, and though the hearts of the wicked were stirred up in bitterness against me, the Spirit of God was with me, and at the close of the meeting I baptized three persons. One of these was Mrs. Abigail Carver, the mother of Ebenezer Carver, who was seventy years of age and in poor health. She had not so much as visited a neighbor's house for six years, but upon this occasion she walked with boldness to the seashore and I baptized her, and she returned rejoicing.

On the 11th of April I had the happy privilege of again meeting with Elders Milton Holmes, James Townsend and Abner Rogers, who had come to the islands to attend conference with me.

We held our conference on the 13th of April, on North Fox Island, and had a representation of the different branches on the islands. We also preached and bore our testimony, ordained several and baptized one person at the close of the meeting.

On the 17th of April Mrs. Woodruff left the island to return to her father's home in Scarboro, Maine, and a few days afterwards I called the Saints of the North Island together and communed with and instructed them. I also informed them that the Spirit of God bore record to me that it was our duty to leave the islands for a season and take a western mission. They had been faithfully warned, and the Saints were established in the truth, while the wicked were contending against us, and some were disposed to take our lives if they had the power.

CHAPTER XV

ON THE 28th of April we left the island in an open sailboat and made our way to Owl's Head, and then walked twenty miles. The following day we walked forty miles and suffered some with weary limbs and blistered feet, but we felt that it was for the gospel's sake and did not choose to complain. The next day a walk of thirty miles brought us to Scarboro, where we spent the night at Father Carter's.

On the 8th of May I parted with Mrs. Woodruff and Father Carter and family, and in company with Milton Holmes walked thirty-three miles toward Portsmouth, which city we reached the following day and spent several hours there, visiting the navy yard. We then walked to Georgetown, formerly New Rowley, and spent the night with Father Nathaniel Holmes.

On the 11th of May I visited Charleston and Bunker Hill monument, and also spent several hours in the city of Boston, which then contained a population of one hundred thousand. I ascended to the cupola of the court-house, from which I had a fine view of the city. I visited several of the Saints in the city, and walked over the long bridge to Cambridge and Cambridgeport.

I visited the jail there in order to have an interview with Brother A. P. Rockwood, who had been cast into prison on the plea of debt, in order to trouble and distress him, because he was a "Mormon." This was the first time we had ever met. The jailor permitted me to enter the room where he was. It was the first time in my life I had ever entered a prison. The jailor turned the key upon us and locked us both in.

I found Brother Rockwood strong in the faith of the gospel. He had the Bible, Book of Mormon, Voice of Warning, and *Evening and Morning Star* as his companions, which he read daily.

We conversed together for three hours in this solitary abode. He informed me of many things which had transpired while he was confined there as a prisoner. Among other things, he mentioned that the jail had taken fire a few days previous to my visit. He said it looked a little like a dark hour. The fire was roaring over his head, while uproar and confusion were upon every hand. Fire engines were rapidly playing around the building, with water pouring into every room. The people were hallooing in the streets. Prisoners were begging for mercy's sake to be let out, or they would be consumed in the fire. One was

struggling in the agonies of death, while others were curs-
ing and swearing. Brother Rockwood said he felt composed in the midst of it until the fire was extinguished.

At eight o'clock the jailor unlocked the prison door to
let me out, and I gave the parting hand to the prisoner of
hope.

We had spent a pleasant time together, and he rejoiced at my visit; and who would not, to meet with a
friend in a lonely prison? I left him in good spirits, and
wended my way back to Boston.

I spent several days in Boston, holding meetings with
the Saints there, and then walked to Providence, Rhode
Island, preaching by the way.

I there took steamer and arrived in New York on the
18th of May, where I met with Elder Orson Pratt and his
family, and Elijah Fordham, and near one hundred Saints
who had been baptized in the city of New York.

I spent three days in New York visiting the Saints and
holding meetings. Several new converts were baptized
while I was there.

Leaving New York, I traveled through New Jersey,
and returned to Farmington, Connecticut, the residence
of my father. I arrived at his house on the 12th of June.

It was with peculiar sensations that I walked over my
native land, where I spent my youth, and cast my eyes
over the Farmington meadows and the hills and dales
where I had roamed in my boyhood with my father, step-
mother, brothers and half-sister.

On my arrival at my father's home I had the happy
privilege of once more taking my parents and sister by the
hand, also my uncle, Ozem Woodruff, who was among the
number I had baptized the year before.

After spending an hour in conversation, we sat down around our father's table and supped together and were refreshed. Then we bowed upon our knees together in the family circle and offered up the gratitude of our hearts to God for preserving our lives and reuniting us.

I spent the next eighteen days in Farmington and Avon, visiting my father's household, my uncles, aunts, cousins, neighbors and friends, preaching the gospel of Jesus Christ unto them and striving to bring them into the kingdom of God.

On the 1st of July, 1838, one of the most interesting events transpired of my whole life in the ministry.

When Father Joseph Smith gave me my patriarchal blessing, among the many wonderful things of my life, he promised me that I should bring my father's household into the kingdom of God, and I felt that if I ever obtained the blessing, the time had come for me to perform it.

By the help of God, I preached the gospel faithfully to my father's household and to all that were with him, as well as to my other relatives, and I had appointed a meeting on Sunday, the 1st of July, at my father's home.

My father was believing my testimony, as were all in his household, but upon this occasion the devil was determined to hinder the fulfillment of the promise of the patriarch unto me.

It seemed as though Lucifer, the son of the morning, had gathered together the hosts of hell and exerted his powers upon us all. Distress overwhelmed the whole household, and all were tempted to reject the work. And it seemed as though the same power would devour me. I had to take to my bed for an hour before the time of meeting. I there prayed unto the Lord with my whole soul for deliverance, for I knew the power of the devil was exercised to hinder me from accomplishing what God had promised me.

The Lord heard my prayer and answered my petition, and when the hour of meeting had come I arose from my bed, and could sing and shout for joy to think I had been delivered from the power of the evil one.

Filled with the power of God, I stood up in the midst of the congregation and preached the gospel of Jesus Christ unto the people in great plainness.

At the close of the meeting we assembled on the banks of the Farmington river, "because there was much water there," and I led six of my friends into the river and baptized them for the remission of their sins.

All of my father's household were included in this number, according to the promise of the Patriarch. They were all relatives except Dwight Webster, who was a Methodist class-leader and was boarding with my father's family.

I organized the small number of nine persons, eight of whom were my relatives, into a branch of the Church, and ordained Dwight Webster to the office of a Priest and administered the sacrament unto them.

It was truly a day of joy to my soul. My father, stepmother and sister were among the number baptized. I afterwards added a number of relatives. I felt that this day's work alone amply repaid me for all my labor in the ministry.

Who can comprehend the joy, the glory, the happiness and consolation that an Elder of Israel feels in being an instrument in the hands of God of bringing his father, mother, sister, brother, or any of the posterity of Adam through the door that enters into life and salvation? No man can, unless he has experienced these things, and possesses the testimony of Jesus Christ and the inspiration of Almighty God.

CHAPTER XVI

NOW, as my mission to my native land was accomplished, which I felt impressed to take while upon the islands, I felt it my duty to return here.

Monday, July 2nd, 1838, was the last day and night I spent at my father's home while upon this mission. At the setting of the sun I took the last walk with my sister I ever had with her while in my native State. We walked by the canal and viewed the river and fields, and conversed upon our future destiny.

After evening prayer with the family, my father retired to rest, and I spent a season with my step-mother who had reared me from my infancy. In conversation we felt sensibly the weight of the power of temptation, out of which the Lord had delivered us.

I also spent a short time with my sister Eunice, the only sister I was ever blessed with in my father's family. I had baptized her into the Church and Kingdom of God and we mingled our sympathies, prayers and tears together before the throne of grace.

How truly are the bonds of consanguinity and of the blood of Christ united in binding the hearts of the Saints of God together, and "how blessings brighten as they take their flight!"

This being the last night I was to spend beneath my father's roof while upon this mission, I felt the weight of it, and my prayer was, "O, Lord, protect my father's house, and bring him to Zion!" (which prayer was granted).

On the morning of July 3rd, I took leave of my relatives and my native land, and started on my return to Maine.

I arrived in Scarboro on the 6th, and on the 24th my first child—a daughter—was born, at Father Carter's house. We named her Sarah Emma.

On the 30th of July I left my wife and child at Father Carter's and started once more to visit Fox Islands.

While holding meeting with the Saints at North Vinal Haven on the 9th of August I received a letter from Thomas B. Marsh, who was then President of the Twelve Apostles, informing me that Joseph Smith, the Prophet, had received a revelation, naming as persons to be chosen to fill the places of those who had fallen: John E. Page, John Taylor, Wilford Woodruff and Willard Richards.

President Marsh added, in his letter, "Know then, Brother Woodruff, by this, that you are appointed to fill the place of one of the Twelve Apostles, and that it is agreeable to the word of the Lord, given very lately, that you should come speedily to Far West, and, on the 26th of April next, take your leave of the Saints here and depart for other climes across the mighty deep."

The substance of this letter had been revealed to me several weeks before, but I had not named it to any person.

The time having now come for me to prepare for leaving the islands, I had a desire to take with me all the Saints I could get to go to Zion. There had already been a line drawn upon the islands between the Saints and those who had rejected the gospel, and the enemies were very bitter against me and the work of God I had labored to establish. They threatened my life, but the Saints were willing to stand by me.

I spent four days with the Saints, visiting them, holding meetings and encouraging them, while the devil was raging upon every hand.

I had baptized and organized into the Church nearly one hundred persons while upon the islands, and there seemed a prospect of gathering about half of them with me, but the devil raged to such an extent that quite a number were terrified.

The inhabitants of the islands had but little acquaintance with the management of horses or wagons; in fact, most of them knew more about handling a shark than a horse. However, in company with Nathaniel Thomas, who had sold his property and had money, I went to the mainland and purchased ten new wagons, ten sets of harness and twenty horses. When I got everything prepared for the company to start, I left the affairs with Brother Thomas, and went on ahead of the company to Scarboro, to prepare my own family for the journey.

The outfit which I purchased for the company cost about $2,000.00.

Before leaving Brother Thomas, I counseled him in regard to the course to pursue, and charged him not to be later than the 1st of September in starting for the mainland.

I arrived at Father Carter's on the 19th of August, and waited with great anxiety for the arrival of the company from the islands, but instead of reaching there by the 1st of September they did not arrive till the 3rd of October; and when they did arrive the wagon covers were all flying in the breeze. It took a good day's work to nail down the covers, paint the wagons and get prepared for the journey.

CHAPTER XVII

O N THE afternoon of the 9th of October, we took leave of Father Carter and family, and started upon our journey of 2,000 miles at this late season of the year, taking my wife with a suckling babe at her breast with me, to lead a company of fifty-three souls from Maine to Illinois, and to spend nearly three months in traveling in wagons, through rain, mud, snow and frost. It was such a trial as I never before had attempted during my experience as a minister of the gospel.

On our arrival at Georgetown we were joined by Elder Milton Holmes. We traveled each day as far as we could go, and camped wherever night overtook us.

On the 13th of October, while crossing the Green Mountains, I was attacked with something resembling the cholera. I was very sick. I stopped at a house for about two hours, but the Elders administered to me, and I revived.

On the 24th I was again taken sick, and my wife and child were also striken down. We had several others sick in the company, through the exposure of the journey.

On the 31st we had our first snow-storm, and the horses dragged our wagons all day through mud, snow and water.

On the 2nd of November Elder Milton Holmes left us, and took steamer for Fairport; and two days afterwards a little boy of Nathaniel Holmes', about six years of age, died, and we had to bury him at Westfield.

The roads finally became so bad and the cold so severe that Nathaniel Thomas and James Townsend concluded to stop for the winter. We parted with them on the 21st of November, near New Portage, Ohio.

On the 23rd of November my wife, Phoebe, was attacked with a severe headache, which terminated in brain fever. She grew more and more distressed daily as we continued our journey. It was a terrible ordeal for a woman to travel in a wagon over rough roads, afflicted as she was. At the same time our child was also very sick.

The 1st of December was a trying day to my soul. My wife continued to fail, and in the afternoon, about 4 o'clock, she appeared to be struck with death. I stopped my team, and it seemed as though she would breathe her last lying in the wagon. Two of the sisters sat beside her, to see if they could do anything for her in her last moments.

I stood upon the ground, in deep affliction, and meditated. I cried unto the Lord, and prayed that she might live and not be taken from me. I claimed the promises the Lord had made unto me through the prophets and patriarchs, and soon her spirit revived, and I drove a short distance to a tavern, and got her into a room and worked over her and her babe all night, and prayed to the Lord to preserve her life.

In the morning the circumstances were such that I was under the necessity of removing my wife from the inn, as there was so much noise and confusion at the place that she could not endure it. I carried her out to her bed in the wagon and drove two miles, when I alighted at a house and carried my wife and her bed into it, with a determination to tarry there until she either recovered her health or passed away. This was on Sunday morning, December 2nd.

After getting my wife and things into the house and wood provided to keep up a fire, I employed my time in taking care of her. It looked as though she had but a short time to live.

She called me to her bedside in the evening and said she felt as though a few moments more would end her existence in this life. She manifested great confidence in the cause she had embraced, and exhorted me to have confidence in God and to keep His commandments.

To all appearances, she was dying. I laid hands upon her and prayed for her, and she soon revived and slept some during the night.

December 3rd found my wife very low. I spent the day in taking care of her, and the following day I returned to Eaton to get some things for her. She seemed to be gradually sinking and in the evening her spirit apparently left her body, and she was dead.

The sisters gathered around her body, weeping, while I stood looking at her in sorrow. The spirit and power of God began to rest upon me until, for the first time during her sickness, faith filled my soul, although she lay before me as one dead.

I had some oil that was consecrated for my anointing while in Kirtland. I took it and consecrated it again before the Lord for anointing the sick. I then bowed down before the Lord and prayed for the life of my companion, and I anointed her body with the oil in the name of the Lord. I laid my hands upon her, and in the name of Jesus Christ I rebuked the power of death and the destroyer, and commanded the same to depart from her, and the spirit of life to enter her body.

Her spirit returned to her body, and from that hour she was made whole; and we all felt to praise the name of God, and to trust in Him and to keep His commandments.

While this operation was going on with me (as my wife related afterwards) her spirit left her body, and she saw it lying upon the bed, and the sisters weeping. She looked at them and at me, and upon her babe, and, while gazing upon this scene, two personages came into the room carrying a coffin and told her they had come for her body. One of these messengers informed her that she could have her choice: she might go to rest in the spirit world, or, on one condition she could have the privilege of returning to her tabernacle and continuing her labors upon the earth. The condition was, if she felt that she could stand by her husband, and with him pass through all the cares, trials, tribulation and afflictions of life which he would be called to pass through for the gospel's sake unto the end. When she looked at the situation of her husband and child she said: "Yes, I will do it!"

At the moment that decision was made the power of faith rested upon me, and when I administered unto her, her spirit entered her tabernacle, and she saw the messengers carry the coffin out at the door.

On the morning of the 6th of December, the Spirit said to me: "Arise, and continue thy journey!" and through the mercy of God my wife was enabled to arise and dress herself and walked to the wagon, and we went on our way rejoicing.

On the night of the 11th I stopped for the night at an inn, the weather being very cold. I there learned of the sudden death of my brother, Asahel H. Woodruff, a merchant of Terre Haute, Ind.

I had anticipated a joyful meeting with this brother on the following day. Instead of this, I only had the privilege of visiting his grave, in company with my wife, and examining a little into his business.

I was offered the position of administrator of his affairs, but I was leading a company of Saints to Zion, and could not stop to attend to his temporal business. Strangers settled his affairs, and took possession of his property. His relatives obtained nothing from his effects except a few trifling mementos.

I left this place and crossed into Illinois on the 13th of December, and arrived at Rochester on the 19th, and, getting information of the severe persecutions of the Saints in Missouri and the unsettled state of the Church at that time, we concluded to stop at Rochester and spend the winter.

Thus ended my journey of two months and sixteen days, leading the Fox Island Saints to the west, through all the perils of a journey of nearly two thousand miles, in the midst of sickness and great severity of weather.

I took my family in the spring and removed to Quincy, Illinois, where I could mingle with my brethren, and I felt to praise God for His protecting care over me and my family in all our afflictions.

CHAPTER XVIII

JOSEPH SMITH, the Prophet, asked the Lord what His will was concerning the Twelve, and the Lord answered in a revelation, given July 8th, 1838, in which He says: "Let them take leave of my Saints in the city Far West, on the 26th day of April next, on the building spot of my house, saith the Lord. Let my servant John Taylor, and also my servant John E. Page, and also my servant Wilford Woodruff, and also my servant Willard Richards, be appointed to fill the places of those who have fallen, and be officially notified of their appointment."

It will be observed that this differs from nearly all other revelations in this respect: a fixed day and a stated place were given for the commencement of the mission. When the revelation was given, all was peace and quietude in Far West, Missouri, the city where most of the Latter-day Saints dwelt; but before the time came for its fulfillment, the Saints of God had been driven out of the State of Missouri into the State of Illinois, under the edict of Governor Boggs, and the Missourians had sworn that if all the other revelations of Joseph Smith were fulfilled, that should not be. It stated that the day and the place where the Twelve Apostles should take leave of the Saints, to go on their missions across the great waters, and the mobocrats of Missouri had declared that they would see that it should not be fulfilled.

It seemed as though the Lord, having a foreknowledge of what would take place, had given the revelation in this manner to see whether the Apostles would obey it at the risk of their lives.

When the time drew near for the fulfillment of this commandment of the Lord, Brigham Young was the President of the Twelve Apostles; Thos. B. Marsh, who was the senior Apostle, had fallen. Brother Brigham called together those of the Twelve who were then at Quincy, Illinois, to see what their minds would be about going to Far West, to fulfill the revelation. The Prophet Joseph and his brother Hyrum, Sidney Rigdon, Lyman Wight and Parley P. Pratt were in prison in Missouri, at the time; but Father Joseph Smith, the Patriarch, was at Quincy, Illinois. He and others who were present did not think it wisdom for us to attempt the journey, as our lives would be in great jeopardy. They thought the Lord would take the will for the deed. But when President Young asked the Twelve what our feelings were upon the subject, we all of us, as the voice of one man, said the Lord God had spoken, and it was for us to obey. It was the Lord's business to take care of His servants, and we would fulfill the commandment, or die trying.

To fully understand the risk the Twelve Apostles ran in making this journey, my readers should remember that Lilburn W. Boggs, governor of the State of Missouri, had issued a proclamation, in which all the Latter-day Saints were required to leave that State or be exterminated. Far West had been captured by the militia, who were really only an organized mob; the citizens had been compelled to give up their arms; all the leading men who could be got hold of had been taken prisoners; the rest of the Saints—men, women and children—had to flee as best they could out of the State to save their lives, leaving all their houses, lands and other property which they could not carry with them to be taken by the mob. In fact they shot down the cattle and hogs of the Saints wherever they could find them, and robbed them of nearly everything they could lay their hands upon. Latter-day Saints were treated with merciless cruelty and had to endure the most outrageous abuses. It was with the greatest difficulty that many of them got out of the State, especially the prominent men; for there were many men of that State at that time, who acted as though they thought it no more harm to shoot a "Mormon" than a mad dog. From this brief explanation you will be able to understand why some of the brethren thought we were not required to go back to Far West to start from there upon our mission across the ocean to Europe.

Having determined to carry out the requirement of the revelation, on the 18th of April, 1839, I took into my wagon Brigham Young and Orson Pratt; and Father Cutler took into his wagon John Taylor and George A. Smith, and we started for Far West.

On the way we met John E. Page, who was going with his family, to Quincy, Illinois. His wagon had turned over, and when we met him he was trying to gather up a barrel of soft soap with his hands. We helped him get up his wagon. He drove down into the valley below, left his wagon, and accompanied us on our way.

On the night of the 25th of April, we arrived at Far West, and spent the night at the home of Morris Phelps, who was not there, however, himself; he, having been taken prisoner by the mob, was still in prison.

On the morning of the 26th of April, 1839, notwithstanding the threats of our enemies that the revelation which was to be fulfilled this day should not be, and notwithstanding that ten thousand of the Saints had been driven out of the State by the edict of the governor, and though the Prophet Joseph and his brother, Hyrum Smith, with other leading men were in the hands of our enemies, in chains, and in prison, we moved on to the temple grounds in the city of Far West, and held a council, and fulfilled the revelation and commandment given unto us, and we performed many other things at this council.

We excommunicated from the Church thirty-one persons, who had apostatized and become its enemies.

The "Mission of the Twelve" was sung, and we then repaired to the south-east corner of the temple ground, and, with the assistance of Elder Alpheus Cutler, the master workman of the building committee, laid the southeast chief corner stone of the temple, according to revelation.

There were present of the Twelve Apostles: Brigham

Young, Heber C. Kimball, Orson Pratt, John E. Page
and John Taylor, who proceeded to ordain Wilford
Woodruff and George A. Smith, to the apostleship, and
as members of the quorum of the Twelve, in the places of
those who had fallen, as they had been called by revelation.

Darwin Chase and Norman Shearer, who had just
been liberated from Richmond prison, were also ordained
to the office of Seventies. The Twelve then offered up
vocal prayer in the following order: Brigham Young,
Heber C. Kimball, Orson Pratt, John E. Page, John
Taylor, Wilford Woodruff and George A. Smith, after
which we sang "Adam-ondi-Ahman."

The Twelve then took their leave of, and gave the
parting hand to, the following Saints, agreeable to reve-
lation: A. Butler, Elias Smith, Norman Shearer, Wm.
Burton, Stephen Markham, Shadrach Roundy, Wm. O.
Clark, John W. Clark, Hezekiah Peck, Darwin Chase,
Richard Howard, Mary Ann Peck, Artimesia Granger,
Martha Peck, Sarah Granger, Theodore Turley, Hiram
Clark, and Daniel Shearer.

Bidding good-by to the small remnant of the Saints
who remained on the temple ground to see us fulfill the
revelation and commandments of God, we turned our
backs on Far West and Missouri, and returned to Illinois.
We had accomplished the mission without a dog moving
his tongue at us, or any man saying, "Why do you do so?"

We crossed the Mississippi river on the steam ferry,
entered Quincy on the 2nd of May, and all had the joy of
reaching our families once more in peace and safety.

There was an incident connected with our journey that
is worthy of record. While we were on our way to fulfill
the revelation, Joseph, the Prophet, and his companions in
chains had been liberated, through the blessings of God,

from their enemies and prison, and they passed us. We were not far distant from each other, but neither party knew it. They were making their way to their families in Illinois, while we were traveling to Far West into the midst of our enemies. So they came home to their families and friends before our return.

May the 3rd was a very interesting day to me, as well as to others. In company with five others of the quorum of the Twelve, I rode four miles out of town to Mr. Cleveland's, to visit Brother Joseph Smith and his family.

Once more I had the happy privilege of taking Brother Joseph by the hand. Two years had rolled away since I had seen his face. He greeted us with great joy, as did Hyrum Smith and Lyman Wight, all of whom had escaped from their imprisonment together. They had been confined in prison six months, and had been under sentence of death three times; yet their lives were in the hands of God, and He had delivered them, and they were now mingling with their wives, children and friends, and out of the reach of the mob. Joseph was frank, open and familiar as usual, and our rejoicing was great.

No man can understand the joyful sensations created by such a meeting, except those who have been in tribulation for the gospel's sake.

After spending the day together, we returned to our families at night.

On the day following, May 4th, we met in conference at Quincy, the Prophet Joseph presiding, which caused great joy and rejoicing to all the Saints.

On Sunday, May 5th, Joseph Smith addressed the assembly, followed by Sidney Rigdon and the Twelve Apostles. The Spirit of the Lord was poured out upon us, and we had a glorious day.

On May 6th, I met with the Seventies, and we ordained sixty men into the quorums of Elders and Seventies. Brother Joseph met with the Twelve, Bishops and Elders, at Bishop Partridge's house; and there were a number with us who were wounded at Haun's Mill. Among them was Isaac Laney, who had been, in company with about twenty others, at the mill, when a large armed mob fired among them with rifles and other weapons, and shot down seventeen of the brethren, and wounded more. Brother Laney fled from the scene, but they poured a shower of lead after him, which pierced his body through and through. He showed me eleven bullet holes in his body. There were twenty-seven in his shirt, seven in his pantaloons, and his coat was literally cut to pieces. One ball entered one arm-pit and came out at the other.

Another entered his back and came out at the breast. A ball passed through each hip, each leg and each arm. All these shots were received while he was running for life, and, strange as it may appear, though he had also one of his ribs broken, he was able to outrun his enemies, and his life was saved. We can only acknowledge this deliverance to be by the power and mercy of God.

President Brigham Young was also among the number. He also fled, and although the balls flew around him like hail, he was not wounded. How mysterious are the ways of the Lord!

Before starting on our missions to England, we were under the necessity of settling our families. A place called Commerce, afterwards named Nauvoo, was selected as the place at which our people should settle.

I left Quincy, in company with Brother Brigham Young and our families on the 15th of May, and arrived in Commerce on the 18th. After an interview with Joseph we crossed the river at Montrose, Iowa. President Brigham Young and myself, with our families, occupied one room about fourteen feet square. Finally Brother Young obtained another room and moved his family into it. Then Brother Orson Pratt and family moved into the same room with myself and family.

CHAPTER XIX

WHILE I was living in this cabin in the old barracks, we experienced a day of God's power with the Prophet Joseph. It was a very sickly time and Joseph had given up his home in Commerce to the sick, and had a tent pitched in his door-yard and was living in that himself. The large number of Saints who had been driven out of Missouri, were flocking into Commerce; but had no homes to go into, and were living in wagons, in tents, and on the ground. Many, therefore, were sick through the exposure they were subjected to. Brother Joseph had waited on the sick, until he was worn out and nearly sick himself.

On the morning of the 22nd of July, 1839, he arose, reflecting upon the situation of the Saints of God in their persecutions and afflictions, and he called upon the Lord in prayer, and the power of God rested upon him mightily, and as Jesus healed all the sick around Him in His day, so Joseph, the Prophet of God, healed all around on this occasion. He healed all in his house and door-yard, then, in company with Sidney Rigdon and several of the Twelve, he went among the sick lying on the bank of the river and he commanded them in a loud voice, in the name of Jesus Christ, to come up and be made whole, and they were all healed. When he healed all that were sick on the east side of the river, they crossed the Mississippi river in a ferry-boat to the west side, to Montrose, where we were. The first house they went into was President Brigham Young's. He was sick on his bed at the time. The Prophet went into his house and healed him, and they all came out together. As they were passing by my door, Brother Joseph said: "Brother Woodruff, follow me." These were the only words spoken by any of the company from the time they left Brother Brigham's house till we crossed the public square, and entered Brother Fordham's house. Brother Fordham had been dying for an hour, and we expected each minute would be his last.

I felt the power of God that was overwhelming His Prophet.

When we entered the house, Brother Joseph walked up to Brother Fordham, and took him by the right hand; in his left hand he held his hat.

He saw that Brother Fordham's eyes were glazed, and that he was speechless and unconscious.

After taking hold of his hand, he looked down into the dying man's face and said: "Brother Fordham, do you not know me?" At first he made no reply; but we could all see the effect of the Spirit of God resting upon him.

He again said: "Elijah, do you not know me?"

With a low whisper, Brother Fordham answered, "Yes!"

The Prophet then said, "Have you not faith to be healed?"

The answer, which was a little plainer than before, was: "I am afraid it is too late. If you had come sooner, I think I might have been."

He had the appearance of a man waking from sleep. It was the sleep of death.

Joseph then said: "Do you believe that Jesus is the Christ?"

"I do, Brother Joseph," was the response.

Then the Prophet of God spoke with a loud voice, as in the majesty of the Godhead: "Elijah, I command you, in the name of Jesus of Nazareth, to arise and be made whole!"

The words of the Prophet were not like the words of man, but like the voice of God. It seemed to me that the house shook from its foundation.

Elijah Fordham leaped from his bed like a man raised from the dead. A healthy color came to his face, and life was manifested in every act.

His feet were done up in Indian meal poultices. He kicked them off his feet, scattered the contents, and then called for his clothes and put them on. He asked for a bowl of bread and milk, and ate it; then put on his hat and followed us into the street, to visit others who were sick.

The unbeliever may ask: "Was there not deception in this?"

If there is any deception in the mind of the unbeliever, there was certainly none with Elijah Fordham, the dying man, nor with those who were present with him, for in a few minutes more he would have been in the spirit world, had he not been rescued. Through the blessing of God, he lived up till 1880, in which year he died in Utah, while all who were with him on that occasion, with the exception of one, are in the spirit world.

Among the number, were Joseph and Hyrum Smith, Sidney Rigdon, Brigham Young, Heber C. Kimball, George A. Smith, Parley P. Pratt and Orson Pratt. Wilford Woodruff is the only one living who was present at the time, and he will soon mingle with those who have gone.

As soon as we left Brother Fordham's house, we went

into the house of Joseph B. Noble, who was very low and dangerously sick.

When we entered the house, Brother Joseph took him by the hand, and commanded him, in the name of Jesus Christ, to arise and be made whole. He did arise and was immediately healed.

While this was going on, the wicked mob in the place, led by one Kilburn, had become alarmed, and followed us into Brother Noble's house.

Before they arrived there, Brother Joseph had called upon Brother Fordham to offer prayer.

While he was praying the mob entered, with all the evil spirits accompanying them.

As soon as they entered, Brother Fordham, who was praying, fainted and sank to the floor.

When Joseph saw the mob in the house, he arose and had the room cleared of both that class of men and their attendant devils. Then Brother Fordham immediately revived and finished his prayer.

This shows what power evil spirits have upon the tabernacles of men. The Saints are only saved from the power of the devil by the power of God.

This case of Brother Noble's was the last one of healing upon that day. It was the greatest day for the manifestation of the power of God through the gift of healing since the organization of the Church.

When we left Brother Noble, the Prophet Joseph went with those who accompanied him from the other side, to the banks of the river, to return home.

While waiting for the ferry-boat, a man of the world, knowing of the miracles which had been performed, came to him and asked him if he would not go and heal two twin children of his, about five months old, who were both lying sick nigh unto death.

They were some two miles from Montrose.

The Prophet said he could not go; but, after pausing some time, he said he would send some one to heal them; and he turned to me and said: "You go with the man and heal his children."

He took a red silk handkerchief out of his pocket and gave it to me, and told me to wipe their faces with the handkerchief when I administered to them, and they should be healed. He also said unto me: "As long as you will keep that handkerchief, it shall remain a league between you and me."

I went with the man, and did as the Prophet commanded me, and the children were healed.

I have possession of the handkerchief unto this day.

CHAPTER XX

ON THE first of July, 1839, Joseph Smith and his counselors, Sidney Rigdon and Hyrum Smith, crossed the river to Montrose, to spend the day with the Twelve, and set them apart and bless them, before they started upon their missions. There were twelve of us who met there, and we all dined in my house.

After dinner, we assembled at Brother Brigham Young's house for our meeting.

Brother Hyrum Smith opened by prayer; after which the Presidency laid their hands upon our heads and gave each of us a blessing.

President Rigdon was mouth in blessing me, and also blessed Sisters Young, Taylor and Woodruff.

The Prophet Joseph promised us if we would be faithful, we should be blessed upon our mission, have many souls as seals of our ministry, and return again in peace and safety to our families and friends; all of which was fulfilled.

Brother Hyrum advised me to preach the first principles of the gospel; he thought that was about as much as this generation could endure.

Then Joseph arose and preached some precious things of the Kingdom of God unto us, in the power of the Holy Ghost; some of which I here copy from my journal:

"Ever keep in exercise the principle of mercy, and be ready to forgive our brethren on the first intimation of their repentance and desire for forgiveness; for our Heavenly Father will be equally as merciful unto us. We also ought to be willing to repent of and confess our sins, and keep nothing back. Let the Twelve be humble and not be exalted, and beware of pride and not seek to excel one another, but act for each other's good, and honorably make mention of each other's names in prayer before the Lord and before your fellow-men. Do not backbite or devour a brother. The Elders of Israel should seek to learn by precept and example in this late age of the world and not be obliged to learn everything we know by sad experience. I trust the remainder of the Twelve will learn wisdom and not follow the example of those who have fallen. When the Twelve or any other witnesses of Jesus Christ, stand before the congregations of the earth, and they preach in the power and demonstration of the Holy Ghost, and the people are astonished and confounded at the doctrine, and say, 'That man has preached a powerful sermon'; then let that man or those men take care that they do not ascribe the glory unto themselves, but be careful that they are humble, and ascribe the glory to God and the Lamb; for it is by the power of the Holy Priesthood and the Holy Ghost that they have power thus to speak.

"Who art thou, O man, but dust, and from whom dost thou receive thy power and blessings, but from God?

"Then let the Twelve Apostles and Elders of Israel observe this key, and be wise: *Ye are not sent out to be taught but to teach.*

"Let every man be sober, be vigilant, and let all his words be seasoned with grace, and keep in mind it is a day of warning, and not of many words.

"Act honestly before God and man; beware of sophistry, such as bowing and scraping unto men in whom you have no confidence. Be honest, open and frank in all your intercourse with mankind.

"I wish to say to the Twelve and all the Saints to profit by this important key, that in all your trials, troubles, temptations, afflictions, bonds, imprisonments and deaths, see to it that you do not betray Jesus Christ, that you do not betray the revelations of God, whether in the Bible, Book of Mormon, or Doctrine and Covenants, or any of the words of God.

"Yea, in all your troubles, see that you do not this thing, lest innocent blood be found upon your skirts, and ye go down to hell.

"We may ever know by this sign that there is danger of our being led to a fall and apostasy when we give way to the devil, so as to neglect the first known duty; but whatever you do, do not betray your friend."

The foregoing are some of the instructions given to the Twelve by the Prophet Joseph, before they started upon their missions.

Inasmuch as the devil had been in a measure thwarted

by the Twelve going to Far West, and returning without harm, it seemed as though the destroyer was determined to make some other attempt upon us to hinder us from performing our missions; for it seemed that as soon as any one of the Apostles began to prepare for starting, he was smitten with chills and fever or sickness of some kind.

Nearly all of the quorum of the Twelve or their families began to be sick, so it still required the exercise of a good deal of faith and perseverance to start off on a mission.

On the 25th of July, for the first time in my life, I was attacked with chills and fever; and this I had every other day, and, whenever attacked, I was laid prostrate.

My wife, Phoebe, was also soon taken down with the chills and fever, as were quite a number of the Twelve.

I passed thirteen days in Montrose with my family, after I was taken sick, before I started on my mission.

The 7th of August was the last day I spent at home in Montrose, and although sick with the chills and fever the most of the day, I made what preparations I could to start on the morrow on a mission of four thousand miles, to preach the gospel to the nations of the earth, and this, too, without purse or scrip, with disease resting upon me, and a stroke of fever and ague once every two days.

Yet I did this freely, for Christ's sake, trusting in Him for the recompense or reward. My prayer was: "May the Lord give me grace according to my day and souls for my hire, and a safe return to my family and friends, which favor I ask in the name of Jesus Christ. Amen."

CHAPTER XXI

EARLY upon the morning of the 8th of August, 1839, I arose from my bed of sickness, laid my hands upon the head of my sick wife, Phoebe, and blessed her. I then departed from the embrace of my companion, and left her almost without food or the necessaries of life.

She parted from me with the fortitude that becomes a Saint, realizing the responsibilities of her companion. I quote from my journal:

"Phoebe, farewell! Be of good cheer; remember me in your prayers. I leave these pages for your perusal when I am gone. I shall see thy face again in the flesh. I go to obey the commands of Jesus Christ."

Although feeble, I walked to the banks of the Mississippi river. There President Brigham Young took me in a canoe (having no other conveyance) and paddled me across the river.

When we landed, I lay down on a side of sole leather, by the post office, to rest.

Brother Joseph, the Prophet of God, came along and looked at me.

"Well, Brother Woodruff," said he, "you have started upon your mission."

"Yes," said I, "but I feel and look more like a subject for the dissecting room than a missionary."

Joseph replied: "What did you say that for? Get up, and go along; all will be right with you!"

I name these incidents that the reader may know how the brethren of the Twelve Apostles started upon their missions to England, in 1839.

Elder John Taylor was going with me, and we were

the first two of the quorum of the Twelve who started on their mission.

Brother Taylor was about the only man in the quorum that was not sick.

Soon a brother came along with a wagon, and took us in. As we were driving through the place, we came to Parley P. Pratt, who was stripped to the shirt and pants with his head and feet bare. He was hewing a log, preparing to build a cabin.

He said: "Brother Woodruff, I have no money, but I have an empty purse, which I will give you." He brought it to me, and I thanked him for it.

We went a few rods further, and met Brother Heber C. Kimball, in the same condition, also hewing a log, towards building a cabin.

He said: "As Parley has given you a purse, I have got a dollar I will give you to put in it."

He gave me both a dollar and a blessing.

We drove sixteen miles across a prairie, and spent the night with a Brother Merrill. The day following we rode ten miles, to a Brother Perkins', and he took us in his wagon to Macomb, and from thence to Brother Don Carlos Smith's.

I rode four hours during the day over a very rough road of stones and stumps, lying on my back in the bottom of the wagon, shaking with the ague, and I suffered much.

We held a meeting in a grove near Don Carlos Smith's and here Elder Taylor baptized George Miller, who afterwards was ordained a Bishop.

At the meeting the Saints gave us nine dollars, and George Miller gave us a horse to help us on our journey.

I rode to Rochester with Father Coltrin, where I had an interview with several families of the Fox Island Saints, whom I had brought up with me from Fox Islands, in 1838. I spent several days with them and at Springfield, where Elder Taylor published fifteen hundred copies, in pamphlet form, of a brief sketch of the persecutions and sufferings of the Latter-day Saints, inflicted by the inhabitants of Missouri.

We sold our horse and in company with Father Coltrin, Brother Taylor and myself left Springfield, and continued our journey.

I had the chills and fever nearly every other day, which made riding in a lumber wagon very distressing to me, especially when I shook with the ague.

On the 24th of August, we rode to Terre Haute, and spent the night with Dr. Modisett. I suffered much with the chills and fever.

Elder John Taylor up to this time had appeared to enjoy excellent health, but the destroyer did not intend to make him an exception to the rest of the Apostles. On the 28th of August, he fell to the ground as though he had been knocked down. He fainted away, but soon revived. On the following day, however, the enemy made a powerful attack upon his life. He fainted away several times, and it seemed as though he would die. We stopped several hours with him at a house by the wayside. We then took him into the wagon and drove to Horace S. Eldredge's, and spent the remainder of the day and night doctoring him.

In the morning Brother Taylor was so far recovered that he thought he would be able to ride. So we started on our journey on the morning of the 30th, and we traveled forty miles, to Louisville, and spent the night with the family of Brother James Townsend.

We felt terribly shaken up, being in such a weak state. Brother Townsend was away from home, but we were kindly entertained by Sister Townsend.

In the morning, Elder Taylor, though very weak, felt disposed to continue his journey. We traveled fourteen miles to Germantown. He was quite sick at night, and the bilious fever seemed to settle upon him. I was also very feeble myself.

On the day following, September 1st, being Sunday, Brother Taylor concluded to remain there for the day, and hold a meeting.

It was a German settlement. He wished me to speak, and I spoke upon the first principles of the gospel. He followed me, and spoke until he was exhausted.

After we returned to the inn where we were stopping, I was taken with a chill and fever, and had a very bad night. Brother Taylor was also very sick.

The following day, September 2nd, was a painful day to my feelings. It was evident that Brother Taylor had a settled fever upon him, and would not be able to travel.

Father Coltrin was resolved to continue his journey, and, in conversing with Brother Taylor, he thought it better for one sick man to be left than for two, as I was so sick with the chills and fever that I was not able to render him any assistance, nor, indeed, to take care of myself. Under these circumstances, Brother Taylor advised me to continue my journey with Brother Coltrin, and make the best of my way to New York.

CHAPTER XXII

AFTER committing Elder Taylor into the hands of the Lord, though painful to me, I gave him the parting hand, and started. I left him in Germantown, Wayne County, Indiana, in the hands of a merciful God and a kind and benevolent family, who promised to do everything in their power to make him comfortable until his recovery.

This they did, though he passed through a severe course of bilious fever, and was sick nigh unto death. Through the mercy of God, however, he recovered from his sickness and continued his journey. We next met in the city of New York.

I continued my journey with Father Coltrin, and we reached Cleveland on the 18th of September. We there took steamer for Buffalo, but were three days and a night in a storm before we made the harbor. We landed at midnight, and in doing so we ran into a schooner, and stove it in.

From Buffalo I traveled to Albany in a canal boat, and had a stroke of the ague daily.

While on my journey, at Albany, I took a stage in the night, and rode to my father's home in Farmington, on the 21st of September.

I was glad to meet with my father's family and the other members of the small branch of the Church which existed there upon this occasion, as I found them all strong in the faith of the gospel, and glad to meet with me.

I was still suffering with the ague daily.

On the 27th of September, my grandmother (on my mother's side) Anna Thompson, died at Avon. She was eighty-four years of age.

It was a singular coincidence that she, with her husband, Lot Thompson, also Mercy Thompson and Samuel Thompson, all of one family, died when they were eighty-four years of age. I was not able to attend my grandmother's funeral.

On the 4th of October, 1839, my uncle, Adna Hart, died, aged forty-three years. I had visited him in his sickness, and preached the gospel to him, and he was believing. I had also been associated with him from my youth up.

On his death bed he sent me a request that I would preach his funeral sermon.

I was having the chills and fever daily at the time, attended with a very severe cough, so much so that my father thought that I would never leave his home alive. But when they brought me the request of my dying uncle, and the day came for his burial, I told my father to get his horse and buggy ready, for I was going to attend the funeral.

He thought I was very reckless in regard to my own life, as I had suffered with the chills and fever some fifteen days, and to attempt to speak in my weak state, and to begin at the same hour that my chill was to come on, seemed to him foolhardy.

My parents were quite alarmed, yet according to my request my father got up his team, and I rode with him and my stepmother five miles, through a cold, chilly wind, and I commenced speaking to a large congregation, at the same hour that my chill had been in the habit of coming on.

I spoke over an hour with great freedom, and my chill left me from that hour, and I had no more attacks for many days.

On the Monday following, October 17th, I felt sufficiently restored to health to continue my journey. I took
leave of my father and sister, and left for New York,
where I arrived on the morning of the 8th of November.

I spent two months and seven days after my arrival in
New York, in traveling and preaching in that city, New
Jersey and Long Island, a portion of the time with Parley
and Orson Pratt. I had frequent attacks during this time
of the chills and fever, but I preached almost daily.

On the 13th of December I attended our conference in
New York City with Parley P. Pratt, and on this day
Elder John Taylor arrived in our midst, and it was a hap-
py meeting.

He had passed through a severe siege of sickness after
we parted, but through the mercy of God had been preserved, and was able to continue his journey. He also informed us that others of the quorum of the Twelve had
suffered a great deal of sickness, and that it was with difficulty that they could travel.

After spending six days in New York, Elder John
Taylor in company with Elder Theodore Turley and myself sailed out of New York Harbor, for Liverpool, on
board the packet ship *Oxford*, on the 19th of December,
1839.

We took the steerage passage, which cost fifteen dollars each. We had storms and rough weather, but most of
the winds were favorable for a quick passage.

While on the ship a Methodist minister got into a discussion with some Catholics who were in the company, and
the arguments of the minister ran rather more into abuse
than sound argument.

Elder Taylor told the Methodist minister that he did
not think it was becoming in the daughter to find so much

fault with the mother, for as the Methodists were the off-spring of the Catholics, Elder Taylor thought the mother had as much right to enjoy her religion unmolested as the daughter had. That ended the argument.

Our company consisted of one hundred and nine souls, composed of Americans, English, Scotch, Irish, Welsh and Dutch.

We arrived in Liverpool dock on the 11th day of January, 1840, having made the voyage from New York in twenty-three days.

CHAPTER XXIII

ON JANUARY 13th, 1840, after visiting Mr. George Cannon, the father of President George Q. Cannon, and his family, we took cars in the evening and arrived in the midst of the Preston branch of the Saints, built up in 1837, by Elders Heber C. Kimball, Orson Hyde and Willard Richards.

We very soon had a pleasant interview with Elder Willard Richards, who had remained in Preston to take care of the Church, while the rest had returned home to America.

We spent three days at Preston in visiting the Saints and on the 17th we held a council at Elder Richards' home in that place.

After consulting upon the best course for us to pursue, it was finally resolved that Elder John Taylor and Joseph Fielding go to Liverpool, Elder Woodruff to Staffordshire Potteries, Theodore Turley to Birmingham, Elder Richards wherever the Spirit might direct him, and that Wm. Clayton preside over the branch in Manchester.

After various principles of the Church had been expounded by the Apostles present, the council adjourned.

Elder Willard Richards had been called to be one of the quorum of the Twelve Apostles, but had not yet received his ordination.

On the day following I parted with Elders Taylor and Fielding, who went to Liverpool, and with Elder Richards, who tarried in Preston. Elder Turley and I went to Manchester.

It was the first time I ever visited that city. I here first met with Elder Wm. Clayton. As soon as I had an introduction to him, he informed me that one of the sisters in that place was possessed of the devil, and he asked me to go and cast it out of her, thinking that one of the Twelve Apostles could do anything in this line he might wish to.

However, I went with him to the house where the woman lay, in the hands of three men, in a terrible rage, and trying to tear her clothing from her.

I also found quite a number of Saints present, and some unbelievers, who had come to see the devil cast out and a miracle wrought.

If I had acted upon my own judgment I should not have attempted to administer to her with the company present, but as I was a stranger there, and Brother Clayton presided over the branch, I joined him in administering to the woman. But the unbelief of the wicked present was so great, we could not cast the devil out of her, and she raged worse than ever.

I then ordered the room to be cleared, and when the company left the house, except the few attending to her, we laid hands upon her, and I commanded the devil to come out of her, in the name of Jesus Christ. The devil left her and she was entirely cured and fell asleep.

The next day being the Sabbath, she came before a large congregation of people, and bore testimony to what the Lord had done for her. We had a large assemblage through the day and evening, to whom I preached the gospel.

On Monday morning, the devil, not being satisfied with being cast out of the woman, entered into her little child, which was but a few months old.

I was called upon to visit the child. I found it in great distress, writhing in its mother's arms. We laid hands upon it and cast the devil out of it, and the evil spirits had no power over the household afterwards.

This was done by the power of God, and not of man. We laid hands upon twenty in Manchester who were sick, and they were mostly healed.

On the 21st, I arrived in Burslem by coach, and met, for the first time, with Elder Alfred Cordon. This being my field of labor, I stopped and commenced work.

Elder Turley stopped in the pottery district some eight days, then went to Birmingham, his field of labor.

I received a letter on the 10th of February, from Elder John Taylor, who was at Liverpool, saying they had commenced there and baptized ten persons.

I labored in the Staffordshire Potteries, in Burslem, Hanley, Stoke, Lane End, and several other villages, from the 22nd of January until the 2nd of March, preaching every night in the week and two or three times on the Sabbath.

I baptized, confirmed and blessed many, and we had a good field open for labor. Many were believing and it appeared as though we had a door open to bring many into the Church in that part of the vineyard.

March 1st, 1840, was my birthday, when I was thirty-three years of age. It being Sunday I preached twice through the day to a large assembly in the City Hall, in the town of Hanley, and administered the sacrament unto the Saints.

In the evening I again met with a large assembly of the Saints and strangers, and while singing the first hymn the Spirit of the Lord rested upon me, and the voice of God said to me, "This is the last meeting that you will hold with this people for many days."

I was astonished at this, as I had many appointments out in that district.

When I arose to speak to the people, I told them that it was the last meeting I should hold with them for many days. They were as much astonished as I was.

At the close of the meeting four persons came forward for baptism, and we went down into the water and baptized them.

In the morning I went in secret before the Lord, and asked Him what His will was concerning me.

The answer I got was, that I should go to the south, for the Lord had a great work for me to perform there, as many souls were waiting for the word of the Lord.

CHAPTER XXIV

ON THE 3rd of March, 1840, in fulfillment of the word of the Lord to me, I took coach and rode to Wolverhampton, twenty-six miles, and spent the night there.

On the morning of the 4th I again took coach, and rode through Dudley, Stourbridge, Stourport and Worcester, and then walked a number of miles to Mr. John Benbow's, Hill Farm, Castle Frome, Ledbury, Herefordshire. This was a farming country in the south of England, a region where no Elder of the Latter-day Saints had visited.

I found Mr. Benbow to be a wealthy farmer, cultivating three hundred acres of land, occupying a good mansion, and having plenty of means. His wife, Jane, had no children.

I presented myself to him as a missionary from America, an Elder of the Church of Jesus Christ of Latter-day Saints, who had been sent to him by the commandment of God as a messenger of salvation, to preach the gospel of life unto him and his household, and the inhabitants of the land.

Mr. Benbow and his wife received me with glad hearts and thanksgiving. It was in the evening when I arrived, having traveled forty-eight miles by coach and on foot during the day, but after receiving refreshments we sat down together, and conversed until two o'clock in the morning.

Mr. Benbow and his wife rejoiced greatly at the glad tidings which I brought unto them of the fullness of the everlasting Gospel, which God had revealed through the mouth of His Prophet, Joseph Smith, in these last days.

I rejoiced greatly at the news that Mr. Benbow gave me, that there was a company of men and women—over six hundred in number—who had broken off from the Wesleyan Methodists, and taken the name of United Brethren. They had forty-five preachers among them, and had chapels and many houses that were licensed according to the law of the land for preaching in.

This body of United Brethren were searching for light and truth, but had gone as far as they could, and were continually calling upon the Lord to open the way before them, and send them light and knowledge that they might know the true way to be saved.

When I heard these things I could clearly see why the Lord had commanded me, while in the town of Hanley, to leave that place of labor and go to the south, for in Herefordshire there was a great harvest-field for gathering many Saints into the kingdom of God.

I retired to my bed with joy after offering my prayers and thanksgiving to God, and slept sweetly until the rising of the sun.

I arose on the morning of the 5th, took breakfast, and told Mr. Benbow I would like to commence my Master's business, by preaching the gospel to the people.

He had a large hall in his mansion which was licensed for preaching, and he sent word through the neighborhood that an American missionary would preach at his house that evening.

As the time drew nigh, many of the neighbors came in, and I preached my first gospel sermon in the house. I also preached on the following evening at the same place, and baptized six persons, including Mr. John Benbow and his wife, and four preachers of the United Brethren.

I spent most of the following day in clearing out a pool of water, and preparing it for baptizing in, as I saw many to be baptized there. I afterwards baptized six hundred in that pool of water.

On Sunday, the 8th, I preached at Frome's Hill in the morning, at Standley Hill in the afternoon, and at John Benbow's Hill Farm, in the evening.

The parish church that stood in the neighborhood of Brother Benbow's, presided over by the rector of the parish, was attended during the day by only fifteen persons, while I had a large congregation, estimated to number a thousand, attend my meeting through the day and evening.

When I arose in the evening to speak at Brother Benbow's house, a man entered the door and informed me that he was a constable, and had been sent by the rector of the parish with a warrant to arrest me.

I asked him "For what crime?"

He said, "For preaching to the people."

I told him that I, as well as the rector, had a license for preaching the gospel to the people, and that if he would take a chair I would wait upon him after meeting.

He took my chair and sat beside me. I preached the first principles of the everlasting gospel for an hour and a quarter. The power of God rested upon me, the Spirit filled the house, and the people were convinced.

At the close of the meeting I opened a door for baptism, and seven offered themselves. Among the number were four preachers and the constable.

The latter arose and said, "Mr. Woodruff, I would like to be baptized."

I told him I would like to baptize him. I went down to the pool and baptized the seven. We then met together and I confirmed thirteen, and broke bread unto the Saints and we all rejoiced together.

The constable went to the rector and told him if he wanted Mr. Woodruff taken up for preaching the gospel, he must go himself and serve the writ, for he had heard him preach the only true gospel sermon he had ever listened to in his life.

The rector did not know what to make of it, so he sent two clerks of the Church of England as spies, to attend our meeting, and find out what we did preach.

But they were both pricked in their hearts and received the word of the Lord gladly, and were baptized and confirmed members of the Church of Jesus Christ of Latter-day Saints.

The rector became alarmed and did not dare to send anybody else.

The ministers and rectors of the South of England called a convention and sent a petition to the Archbishop of Canterbury, to request Parliament to pass a law prohibiting the "Mormons" from preaching in the British dominion.

In this petition the rector stated that one "Mormon" missionary had baptized fifteen hundred persons, mostly members of the English church, during the last seven months.

But the archbishop and council, knowing well that the laws of England gave free toleration to all religions under the British flag, sent word to the petitioners that if they had the worth of souls at heart as much as they had the ground where hares, foxes and hounds ran, they would not lose so many of their flock.

I continued to preach and baptize daily.

On the 21st day of March I baptized Elder Thomas Kingston. He was the superintendent of both preachers and members of the United Brethren.

The first thirty days after my arrival in Herefordshire, I had baptized forty-five preachers and one hundred and sixty members of the United Brethren, who put into my hands one chapel and forty-five houses, which were licensed according to law to preach in.

This opened a wide field of labor, and enabled me to bring into the Church, through the blessing of God, over eight hundred souls during eight months, including all of the six hundred United Brethren except one person, also including some two hundred preachers of various denominations.

This field of labor embraced Herefordshire, Gloucestershire, and Worcestershire, and formed the conferences of Garway, Godfield Elm and Frome's Hill.

I was visited by President Young and Dr. Richards.

Brother Benbow furnished us with £300 to print the first Book of Mormon that was published in England; and on the 20th of May, 1840, Brigham Young, Willard Richards and I held a council on the top of Malvern Hill, and there decided that Brigham Young go direct to Manchester and publish 3,000 copies of the Hymn Book and 3,000 copies of the Book of Mormon, this being the first publication of these books in England.

The power of God rested upon us and upon the mission.

The sick were healed, devils were cast out, and the lame were made to walk.

One case I will mention: Mary Pitt, who died in Nauvoo, sister of Wm. Pitt, who died in Salt Lake City, had not walked upon her feet for eleven years. We carried her into the water and I baptized her.

On the evening of the 18th of May, 1840, at Brother Kingston's house in Dymock, Elders Brigham Young, Willard Richards and I laid hands upon her head and confirmed her.

Brigham Young, being mouth, rebuked her lameness, and commanded her to arise and walk, in the name of the Lord. The lameness then left her, and she never afterwards used a staff or crutch.

She walked through the town of Dymock next day, which created a stir among the people; but the wicked did not feel to give God the glory.

The whole history of this Herefordshire mission shows the importance of listening to the still small voice of the Spirit of God and the revelations of the Holy Ghost.

The Lord had a people there prepared for the gospel. They were praying for light and truth, and the Lord sent me to them, and I declared the gospel of life and salvation unto them, and some eight hundred souls received it, and many of them have been gathered to Zion in these mountains. Many of them have also been called to officiate in the bishopric, and have done much good in Zion. But in all these things we should ever acknowledge the hand of God, and give Him the honor, praise and glory, forever and ever. Amen.

CHAPTER XXV

IN ORDER to obtain revelation from God, and in order to know when we do obtain revelation, whether it is from God or not, we must follow the teachings of the revelations of God unto us. St. James says: "If any man lack wisdom, let him ask of God, that giveth to all men liberally, and upbraideth not; and it shall be given him." Again, it is said, "Ask, and it shall be given you; seek, and ye shall find; knock, and it shall be opened unto you."

It was upon this promise that Joseph Smith went before the Lord and prayed in the name of Jesus Christ, and asked for knowledge, wisdom and understanding in order to know what to do to be saved; and he proved the promises of St. James before the Lord, and the heavens were opened to his view, and the Father and Son were revealed unto him, and the voice of the great Eloheim unto him was: "This is my beloved Son, hear ye Him."

This was the first revelation of God to him. He did hearken to the voice of Jesus Christ all his life afterwards, and received a code of revelations and the word of the Lord unto him as long as he dwelt in the flesh.

Joseph Smith left as strong a testimony as was ever given to the human family, and sealed that testament with his own life and blood.

We all have to pursue the very same course in order to obtain revelations from God. But I wish to impress this truth upon the rising generation and all who read this testimony, that the Lord does not give revelations or send angels to men or work miracles to accommodate the notions of any man who is seeking for a sign.

When we have the principles of the gospel revealed to us through the mouth of the Savior, or by inspired prophets or apostles, we have no need to ask the Lord to reveal that unto us again. While the priesthood is restored to the earth, and the revelations of God are revealed to us through the mouths of prophets and apostles concerning the fullness of the gospel—doctrines, ordinances and principles—we should study them, and treasure up knowledge by faith. We should study out of the best books, and the Holy Ghost will bring to our remembrance those things which we stand in need of, in the selfsame hour that we are called to teach the people.

But when any priest, elder, prophet, apostle, or messenger is sent of God to preach the gospel, gather the Saints, work in temples or perform any work for the Lord, and that man is faithful and humble before the Lord in his prayers and duty, and there is any snare or evil in his path, or the righteous to be sought out, or danger to the emigration of the Saints either by sea or land, or knowledge needed in a temple, then the Lord will reveal to him all that is necessary to meet the emergency.

The teachings of the Prophet Joseph Smith to President John Taylor and the rest of us was to obtain the Holy Spirit, get acquainted with it and its operations, and listen to the whisperings of that Spirit and obey its voice, and it soon will become a principle of revelation unto us.

We have found this true in our experience, and in order to prove whether a revelation is from God or not we follow out the principles revealed to us, and if we find that which was manifested to us proves true, we know it is from God; for truth is one of His attributes, and the Holy Ghost deceiveth no man. When a man becomes acquainted with the whisperings of the Holy Ghost, which is revelation, he should be very careful to obey it, for his life may depend upon it. Revelation is one of the gifts of the Holy Ghost, and for the benefit of my young friends who may read this work, I will give an account of a few instances from my own experience of listening to the revelations of the Holy Ghost to me.

In 1848, after my return to Winter Quarters from our pioneer journey, I was appointed by the Presidency of the Church to take my family and go to Boston, to gather up the remnant of the Saints and lead them to the valleys of the mountains.

While on my way east I put my carriage into the yard of one of the brethren in Indiana, and Brother Orson Hyde set his wagon by the side of mine, and not more than two feet from it.

Dominicus Carter, of Provo, and my wife and four children were with me. My wife, one child, and I went to bed in the carriage, the rest sleeping in the house.

I had been in bed but a short time, when a voice said to me, "Get up, and move your carriage."

It was not thunder, lightning nor an earthquake, but the still, small voice of the Spirit of God — the Holy Ghost.

I told my wife I must get up and move my carriage. She asked: "What for?"

I told her I did not know, only the Spirit told me to do it.

I got up and moved my carriage several rods, and set it by the side of the house.

As I was returning to bed, the same Spirit said to me, "Go and move your mules away from that oak tree," which was about one hundred yards north of our carriage.

I moved them to a young hickory grove and tied them up. I then went to bed.

In thirty minutes a whirlwind caught the tree to which my mules had been fastened, broke it off near the ground and carried it one hundred yards, sweeping away two fences in its course, and laid it prostrate through that yard where my carriage stood, and the top limbs hit my carriage as it was.

In the morning I measured the trunk of the tree which fell where my carriage had stood, and I found it to be five feet in circumference. It came within a foot of Brother Hyde's wagon, but did not touch it.

Thus by obeying the revelation of the Spirit of God to me I saved my life, the lives of my wife and child, as well as my animals.

In the morning I went on my way rejoicing.

While returning to Utah in 1850, with a large company of Saints from Boston and the east, on my arrival at Pittsburg, I engaged a passage for myself and company on a steamer to St. Louis. But no sooner had I engaged the passage than the Spirit said to me, "Go not on board of that steamer, neither you nor your company."

I obeyed the revelation to me, and I did not go on board, but took another steamer.

The first steamer started at dark, with two hundred passengers on board. When five miles down the Ohio river it took fire and burned the tiller ropes, so that the vessel could not reach the shore, and the lives of nearly all on board were lost either by fire or water. We arrived in safety at our destination, by obeying the revelation of the Spirit of God to us.

In another instance, after attending a large annual conference in Salt Lake City, and having a good deal of business to attend to, I was somewhat weary, and at the close of the conference I thought I would repair to my home and have a rest.

As I went into the yard the Spirit said to me, "Take your team and go to the farm," which is some three miles south of the Tabernacle.

As I was hitching the horse to the wagon Mrs. Woodruff asked where I was going.

I said, "To the farm."

"What for?" she asked.

"I do not know," I replied; but when I arrived there I found out.

The creek had overflowed, broken through my ditch, surrounded my home, and filled my barnyard and pig pen.

Through my own exertions I soon turned it and prevented much damage that might have occurred had I not obeyed the voice of the Spirit.

This same Spirit of revelation has been manifested to many of my brethren in their labors in the kingdom of God, one of which I will here name.

Elder Charles C. Rich was going from Sacramento to San Bernardino with a company of brethren. He had in his possession a large amount of money to make payment on their land purchase. This was known to some road agents in the vicinity, who gathered a company of robbers and went on ahead of Brother Rich and lay in ambush, intending to kill the "Mormons" and rob them of their money.

Before reaching the company of robbers Brother Rich came to a by-path or trail. The Spirit then told him to take that path.

The brethren with him marveled at his course, not knowing that enemies awaited them, but they arrived in safety at San Bernardino with their lives and their money, while the robbers wondered why their prey did not come.

CHAPTER XXVI

I WILL now give an example from my own experience of the result of not obeying the voice of the Spirit.

Some years since I had part of my family living in Randolph, Rich County. I was there on a visit, with my team in the month of December.

One Monday morning my monitor, the Spirit watching over me, said: "Take your team and go home to Salt Lake City."

When I named it to my family who were at Randolph they urged me strongly to stop longer.

Through their persuasion I stayed until Saturday morning, with the Spirit continually prompting me to go home. I then began to feel ashamed to think that I had not obeyed the whisperings of the Spirit to me before.

I took my team and started early on Saturday morning. When I arrived at Woodruff, the Bishop urged me to stop until Monday and he would go with me.

I told him, "No, I have tarried too long already."

I drove on sprightly, and when within fifteen miles of Wasatch, a furious storm overtook me, the wind blowing heavily in my face.

In fifteen minutes I could not see any road whatever, and knew not how or where to guide my horses.

I left my lines loosely on my animals, went inside my wagon, tied down my cover, and committed my life and guidance into the hands of the Lord, trusting to my horses to find the way, as they had twice before passed over that road.

I prayed to the Lord to forgive my sin in not obeying the voice of the Spirit to me, and implored Him to preserve my life.

My horses brought me into the Wasatch station at 9 o'clock in the evening, with the hubs of my wagon dragging in the snow.

I got my horses under cover and had to remain there until next Monday night, with the snow six feet deep on the level and still snowing.

It was with great difficulty at last that I saved the lives of my horses by getting them into a box car and taking them to Ogden; while, if I had obeyed the revelation of the Spirit of God to me, I should have traveled to Salt Lake City over a good road without any storm.

As I have received the good and the evil, the fruits of obedience and disobedience, I think I am justified in exhorting all my young friends to always obey the whisperings of the Spirit of God, and they will always be safe.

The Spirit of God will rule over and guide all men who will permit it and seek for it, and this is especially necessary for young Elders who are laboring in the vineyard of the Lord. For the Lord knows where the righteous, honest and meek of the earth are, and will lead the Elders to them.

I have already related a remarkable instance of this in my own experience; when the voice of the Lord came to me in the town of Hanley, England, in 1840.

In that case it dictated me quite contrary to my expectations, for I had appointments out for a week ahead. But I obeyed the voice of the Spirit, went south as I was directed, and my readers know the result.

I will refer to one more instance in my experience upon the subject of revelation:

All the Latter-day Saints understand that we build temples for the purpose of administering ordinances for the dead as well as for the living. The Lord has opened the way in a remarkable manner for many of the members of the Church to obtain records of the names of their dead for several generations.

I had also obtained a record of somewhat over three thousand of my father and mother's families.

After the dedication of the temple at St. George, President Young appointed me to preside over it. When we commenced work in the temple I began to reflect: "How can I redeem my dead? I have some three thousand names of the dead who have been baptized for, and how can I get endowments for them?"

I had none of my family there, and if any had been there they would not have been able to get endowments for so many.

While praying to the Lord to show me how to redeem my dead, the Spirit of God rested upon me, and the voice of the Spirit said to me, "Go and call upon the sons and daughters of Zion in St. George, to come into the temple of the Lord and get endowments for your dead; and it shall be acceptable unto me, saith the Lord."

This filled my soul with joy, and I saw that it opened a field as wide as eternity for the salvation of our dead and the redemption of man, that we might magnify our calling as saviors upon Mount Zion.

On my birthday, March 1, 1877, the day that I was seventy years old, one hundred and fifty-four sisters at St. George went into the temple to get endowments for the same number of the female portion of my dead.

This principle was received by President Young and adopted from that hour, and through the kindness of friends I have had nearly two thousand of my friends receive endowments in the temple of the Lord, and thousands of others have received the same blessings in the same way.

President Young received revelations in the temple, and there are yet many revelations to be received in the last days, concerning the redemption of the dead and many other subjects but they will all be manifest in due time, through the proper authority unto the Church and Kingdom of God.

There are many other manifestations of the power of God and the revelations of Jesus Christ to us in our lives. We have been called by revelation to give endowments for many persons now dead, who, when living were honorable men of the earth, and some who were prominent in our nation, but who were not members of our family.

But I have said sufficient upon this branch of the subject.

CHAPTER XXVII

THE duty of a Patriarch is to bestow blessings upon his posterity and the children of men.

In a revelation (*Doc. and Cov.*, sec. 107) the Lord says that "Three years previous to the death of Adam, he called Seth, Enos, Cainan, Mahalaleel, Jared, Enoch and Methuselah, who were all High Priests, with the residue of his posterity who were righteous into the valley of Adam-ondi-Ahman, and there bestowed upon them his last blessings. * * And Adam * * predicted whatsoever should befall his posterity unto the last generation. These things are all written in the book of Enoch, and are to be testified of in due time."

Abraham, Isaac and Jacob were patriarchs, and blessed their posterity. All that Jacob said and sealed upon the heads of his twelve sons has been fulfilled to the very letter, so far as time has permitted.

We also have patriarchs in our day. Father Joseph Smith, the father of the Prophet Joseph Smith, was the first Patriarch of the Church of Jesus Christ of Latter-day Saints. He gave a great many blessings unto the Saints, which are recorded, and many of them have seen their fulfillment.

When he put his hands on the head of a person to bless him, it seemed as though the heavens were opened, and he could reveal the whole life of that person.

He gave me my patriarchal blessing in the Temple of the Lord at Kirtland, on the 15th day of April, 1837.

Many marvelous things which he sealed upon my head, for which I could then see no earthly chance of fulfillment, have already been fulfilled to the very letter.

One or two instances I will name. He said I should have access to the treasures hid in the ground to assist me in getting myself and others to Zion.

In 1850, while I was in Cambridgeport gathering up the Saints, Alexander Badlam went to California on business, and the Saints who were digging gold there filled a little sack with gold dust and sent it to me to assist me on my mission.

By the sale of this treasure from California I was enabled to emigrate myself, family and a number of others to Zion in the mountains.

He also said I should have power to bring my father and his family into the Church. This was fulfilled when I visited them during my mission to the Fox Islands, as previously related.

My father gathered to Salt Lake City with the Saints, and he died there, aged eighty-three years.

The Patriarch also said that I should be wrapped in the visions of heaven, and the angels of God should teach me many things. This was literally fulfilled.

Again, he told me I should be delivered from my enemies (who would seek my destruction) by the mighty power of God and the administrations of angels. This was marvelously fulfilled while in the city of London, in 1840. Brothers Heber C. Kimball, George A. Smith and I went to London together in the winter of 1840, being the first Elders who had attempted to establish the gospel in that great and mighty city.

As soon as we commenced, we found the devil was manifest; the evil spirits gathered for our destruction, and at times they had great power.

They would destroy all the Saints if they were not restrained by the power of God.

Brother Smith and I were together, and had retired to our rest, each occupying a cot and but three feet apart.

We had only just lain down, when it seemed as if a legion of devils made war upon us to destroy us, and we were struggling for our lives in the midst of this warfare of evil spirits until we were nearly choked to death.

I began to pray the best I could in the midst of this struggle, and asked the Father in the name of Jesus Christ to spare our lives.

While thus praying three personages entered the room, clothed in white and encircled with light.

They walked to our bedside, laid hands upon our heads and we were instantly delivered; and from that time forth we were no more troubled with evil spirits while in the city of London.

As soon as they administered unto us they withdrew from the room, the lights withdrew with them and darkness returned.

Many other sayings of the Patriarch Joseph Smith in my blessing have been fulfilled in my experience, but I have said sufficient on this subject. All the blessings that are sealed upon our heads will be fulfilled, and many more if we are faithful and live for them.

In closing my testimony I wish to say that I do not think that the Lord ever sends an angel to the earth to visit the children of men, unless it is necessary to introduce a dispensation of the gospel, or deliver a message or perform a work that cannot be done otherwise.

It required an angel of God to deliver the gospel to Joseph Smith, because it was not then upon the earth, and that was in fulfillment of the word of the Lord through John the Revelator (*Revelation* xiv:6). And so in regard to the administrations of angels in all ages of the world; it is to deliver a message and perform a work which cannot otherwise be acomplished.

MY FIRST MISSION

By GEORGE Q. CANNON

GEORGE Q. CANNON

GEORGE Q. CANNON

was born in Liverpool, England, January 11, 1827.
His parents joined the Church in 1840, through
the missionary work of John Taylor. On June 18,
1840, George Q. Cannon was baptized, when thirteen years of age. In the fall of 1842 the Cannon
family left Liverpool on their way to Nauvoo.
While crossing the Atlantic the mother died and
was buried in the ocean. Two years later the father
died in St. Louis, where he had gone on a short
business trip. The children were now orphans, the
eldest, George Q., being seventeen. However, they
all made their way across the plains to Utah. In
1850 he was called on a mission to the Hawaiian
Islands. Here he remained for four years, and the
wonderful events described in his book, "My First
Mission," took place. Returning to Utah in 1854
he was requested by Brigham Young to go to San
Francisco and print the Book of Mormon in the
Hawaiian language, a work which he had translated
while on the Islands. In 1860 he was ordained an
Apostle by Brigham Young. Six weeks later he
was sent to Liverpool to preside over the European
Mission. He returned in 1864 to Salt Lake City.
In 1872 he was elected to Congress from the Territory of Utah. After the death of Brigham Young
in 1877, George Q. Cannon became the first counselor to President John Taylor. In this capacity
he served for ten years. He then became the first
counselor to President Wilford Woodruff and
served for eleven years. Following the death of
President Woodruff, George Q. Cannon became the
first counselor to President Lorenzo Snow. He was
serving in this capacity at the time of his death,
April 12, 1901. Judged from any standpoint,
George Q. Cannon was one of the greatest men
that the Mormon Church has yet produced.

CHAPTER I

THE writer will probably never forget his first attempts at speaking in public. While yet a youth he was ordained one of the Seventy Elders. The quorum of which he became a member was organized the day he was ordained, and he was chosen to be its clerk. At the meetings of the quorum it was the custom of those of the Presidents who were present to make a few remarks, and then the members were called upon to speak.

On such occasions he would get so nervous that he would have to stop writing some time before it came his turn to speak; and then, when he did get up, he scarcely knew what he said, his fright was so great.

He constantly suffered from this feeling of fear whenever he attempted to speak at quorum meetings, or testimony meetings, and in fact, for some time after starting on a preaching mission.

There was one resolve that he made in the beginning, which he always kept, and which he desires to impress upon every boy and girl in Zion.

He made up his mind that, whenever called upon, he would, with the help of the Lord, always ask a blessing, or pray, or speak, and not try to excuse himself.

No matter how many have been present, nor how awkward and frightened he has felt, he has always done what was requested of him. But how many times he has seen young men and women decline to speak and to pray when called upon! He has both pitied and felt ashamed for them.

Such persons acquire a habit of *balking,* and *balky* men and women are as bad in their places as balky horses are in theirs.

Many persons think that because they are bashful, and are not in the habit of asking a blessing or praying aloud that, therefore, they can excuse themselves when called upon to do so. But right-feeling people admire boys and girls, young men and young women, who have the courage and good manners to comply with a request of this kind, even if they should make awkward blunders, far more than they would if they refused to do so.

What is called bashfulness is frequently nothing more than pride. Those who are troubled with it are generally anxious to appear to advantage; they desire the approbation of their fellows; and the fear that they will say or do something that will not come up to the standard, oppresses them and makes them nervous.

The first time the writer was called upon to speak to a mixed congregation of Saints and inquirers he was in the company of nine Elders. There were only two or three of them who had ever spoken in public; but as he was the youngest of the party, and felt that he was but a boy, he thought they would all be called upon before him. To his surprise, however, the Elder who was presiding called first upon him.

True to his resolve, he arose and commenced. For two or three, or probably five minutes, he did pretty well. Then he got confused, his ideas were in a jumble, and he forgot all he ever knew. If the bottom had dropped out of his memory, it could not have been worse. He sat down, feeling a little ashamed; but not discouraged. He was on a mission, and he was determined not to back down and fail. But it is very mortifying to get up to speak and then break down.

After this, he took a three weeks' voyage to the country to which he was appointed on a mission. After landing, he attended a public meeting of strangers who had never heard the gospel. It was held in a Seamen's Bethel, the minister having kindly offered it to the Elders for their meeting. One of the Elders spoke on the first principles; the writer followed him and bore testimony and made some other remarks. He was much frightened and embarrassed; but he spoke at greater length than he did before.

After this, circumstances required him to go out among the people alone. In that country, where they had no bells to ring, they called the people together by blowing a conch shell. When skillfully blown, one of these can be heard at a long distance. As the hour approached for meeting, it was customary to commence blowing the shell, and then our young missionary would be seized with trembling. The feeling of dread was terrible. He had been in places of peril where life was in danger; but he never felt as he did about preaching. He was alone and a stranger, and among a strange people. But he would not shrink. He knew that the gospel was true, that he had the authority to preach it, that the people had to be warned, and, therefore, with all his fear, he could not hold his tongue. He felt like Paul did when he said to the Corinthians: "Woe is unto me if I preach not the gospel."

About six weeks after he commenced his ministry alone two messengers arrived from a distant town to invite him to come there and preach. They had heard about the doctrine he taught, and the people he had baptized, and they wanted to learn more about the principles. He returned with the messengers. A large meeting house was obtained in which to preach. It was crowded, for the people had never before had the privilege of hearing a sermon delivered by a Latter-day Saint. You can imagine how he felt. Here was a people anxious to hear, and yet how weak he was, and how full of fear and trembling! When he arose to give out the hymn the sound of his voice in that large building scared him. Then he prayed, and afterwards gave out another hymn. He had called mightily upon God for help. When he commenced to speak the Spirit of the Lord rested upon him as it never had done before. The people had faith, and their hearts were prepared to receive the truth. For upwards of an hour he spoke, and he was so carried away in the Spirit, that he was like a man in a trance. Joy filled his heart and the hearts of the people. They wept like children, and that day was the beginning of a good work in that place.

I shall not attempt to describe to you the gladness that our young missionary felt. He had been a slave; but now he was free. God had broken the bands of fear, and he felt to glorify Him for His goodness. From that day to this he has never suffered from those dreadful feelings which oppressed him. Still, there are but few public speakers, especially in this Church, who do not have a nervous feeling when they first arise to speak; and it is frequently the case that when they feel the most nervous they are enabled to speak with the greatest power. They feel their own weakness, and they seek unto God for help.

Many of the readers of this may yet be sent on missions, and a recollection of this sketch may help them to persevere. Never decline to ask a blessing, to pray or to speak when called upon, and God will help you to overcome all feelings of fear.

CHAPTER II

IN EARLY days in California everything was valued at a high price. There were ten of us, Elders, who wanted to get passage from San Francisco to Honolulu, the principal town on the Sandwich Islands. After trying for some days we succeeded in obtaining a passage between decks on the good ship *Imaum of Muscat,* Captain Ritches, commander. We had to find our own bedding; but the captain agreed to furnish us food, which we were told was to be the same as they had in the cabin.

Either this part of the contract was not fulfilled, or they lived poorly in the cabin; for our fare was not very inviting. But we thought we were fortunate in not having to pay more than $40 in gold for the passage and these privileges.

I have seen places that were more comfortable than our quarters between decks. I have been on the sea many times since, and I believe, if I had my choice, I would take a trip as a cabin passenger on a Cunard steamship in preference to a voyage on the *Imaum of Muscat,* with its cabin fare and the privilege of sleeping in my own blankets.

The *Imaum* was low between decks, and then it was so dark there, that for a few minutes after descending, we could see nothing. We had had some rough experience, however, since leaving our homes, and we were not disposed to find fault with our ship or her accommodations.

For one week after embarking, we lay in the bay of San Francisco, head winds preventing our sailing. This was tiresome to us, and did not suit the captain, for he had to feed us, at least a part of the time. Probably this week's delay helped him to conclude that cabin fare was too good for us. As soon as the wind became favorable, the pilot thought it best to get ready for sea, and when the tide turned to go out, about one o'clock in the afternoon, we hoisted sail and started.

My recollections of passing out of the Golden Gate, as the mouth of San Francisco harbor is called, are not very pleasant. We had to beat out, that is, tack from side to side, and the swell came in from the ocean in large, heavy rolling waves. On each side we could see a long line of breakers running seaward, the foam looking in the distance like large banks of snow.

We had not passed through the gate when we began to be sea-sick. Those ocean swells will produce sea-sickness very quickly. There was no place on deck to be sick without being in the way, so we ran below. I vomited freely and felt relieved, and then went on deck again. The sun was declining in the west, and the sky was angry-looking and threatening, giving every indication of a storm. We were outside the heads, and before us stretched the great Pacific; but there were islands around, of which the captain knew but little. He did not like the idea of the pilot leaving him in such a position with darkness approaching and every prospect of a storm.

If the captain was anxious to have the pilot remain, the latter was equally desirous of getting away from the ship before nightfall. He had no wish to remain through the storm and to run the risk of being carried out to sea; so when a pilot boat hove in sight, he hailed it, and descended into the little yawl which came from it for him in such haste that he forgot his water-proof coat.

It was very natural, I suppose, for him, after piloting the ship out of the harbor, to be eager to get back before the storm broke upon us; but I believe we all should have felt better if he had remained with us.

The captain, especially, felt the responsibility of his position. Here he was outside of a strange harbor, on a dangerous coast, with a strong wind blowing directly on shore, and darkness upon him and he ignorant of his surroundings!

We had no time to indulge in many reflections upon the subject. Our time was occupied in another direction, for we were all suffering severely from the effects of seasickness; and notwithstanding the dangers of our situation, the sense of the ridiculous, in my case—only one bucket among us for every purpose—overcame fear, and I could not help laughing.

Many of our Elders and foreign settlers have been in a similar position, and all such can imagine our feelings better than I can describe them . My levity, however, under circumstances so inconvenient and perplexing, offended one of the Elders so much that he reprimanded me for it.

While we were thus engaged, the noise on deck was very great. The captain had as first mate a half-caste East Indian, and the most of his hands were Malays. His orders to the mate, and the latter's cries to the hands, and their chattering to one another, made a clamor that sounded loud above the noise of the storm.

Right in the midst of our sickness we heard the startling cry from the mate of "breakers ahead," and that we were close upon them. At any other time this would have excited us; but we were so sick we did not mind it.

Shortly after this, we felt the vessel strike something solid, and she trembled from stem to stern; this was directly followed by a grating sound, and a thumping at the stern. The first thought was that she had struck a reef;

but as we felt her settle in the trough of the sea, we knew that if she had struck, she had passed over it.

The shock that we felt was caused by a heavy breaker striking us; it had broken the wheel ropes, and the grating noise that we heard was the thumping of the helm. Had the breaker gone over us it would have swept the decks clean, or, had the wheel ropes broken a short time before, it is probable the vessel would have been lost.

In considering our narrow escape, afterwards, we felt to give the glory of our deliverance to God. We were His servants, and on His business, and He had preserved us.

That night was one of great anxiety to the captain, officers and crew. Notwithstanding our sickness, we also realized that we were in a critical position, and exerted all the faith we could.

The captain had his wife with him, and so little hope did he have at one time of saving the vessel, that he told her to prepare for eternity, for he did not think we would ever see daylight in this world again.

At last the morning dawned, the storm died away, and we were enabled to take our course.

Oh, the blessed daylight! How joyfully it was hailed on board that vessel! It did not relieve us from our seasickness, but it did from our peril.

Several days elapsed before the captain recovered from his fatigue and hoarseness, caused by shouting his orders that night.

The *Imaum of Muscat* was bound for the East Indies, but was to touch at the Sandwich Islands. We were glad that we had to go no farther, so it was with positive delight that we learned after being nearly four weeks on board, that we would soon be at the end of our voyage.

The sight of land is most welcome to those who have

been weeks at sea, especially if they have suffered from
sea-sickness. To our eyes, therefore, the rough, moun-
tainous isles of the Hawaiian group were very beautiful.
We longed to tread upon them.

For myself, I was scarcely intended for a sailor. I am
very easily made sick by the motion of a vessel on the
water, and no amount of going to sea prevents this. Some
years since, while crossing the Atlantic, I lay sea-sick in
my berth, and to divert my mind, I tried to recall the number of different times I had been in that condition. I
counted upwards of fifty distinct occasions that I had suffered from this sensation, and I have been sea-sick a number of times since.

During the night we passed the island of Hawaii, the
largest of the group, and the one on which Captain Cook,
the first white man (so far as known) who discovered
these islands, was killed.

The next morning the island of Maui was seen in the
distance; then Molokai and Lanai; and the morning following, when we arose, we were sailing alongside of Oahu,
the island on which the town of Honolulu, the capital of
the kingdom, is situated.

CHAPTER III

HONOLULU is built on an extensive flat, of great
fertility. The town is pretty, and wears a tropical
look; but, since the time of which I write, its buildings and
surroundings have been greatly improved. Groves of cocoa-nut trees, with their long, feathery leaves, and tall,
graceful trunks, were growing here and there in the vicinity of the town, and trees of other kinds were also abun-

dant in and around it. Behind Honolulu stretches what is called the Nuuanu valley, a beautiful country, which, even when we first visited it, was selected as a proper locality for the villas and country residences and gardens of the officers of the government, the missionaries and merchants.

On the right of the harbor of Honolulu is "Punch Bowl Hill," a large hill where once a volcano burned, but which is now extinct. The name is very suitable, for the volcano has left it more in the shape of a punch bowl than anything else.

While yet some miles from the mouth of the harbor we met several canoes, containing natives of the islands, who were out fishing. These canoes were merely logs hollowed out; but they were easily managed, and, with the aid of sails, their progress through the water was very rapid. To prevent their turning over, they had outriggers fastened to their sides.

A coral reef, over which the sea breaks with a tremendous roar, even in calm weather, extends nearly around the harbor of Honolulu. The entrance is very narrow, and seemed difficult of access, and as we entered, guided by a skillful pilot, a man was kept busy throwing the lead to learn the depth of the water. On the reefs were the wrecks of several vessels. The water was beautifully clear, and it was easy to distinguish the bottom as we sailed along.

No sooner was the anchor dropped than the decks were crowded with natives; some trying to sell bananas, oranges, cocoanuts, melons and other fruits (this was in the month of December), and others anxious to take us ashore. The monotonous character of their language, their rapid utterance, their numerous gestures, caused us to watch them with interest. We thought them a strange people. I little thought at that time that I would ever learn their language, or become as familiar with their customs as I afterwards did; for, though we had been sent on missions to the Islands, we supposed our time would be occupied in preaching to the whites.

Our first duty, after securing lodgings, was to repair to a convenient mountain, on the top of which we found a steep knob that rose suddenly and formed a table of thirty or thirty-five feet in width.

On the way up we picked up a rock apiece, with which we formed a rude altar. We then sang a hymn, and each one, in his turn, expressed his desires. The oldest, who was also the president, was selected to be mouth in prayer. He embodied our desires in his prayer. They were that the Lord would make speedy work on those islands, open an effectual door for the preaching of the gospel, confound all opposers, help us to gather out the honest-in-heart, and spare our lives to return home in safety.

Having thus dedicated the island and ourselves to the Lord, one of the Elders spoke in tongues and uttered many comforting promises, and another interpreted. The spirit of the Lord rested powerfully upon us, and we were filled with exceeding great joy. I had the satisfaction, afterwards, of witnessing the fulfillment of the promise made on that occasion.

The sun was sinking low in the heavens when we got through. Our descent was quickly made, for we felt joyful, and when men are joyful and the Spirit of God rests upon them, they feel lithe and active. We had been in the presence of the Lord, and had felt His power, and why should we not be happy?

The president of the mission had chosen as his companion the next oldest man. The most suitable place for them to remain, we all felt, was at Honolulu. But what must the rest do? Scatter among the other islands, or remain on that island—Oahu—until they learned more of the condition of affairs? It was decided that to go to the various islands would be the wiser plan.

There were four islands of importance yet to be occupied, and there were eight of us remaining. But who were to be partners, and how should we decide which island each couple should go to? The president did not like to pair us off, nor to say which of the islands we should go to; but he consented, with his partner, to select four out of the eight to preside, one on each of the islands.

We withdrew while they discussed this matter, and made their selection. To my great surprise, when we returned, I found that I was chosen as one of the four. Never in my life did I feel my weakness more sensibly than on that occasion. I was the youngest of the party, and felt that I was the least able of all to perform the duties assigned me.

The next thing was to select partners and islands; and how do you think we did this? You read in the Bible about casting lots. We cast lots. Four pieces of paper were marked: *one, two, three* and *four.* The one who drew *one* had the first choice of partners; so with the second, third and fourth numbers. Then the islands were marked on slips of paper in the same manner, and we drew for them. Number one fell to my lot. I had the first choice.

My mind had not rested on any one as my choice for partner, and I was at a loss for a few moments whom to select. Then the spirit of the Lord plainly told me to choose Brother James Keeler. I did so.

I was both surprised and pleased at the manner in which he received my choice; for I, being so young, and he so much my senior, had thought that he would prefer a partner of more mature years and experience.

He afterwards told me that when the four were chosen, and he found that I was one of them, he had slipped out and prayed to the Lord that I might be led to select him to go with me. His prayer was heard and answered, and we both were gratified.

In casting lots for islands, Maui fell to us. When we were sailing past it my feelings were drawn towards that island, and I felt that I would like that to be my field of labor. I knew not why this should have been so, except that the Lord gave me the feeling, for I knew nothing concerning it that would make it a desirable place in my eyes.

My joy was very great that evening, because of these precious manifestations of God's goodness. I felt that He was near at hand to hear and answer prayer, and to grant the righteous desires of our hearts; and how could we doubt His providence for and care over us in the future?

Children, I know of no feeling that can fill the human breast with such unspeakable happiness, joy and confidence as faith in God. If God be with us, who can be against us?

As I have already mentioned, there were eight of us Elders, besides the two who were to remain at Honolulu. Their names were Hiram Clark, the president, and his fellow-laborer, Thomas Whittle. The island on which we first landed was to be their field. The four who were chosen to preside on the other islands were: Henry W. Bigler, whose partner was Thomas Morris, and to whom the island of Molokai fell by lot; John Dixon, whose partner was William Farrer, and whose field was the island of Kauai; James Hawkins, who chose Hiram Blackwell as his companion, and to whom the island of Hawaii fell as a field of labor; and George Q. Cannon, whose fellow-laborer was James Keeler, and their field the island of Maui.

As the president counseled Brother Morris to go to work at Honolulu, and Brother Bigler was, therefore, alone, and his island lay convenient to Maui, he concluded to accompany the two last-named Elders to Maui.

The thought of parting from his companions in a foreign land produces lonely feelings in the breast of an Elder, but particularly if he be young and inexperienced. Our consolation on this occasion was that we were taking the plan whereby we might reap more abundant joy.

CHAPTER IV

LAHAINA is the principal town on Maui. It has no harbor, but vessels anchor in what is called the roadstead. Looking from the sea at the town, it is not very imposing. It lies on a level strip of land, and is stretched along the beach, and the houses are almost hidden by the foliage. Groves of cocoa-nut trees are to be seen, which give the place a tropical look.

We had considerable difficulty in procuring a suitable place to stop. There was a hotel and some boarding houses; but we could not live at any of them very long, for our funds were low. We secured a native house of one room, at a rent of four dollars per week.

These native houses are built by putting posts in the ground, on which a board is laid as a plate for the rafters to rest upon. When the frame of posts and rafters is built, poles, about the size of hoop-poles, are lashed horizontally, about six inches apart, on to the posts and rafters. The house is then thatched by fastening a durable grass, which they have in that country, on to the poles. When finished, a house looks, in shape and size, like a well built hay stack.

Such houses are only suited to a warm country where they never have frost. Inside the house they have no board floors. The ground is covered with grass, on which mats are laid. The making of these mats constitutes one of the chief employments of the women, and a good housewife in that country is known by the quantity and fineness of the mats in her home. Such a woman is very particular to have no dirt brought into her house; for the mats answer the purpose of beds, tables and chairs. They sit upon them; when they eat, their food is placed upon them, and they form their bed, though in many houses they have the place of sleeping raised above the ordinary floor; but even then, they have mats spread out, upon which to sleep.

In consideration of our being white men, the man of whom we rented the house procured a table and three chairs for us. We employed him to cook our food, which consisted principally of sweet potatoes and fish, or meat, with occasionally a little bread, bought at a bakery in town. In those days no native thought of using bread as an article of diet. Their food I shall describe more fully to you in a future chapter.

We had an interview with the American consul, Mr. Bunker, and solicited through him an introduction to the governor of the Island. He readily complied with our request, and in our intercourse with Mr. Bunker he treated us very kindly.

Our mission we felt to be of such importance that we wished to introduce it to the highest authority we could find. I made it a rule on those islands never to go into a place without waiting upon the leading and prominent

men, stating my business, testifying to the work which
God had commenced and asking their aid to enable me to
lay the proclamation of which I was the bearer before the
people. In this way I had interviews with princes, nobles,
governors, officers of the government, missionaries and the
leading men in every locality where I visited.

This course might not be a wise one in every nation
and under all circumstances; but I was led to take it there
and the effects were good. I had a fearlessness and
strength given me which I would not have had if I had
kept myself in a corner, and acted as though I was
ashamed of my mission. I gained influence also with the
people, and they learned to respect me; for, however much
men may differ in their views about religion and other
matters, they generally respect sincerity and courage.

The governor was named James Young. He was a
half-white, his father being a friend of Kamehameha the
First, and one of the first white men who settled among
the Hawaiians. We requested the use of the palace, which
was not then occupied by the royal family, to preach in.
He promised to write to his brother, the minister of the
interior, about it. We called a number of times afterwards to see him; but could get no definite answer. It
was very evident to us that he dare not grant us any
favors.

Rev. Mr. Taylor was the chaplain of the Bethel Chapel at Lahaina, where seamen and most of the white resi-
dents went to worship. We introduced ourselves to him,
told him where we were from and our business, and asked
the privilege of holding meeting in his chapel. He held
meetings in the morning and evening. He consented, and
gave out notice to the people in the morning that we would
hold meeting in the afternoon. Elder Henry W. Bigler

delivered the discourse, and Brother Keeler and I bore testimony. We soon became satisfied that if we confined our labors to the whites, our mission to those islands would be a short one.

The white people were not numerous at Lahaina, and there were but very few at any other place on the island of Maui. Preaching to them with the hope of convincing them of the truth seemed a hopeless labor. The question arose directly, "Shall we confine our labors to the white people?" It is true that we had not been particularly told to preach to the natives of the islands, but we were in their midst, had full authority to declare unto them the message of salvation, and if we did not declare it unto them, some other Elders would have to come and do so, in order to fulfill the command of God to His servants.

For my part I felt it to be clearly my duty to warn all men, white and red; and no sooner did I learn the condition of the population than I made up my mind to acquire the language, preach the gospel to the natives and to the whites whenever I could obtain an opportunity, and thus fill my mission. I felt resolved to stay there, master the language and warn the people of those islands, if I had to do it alone; for I felt that I could not do otherwise and be free from condemnation; the spirit of it was upon me. Elders Bigler and Keeler felt the same.

I mention this, because it was a point upon which a difference of opinion afterwards arose, some of the Elders being of the opinion that our mission was to the whites, and that when we had warned them, we were at liberty to return. How do you think such differences of views and opinions can be settled? Had the president of the mission exercised the authority to dictate, he could have decided between these views; but he would not. He left each one to act for himself. We were in a foreign land, far distant from the Apostles and First Presidency, and, therefore, could not appeal to them. Our only resource was to obtain revelation from the Lord for ourselves. This is the privilege of every man and woman in the Church. If Latter-day Saints will seek for knowledge, God will give it to them to guide them in all the details of life, subject, of course, to the presiding authority and its teachings and counsels. By this means we were able, on the Sandwich Islands, to know what course to take.

White men who go to the Sandwich Islands do not always behave themselves as they should. We saw some who acted most disgracefully. They seemed to think that, because they were among the natives, they could abandon all decency. The natives are very close observers. They soon saw that we were not like many of the whites whom they had seen, and they began to take an interest in us. They readily helped us to pronounce and read their language. The want of books was a great drawback at first; but we sent to Honolulu for them.

My desire to learn to speak was very strong; it was present with me night and day, and I never permitted an opportunity of talking with the natives to pass without improving it. I also tried to exercise faith before the Lord to obtain the gift of talking and understanding the language. One evening, while sitting on the mats visiting with some neighbors who had dropped in, I felt an uncommonly great desire to understand what they said. All at once I felt a peculiar sensation in my ears; I jumped to my feet, with my hands at the sides of my head, and exclaimed to Elders Bigler and Keeler who sat at the table, that I believed I had received the gift of interpretation! And it was so.

From that time forward I had but little, if any, difficulty in understanding what the people said. I might not be able at once to separate every word which they spoke from every other word in the sentence; but I could tell the general meaning of the whole. This was a great aid to me in learning to speak the language, and I felt very thankful for this gift from the Lord.

I mention this that my readers may know how willing God is to bestow gifts upon his children. If they should be called to go as missionaries to a foreign nation, whose language they do not understand, it is their privilege to exercise faith for the gifts of speaking and interpreting that language, and also for every other gift which they may need.

CHAPTER V

A LITTLE more than three weeks had passed when our money was paid out, except a very little. Much as we disliked the idea, it seemed necessary for us to separate and seek places to live where we could find them among the natives. We cast lots to learn which direction we should take. Elder Henry W. Bigler drew south; Elder James Keeler, east; and I, north.

I had explained our position to the man of whom we rented the house. Of course my explanations were not perfect, for three weeks' residence had not made us masters of the language; but he comprehended the situation exactly. He went to a neighboring house, where the family lived who had done our washing, and who had been very friendly and kind, and told the lady how matters stood with us. She came in; but we were so busy making our arrangements to start out that we did not converse with her, and she went away again.

Brother Bigler started off in the direction which had fallen to him, with a piece of paper in his hand, on which sentences in native, such as he would be likely to need, were written, with their meaning in English. Brother Keeler and myself were preparing to go in the directions which had fallen to us, when Brother Keeler suggested that we call upon Na-lima-nui, the old lady of whom I have spoken. Our object was to learn from her, if we could, who there was that would be likely to entertain strangers.

"Na-lima-nui" means in the language of the Sandwich Islands "big hands." *Lima* is the noun *hand,* *nui* is the adjective *large* or *big,* and *na* is the sign of the plural. You see it is a differently constructed language to ours. The sign of the plural precedes the noun, and the qualifying adjective follows it, as "hands large or big."

Na-lima-nui did not know where we could find a man who could entertain us; but she said we were welcome to come and live in her house. We had a long talk with her, and I endeavored to explain our position and what our business was in coming to the Islands. We had no money, I said, but anything that we did have, we should be glad to give her. We felt humble, and would have been pleased to obtain a corner on the floor to sleep in, so that we could live, learn the language and fill our mission.

The kindness of this old lady touched me, and I could not refrain from weeping. Never before in my life did I feel so thankful as I did for the shelter she offered. I praised the Lord therefor; it was He who touched the heart of herself and family.

The thought that we should not have to separate added to our joy, and you can probably imagine with what delight we went to find Brother Bigler. He had succeeded in finding a native who was willing to give him food and a lodging place, if he would milk his cow and do other chores. He was as much rejoiced as we to learn that we could live together.

We did not expect to get any more accomodations than a place to stretch ourselves at night in our blankets; but Na-lima-nui's daughter, who was married to a Spaniard, lived adjoining; and she had arranged for her mother to live in her rooms, and the old lady's room had been prepared for us. They had fixed up the room as well as they could.

Such a profound feeling of thankfulness as I had on our obtaining a shelter in this poor, native woman's hut I never experienced before.

It has been my fortune, since those early days of my life, to travel considerably, and to mingle with our missionaries in many lands. I have seen Elders who were willing to endure everything for the gospel's sake; their hearts were filled with joy and a burning desire to magnify their Priesthood and to fill their missions. What they ate or drank, where they lodged or how they were clothed, were matters of little or no thought to them, so long as they had the Spirit of the Lord and were in the line of duty. Others, I have seen, who felt every little privation to be a dreadful hardship; who thought, if everything did not go smoothly with them, they had to suffer more than was necessary, and who were ready to desert their fields of labor and run home at the first opportunity.

I scarcely need say that men of this latter class are rarely, if ever, successful missionaries. They think too much of their own ease and comfort, and their thoughts are too much upon themselves, to labor under any circumstances of difficulty for the salvation of others. When an Elder has the spirit of his mission, self-comfort is forgotten. He is perfectly happy in declaring the gospel and laboring for the salvation of others, and he gives but little thought to the kind of food he eats, or how he fares in other respects. His bodily wants are swallowed up in his joy in Christ.

These were our feelings at the time of which I write. We were willing to live on any food that would sustain our bodies, however common or even disagreeable it might be; we were glad to get a shelter, however humble, to lie under; our desire was to fill our mission: and because we felt thus, the Lord made up for any lack of comfort by giving us His Holy Spirit.

I had never been so happy in my life before as I was then. When I prayed I could go unto God in faith; He listened to my prayers; He gave me great comfort and joy; He revealed Himself to me as He never had done before, and told me that if I would persevere, I should be blessed, be the means of bringing many to the knowledge of the truth, and be spared to return home after having done a good work.

Many things were revealed to me, during those days, when He was the only Friend we had to lean upon, which were afterwards fulfilled. A friendship was there established between our Father and myself, which, I trust, will never be broken nor diminished, and which I hope has continued to grow stronger from those days to these.

It is not my custom to write thus freely about myself; but I am writing for young people to read, upon whom I would like my experience to make an impression. I desire that they should make God their friend, and seek unto Him with faith for that joy, peace and perfect love which He alone can give.

Shortly after we moved into the house of Na-lima-nui, I was called by letter to go up to Honolulu. The partner of the president of the mission had concluded to return home, and I was requested to remove to Honolulu to act in his place.

This was unexpected news to me, and my parting from my companions was nearly as painful as leaving home had been. Besides the Elder of whose proposed departure I had heard, I found there two others—to whom the island of Kauai had fallen as a field of labor—ready to return home.

There were but few whites on that island, and to them they had preached, but had received no encouragement. They had written to the president of the mission, describing the situation of affairs, and he had counseled them to come to Honolulu.

The idea of leaving the islands, because there were not enough white men to preach the gospel to, was so foreign to the minds of my companions on Maui, and to myself, that when I heard these Elders were there with the intention of returning home, I was surprised.

I did not conceal my feelings from them; I told them that I could not go home under existing circumstances, without feeling condemned. The Lord, in my opinion, I said, would hold me accountable for not doing my duty to that people, if I were to leave them; and the people might rise up in judgment against me at some future day, for not having given them the privilege of hearing the truth. My prayer was that the time might speedily come when all should know the Lord, and when His knowledge would cover the earth as the waters covered the deep; and I believed in uniting works and faith. It would sound bad for ten Elders to be sent out to the islands by Elder Charles C. Rich, one of the Twelve Apostles, to preach and to act as the Spirit and circumstances might dictate, and when we found there were not whites that would receive us, turn around and go home, and leave a whole nation to welter in ignorance, because he did not happen to tell us that we were to preach to them in their own tongue. Much more in this strain I was led to say, which it is not necessary to repeat here.

Brother Whittle had been told by Elder Rich that he could return home after filling a short mission. The president of the mission had done all the preaching at the meetings they had held, and had not even given him an opportunity to bear his testimony. His position had been, and still was, unpleasant; and he saw no way to remedy it. If he could do any good, he was willing to stay; but he thought that, under his circumstances, it was useless.

Brother William Farrer, one of the Elders who had been laboring on Kauai, made up his mind that he would not return home, but stop and devote himself to acquiring the language. His partner, however, would not stop. He was bent upon returning. Being an intimate acquaintance, I talked freely with him upon the subject. He would go home, he said, and gladly take a mission to Europe, if he should be appointed; but to labor there he could not with any pleasure. Besides, he was an old bachelor, he added, and he ought to be married, and so he would return home and take him a wife. He did return home; but, poor fellow, he never obtained a wife. Some time after his return, he, with some other brethren, left the city to go to Parley's Park for lumber. On their way home they were ambushed by Indians, and he was killed.

I often ask myself, after hearing of his death, would it not have been better for him if he had remained? For if he had, I believe he would have still been living.

CHAPTER VI

THE progress I had made in learning the language surprised the Elders at Honolulu. I was able to converse tolerably well with the natives, and understand what they said. When they learned how the Lord had opened our way and aided us in acquiring the language, they felt that it might be wisdom for me to continue my labors there, instead of removing to Honolulu. This, after counseling together, was the decision of the president.

I was much gratified at the privilege of returning to Maui; for, to my view, prospects for accomplishing any great amount of good were not very bright then in Honolulu.

Elder William Farrer sailed with me to Maui, to be a partner to Henry W. Bigler.

We had scarcely reached Lahaina, when Elder Hiram Blackwell called upon us from the Island of Hawaii, where he had been with Elder James Hawkins. He was on his way to Honolulu, and expected, if it was not contrary to counsel, to return home. He was discouraged in trying to learn the language and preach to the natives. He reached Honolulu in time to return with the other Elders.

At this point I may anticipate the order of my narrative by stating that Elder James Hawkins, Brother Blackwell's partner, remained on Hawaii for some time, striving to acquire the language, and to proclaim the gospel to the people. He afterwards came up to Maui and labored there, and filled a good mission before he returned home.

About three weeks after my return from Honolulu, we were surprised at receiving a visit from the president of the mission. He had concluded to leave the Sandwich Islands and to go to the Marquesas Islands; for he thought there was a better field there.

These latter islands, 30° south of where we were then, are inhabited by a race of people whose language is very similar to that spoken by the natives of the Sandwich Islands. They are probably descendants of one common stock. But they are naturally more fierce and savage than the Sandwich Islanders. It is said of some of them, that when they are engaged in war, they have no objections to eating a piece of a roasted man; indeed, they rather relish such a meal at such times, as they think it makes them brave.

Our president's principal motive in coming to see us was to have us go with him. If prospects were no better on Maui than on the island he had been on, he thought we should accompany him. It was not from any fear that the people of the Marquesas group would eat us, that we did not fall in with his proposal; but because we could not see the propriety of it.

Our position, just then, was a peculiar one. Here was our president, the man who had been appointed to counsel and guide us, proposing to us to leave the field to which we had been appointed, and to take a journey of several hundred miles to another land to labor. What were we to do? How far did the obedience which we owed to him require us to go? This was an important question. To disobey a man in the rightful exercise of authority, was an act from which we naturally recoiled; and an act, too, of which we were not in the least disposed to be guilty. But we felt that it would not be right for us to leave that island then.

We had done but little at warning the people, or accomplishing our mission, and why leave them then, any more than on the first day that we landed? We had not been appointed by the authority, which called him and us, to go to the Marquesas Islands; we knew of no opening there, or of any reason why we should go there in preference to any other place on the earth. If we followed our president there, because he told us to come with him, and we should find no opening to preach the gospel, why not follow him to some other country if he should so require us?

Fortunately we were relieved from the necessity of refusing to comply with his counsel. He felt plainly enough that his proposal did not strike us favorably. He had not been many hours with us until he found this out; and he told us that probably it would be better for us to remain where we were until we gave the people a fair trial; and then, if we could not do anything, we could follow him, as he intended to write to us respecting his success. The first we heard from him, he had drifted down to Tahiti, on the Society Islands, where some of our Elders were then laboring. His mission, however, was of no profit to himself.

When an Elder has the spirit of his mission, he cannot rest contented unless he is proclaiming to the people the message with which he is entrusted. Surround him with every comfort his heart can desire, and if he has that spirit, he will still be anxious to go forth among the people, even if he knows he will meet with privations and persecution. This was my feeling before the visit of the president of the mission, and after he left, my anxiety increased, and I told the brethren that I must push out among the natives, and commence preaching to them as well as I could. I had made very good progress in the language, and felt able to explain in part the first principles of the gospel.

About a week after the president's visit I started off, intending, if I did not get an opening, to go around the island. But the Lord had revealed to me that I would find a people prepared to receive the truth; and I started as a man would who was going to meet his friends. Though I had never seen them in the flesh, I knew that when I met them they would not be strangers unto me.

Borrowing Brother Bigler's valise, one which he had carried many a day himself while on a mission in the States, I started, feeling as proud of the privilege of swinging it across my shoulder as any knight ever was at wearing, for the first time, his gold spurs.

The great desire of my heart from my early boyhood had been to have the Priesthood and the privilege of preaching the gospel. This desire was now about to be gratified, and though I was timid and very bashful, I felt that God would carry me safely through.

The brethren accompanied me about four miles on my way. We were far from all our friends, and were strangers in a strange land; our parting, therefore, as might be expected, was painful. They remained to continue their study of the language.

It was plain to me that the angel of the Lord was with me; for at whatever place I stopped, I was received most kindly, and the best the people had was at my service.

The principal food of the natives of the Sandwich Islands is called *poi*. This is made out of a root which they call *kalo*. "Kalo" patches are so made that they can be flooded with water; and the ground is never allowed to be uncovered. In planting this root they do not use seed. When a native gathers the "kalo," he carries it to his home, where he cuts off the tops. These are carefully saved, tied up in a bundle, and carried back to the patch. These tops he sticks in the mud at the proper distances apart, and at the end of eleven months he has another crop of "kalo." This is the process of gathering and planting.

The "kalo" bears some resemblance in its leaves and taste to the wild Indian turnips, but its root is much larger; not quite the shape of a tame turnip, but as large as a moderate sized one. There is a variety called the "dry land kalo." It is not so extensively cultivated as the other kind, and is not considered so good eating.

Near every house there is a circular hole. When "kalo" is to be cooked, a fire is built in this, and a quantity of small volcanic rocks are piled on top of it. As the fire burns out these sink to the bottom, and they are spread over the bottom and around the sides of the pit. The "kalo" roots are then laid in, mats are spread over them, then soil, until they are completely covered, excepting a small hole at the top, into which water is poured. That hole is then stopped, and the cooking commences.

"But how do they cook?" you may ask.

When the water is poured in, the rocks, being hot, speedily convert it into steam, and, as it cannot escape, it cooks the roots.

I have seen large hogs cooked in this way, and meat is sweeter cooked in this fashion than by any other method I know anything about. The native men on the Islands do all the cooking.

When the "kalo" has been in long enough to cook, it is uncovered; the skin is washed off, and it is pounded with a stone pestle, on a large, flat slab of wood, until it is like a mass of dough. Then it is put into a calabash, or gourd, and by the next day fermentation has commenced; or, as we would say if it were bread, it has "raised." Water is then added to it, and it is mixed until it is a little thinner than we usually make mush. There is a little sour taste about it the first day. But it is never eaten at that time by the natives, unless they have no other food. They like it best when it is quite sour. This is what they call "poi," and there is no other food that they think can equal it.

Their usual method of eating is worthy of notice. A large calabash of "poi" is placed on the mats; around this the family seat themselves.

In families where they make any pretensions to cleanliness, a small calabash of water is passed around, and each one rinses his or her fingers before commencing to eat.

To keep off the flies, a boy or a girl stands waving a *kahili*, which is made by fastening feathers to a long, slender stick.

In eating, they dip their first two fingers into the calabash, load them with the "poi," and pass them into their mouths. The sucking of the fingers, the gusto with which they eat, and the incessant conversation mingled with laughter which they keep up, would lead a bystander to conclude that they enjoy their food. And they do. If the "poi" be good, and they have plenty of fish or meat to eat with it, they have great pleasure in eating. They think white men who eat together without conversing very unsocial beings. They have an idea that it contributes to health, and to the enjoyment of the food to have pleasant and lively conversation while eating.

Before leaving Lahaina, I had tasted a teaspoonful of "poi"; but the smell of it and the calabash in which it was contained was so much like that of a book-binder's old, sour, paste-pot that when I put it to my mouth I gagged at it, and would have vomited had I swallowed it. But in traveling among the people I soon learned that if I did not eat "poi" I would put them to great inconvenience; for they would have to cook separate food for me every meal. This would make me burdensome to them, and might interfere with my success. I, therefore, determined to learn to live on their food, and, that I might do so, I asked the Lord to make it sweet to me. My prayer was heard and answered; the next time I tasted it, I ate a bowlful, and I positively liked it. It was my food, whenever I could get it from that time as long as I remained on the islands.

It may sound strange, yet it is true, that I have sat down to a table on which bread was placed, and though I had not tasted the latter for months, I took the "poi" in preference to the bread; it was sweeter to me than any food I had ever eaten.

CHAPTER VII

IT WAS during a very wet season that I told the people I was going around the island. They thought it a great undertaking, and tried to persuade me not to go. I evidently had their sympathies; I was boyish-looking, and they called me a *keiki,* which in their language literally means "a child."

Many times as I traveled along they would take my valise from me and carry it; and when I came to a stream of water, they would pack me across it.

I passed through a number of villages, over a very rough, hilly country, and late one night reached the town of Wailuku.

Up to this time, though I had been treated very kindly, I had not met with the persons whom I had been led to expect, by the manifestations of the Spirit, would receive my testimony.

The main part of the town of Wailuku was on the other side of a stream, in attempting to cross which I got wet.

There were some missionaries living here, and as I passed through the town, I hoped that I should get an opportunity of being introduced to them; for I had made it a rule, thus far, not to pass a missionary without bearing testimony to him respecting my mission. But I was dusty and toil-worn, and felt some diffidence about introducing myself.

By this time I had partly come to the conclusion that, as the weather was so unfavorable I would return to Lahaina; and in passing through Wialuku I took a road which I thought led in that direction. I had scarcely got out of the town when I felt impressed to return, the Spirit telling me that if I would do so I should get an opportunity of being introduced to the missionary who resided there.

As I passed the churchyard two half-white women emerged from a house near by, and when they saw me they called to some men who were in the house *"E ka haole!"* which means, "Oh, the white man!" This they repeated two or three times, calling at the same time one of the men by name.

As I walked along towards the picket fence, three men came out of the house, and stepped up towards the gate. When I got opposite to them I saluted them, being greeted by them in return.

I had passed but a few feet when the leader of the men inquired of me where I was going. I told them I thought of returning to Lahaina, on account of the weather. He said that as this was Saturday, I had better stop until Monday with him.

He inquired of me who and what I was, and upon my informing him, his desire to have me stay was increased. I went into the house with him, and, after some little conversation, and an invitation to eat food, which he offered, he proposed that we should go up and see the missionary.

This was what I wanted, and I embraced his proposal gladly.

The missionary's name was Conde; he was a native of Connecticut, and had been sent out by the American Board of Foreign Missions.

We had a very pleasant conversation, during which he made many inquiries respecting Utah, my object in coming to the islands, and our belief. He said he could not believe anything in modern revelation; but expressed a wish to read some of our works.

I lent him the *Voice of Warning,* though I had little hope of it having any effect on him, as he had condemned the doctrines before he had heard or read them.

The moment I entered into the house of this native and saw him and his two friends, I felt convinced that I had met the men for whom I had been looking.

The man who owned the house was a judge, and a leading man in that section. His name was Jonatana H. Napela. It was he who visited Salt Lake City in 1866, in company with Elder George Nebeker. His companions' names were Uaua and Kaleohano. They were all three afterwards baptized and ordained to be Elders, Napela has since died in the faith, and the others are still members of the Church.

They were graduates of the high school in the country, fine speakers and reasoners, and were men of standing and influence in the community.

Napela was very anxious to know my belief, and wherein our doctrines differed from those taught by the missionaries in their midst. I explained to him, as well as I could, our principles, with which he seemed very well satisfied. But next day after the service in their church, Mr. Conde called Napela and a number of the leading men together, and endeavored to poison their minds against our doctrines, by telling all kinds of lies about the Prophet Joseph and the people of Utah.

I learned this at supper by the inquiries which Napela and a number of his friends who were present, made of me. Their questions were of such a nature as to prove to me that somebody had been telling them lies. I afterwards learned that it was the missionary's work.

The Spirit rested powerfully upon me and I told them I had the truth, and besought them, as they valued their souls, not to reject it until they could understand it for themselves; that I should soon be able to explain it fully unto them; that the principles were contained in the Bible, and were eternal truth. They were melted to tears, and promised me that they would not decide that our principles were false until they had a full opportunity of judging for themselves; which promise, I am happy to say, most of them kept, and I had the pleasure of baptizing them into the Church.

I am particular in mentioning this circumstance to show the boys who may read this work that, when they go on missions, and they are in the line of their duty, it is their privilege to have revelations from the Lord to guide them in all their steps. I was led to expect, before I left Lahaina, that I would find those who would receive me. Up to the time I reached Wailuku, I had not found them, and then when I thought it best to go back by another road, and through other villages, to Lahaina, I was told if I would return into Wailuku that I should obtain my desire in getting an interview with the missionary.

The half-white women who saw me were Napela's wife and her sister. There was something very remarkable in their crying out as they did to him and his companions in the house when they saw me. They met whites very frequently, and it was nothing strange for them to pass as I did. This was often alluded to in conversations which we had afterwards, and they wondered why they should have done so. I know that it was the Lord's doings; for if they had not called out, I should have passed unnoticed and missed them. To my sight, the Lord's hand was plainly visible in it all, and I thanked Him for His mercy and goodness.

CHAPTER VIII

ON THE Monday morning I returned to Lahaina, and received a warm welcome from the brethren. They were much interested in the recital of the incidents of my trip. From that time, however, I stayed but little there. Much as I liked the society of the Elders, I could not be content there, for I felt that I ought to be among the natives, trying to teach them the principles of the gospel, and there seemed to be a better opening for this work in other places than at Lahaina.

There being none of the Elders on the Island of Oahu, it was decided that Elders Bigler and Farrer should go there instead of to the island of Molokai. When they sailed for that island, which they did in a few weeks, Brother James Keeler was left alone with no one to converse with in English, unless he occasionally met a white man. This gave him a better opportunity of acquiring the language than he had when we were all there. After some weeks he also was led to leave there and to travel around the island until he found a people who were willing to receive him and the principles which he taught.

When the Presbyterian missionary at Wailuku saw that I had come back there he was displeased. He used all his influence against me among his congregation, and one Sunday he came out in public and delivered a most abusive discourse against the Prophet Joseph and our principles, in which he gave an entirely false statement of the cause of his death, and also warned the people against me.

I happened to be present when this sermon was delivered. While listening to it a variety of emotions agitated me. My first impulse was to jump upon one of the seats as soon as he had got through, and tell the people he had told them a pack of falsehoods. But this I thought would produce confusion, and result in no good. When the services were over, I walked around to the pulpit where he stood. He knew how short a time we had been on the islands, and, I believed, had no idea that I could understand what he had said; when he saw me, therefore, his face turned pale, and to me he looked like a man who had been caught in a mean, low act.

[*152*]

I told him I wanted to give him correct information respecting the things he had told the people that morning, that he might remove the effect of the lies which he had repeated to them; for, I said, they were base lies, and I was a living witness that they were.

He said he did not believe they were lies, and he should not tell the people anything different to what he had said; he thought he had but done his duty, and if the people had been warned against Mahomet in his day, he would not have got so many disciples.

I bore him a solemn testimony respecting the Prophet Joseph, and the truth of the work, and said that I would stand as a witness against him at the judgment seat of God, for having told that people lies and for refusing to tell them the truth when it had been shown to him.

Much more was said, for our conversation lasted about half an hour, and while we conversed many of the congregation, some of whom understood English, crowded around.

This was the first occurrence of the kind in my experience in which I was personally prominent, and it had an importance in my eyes which it would scarcely have were it to happen today. One of those who listened to and understood this conversation was a brother-in-law of Napela's, a half-white and a circuit judge, and a leading man on that island. He gave a report of the conversation which was very favorable to me, and altogether I think the missionary's sermon did good. He intended it for evil; but the Lord overruled it, as He does all the plots and acts of the wicked, for the advancement of His purposes.

The Lord gave me favor in the sight of the natives, and I had their sympathy, though they dare not avow it, for fear of the consequences.

Another reason of the sermon not having so good an effect was the preacher's allusions to Napela. He had called him by name, as the man at whose house I stopped, and denounced him. This, of course, was distasteful to Napela's relatives and friends, many of whom were present. Thus this man, who fought in this manner against the work of God, did not prosper as he expected, neither then nor afterwards.

The Lord has said in one of the revelations to His servants:

"Verily, thus saith the Lord unto you, there is no weapon that is formed against you shall prosper; and if any man shall lift his voice against you, he shall be confounded in mine own due time."

I have found every word of this to be true.

Napela was not frightened by what the missionary had said. He was threatened with removal from his judgeship and with being cut off from their church; but he manifested no disposition to have me leave his house.

The pressure, however, finally became so strong through the continued efforts of the preacher, that I thought it would be wiser for me to withdraw from Wailuku for awhile. I felt for Napela, for he had a heavy opposition to contend with, and I thought that if I went elsewhere, the persecution would not be so severe.

There was a place called *Kula*, (which means a country near the base of a mountain) where there were a few scattered villages, about eighteen miles from Wailuku, to which I was led to go. It was rather an out-of-the-way place, though just before I went there, a brisk trade in Irish potatoes, which grew spontaneously in that region, had been carried on; the people hauling them in carts, from there to a small port not far distant. These potatoes were carried in schooners to California to supply the gold diggers. But they were of a poor quality, and when the farmers of California began to raise them the trade ceased. The business had begun to fall off when I went there.

I stopped at the house of a man by the name of Pake, who had charge of Napela's affairs in Kula, and to whom he had given me a letter of introduction when he found that I had determined to go there. He received me very kindly, also a man by the name of Maiola, whom I had met in Wailuku. He was a deacon in the Presbyterian church.

CHAPTER IX

KULA, the district where I had gone to live, was visited about once in three months by the Presbyterian missionary who had it in charge. The Sunday after my arrival there was his day to make his quarterly visit, and I went down to the village where he was to hold his meeting. His name was Green, and he and I had met a few weeks previously, and had a conversation in which he grew very angry and said he would curse me.

There was a large attendance of natives at this meeting, and he took for his text the 8th verse of the first chapter of Paul's epistle to the Galatians:

"But though we, or an angel from heaven, preach any other gospel unto you than that which we have preached unto you, let him be accursed."

His whole sermon, as well as his prayer previously, was directed against us, warning the natives about us; but the sermon was the poorest and most childish attempt to show what the gospel of Christ was, that I ever listened to.

After he had finished, I arose and told the people it was best to examine the gospel well, and see what its nature and requirements were, and also for each to learn whether it was in his possession or not. I then commenced to show them what the gospel was.

Up to this time Mr. Green had sat amazed, as it appeared, at my audacity. Such a thing as a person arising in a meeting and questioning what he had said, or attempting to teach anything different, was new in his experience, and he seemed so astonished that he could not speak. But when he saw that I had the attention of the people and they were listening to what I said, he aroused himself, opened a catechism which he called *Ai o ka la,* or "Food of the day," and commenced asking the people questions. He was determined to interrupt me, and to divert the minds of the people from what I said. Some of his deacons helped him; they answered his questions in a loud voice, and confusion began to prevail.

I saw that no further good could be done then, so I told the congregation that I intended to hold meetings, and would have opportunities of more fully explaining to them the principles of the gospel, and I stopped.

He warned the people not to entertain me, nor to salute me; if they did, they would be partakers in my evil deeds.

To this I made a suitable reply and withdrew.

From this time I commenced to labor in a more public manner among the people, speaking in their meeting houses as I could get opportunity, and doing all in my power to give them a knowledge of our principles.

My speaking before Mr. Green had a good effect; the people saw that I preached the doctrines of the Bible, and that I was not afraid to meet the preachers; the moral effect of this boldness upon a simple people like them, I found to be excellent.

And here let me say that courage in advocating and defending the truth, when tempered with wisdom, is a quality men always admire. The fear of man, and the fear of telling that portion of the truth which he is sent to declare, are feelings that no Elder should ever indulge in. The man who suffers this fear to prevail with him is never successful. The fear of God and the fear of doing wrong, is the only fear that a Latter-day Saint should ever feel.

My training during the first two years of our settlement of Salt Lake Valley, when we were pinched for food, was of excellent service to me during the days of which I write. I should have thought the meagre diet we had in the valley, rich living if I had had it then.

The people were very poor, and I did not wish to be a burden to them in the least. I avoided eating anything, therefore, that I thought they relished or that they had only occasionally. I have told you that potatoes grew spontaneously there; but the country was too warm for them; this, together with the lack of cultivation, made them very poor. The potato when good was not a vegetable I liked very much. But there I could get nothing else, excepting whortleberries, which grew wild, and which I frequently picked and ate, until one day they made me sick, after which I could not eat them any more.

I might have eaten the potatoes better if I could have had salt to eat with them; but this article they were out of just then. The only thing eatable besides the potatoes was molasses. I have never liked to eat potatoes and molasses together since then.

I well recollect how I enjoyed a meal of "poi" on one occasion during this time. The "kalo" out of which it was made, had been cooked and pounded at some distance from there ("Kalo" did not grow at that time at the part of the Kula where I was), and packed in the leaves of a shrub called *ki;* when thus packed it was called *poi kalo.* It had been warm when packed, which, with the heat of the weather, had made it sour. But the people had cooked it over again, and made it into "poi."

My potato and molasses diet had removed all my fastidiousness about what I ate, and I thought this "poi" the sweetest food I had ever tasted. I ate this "poi" because it was the best and most palatable food I had tasted for weeks.

But what I lacked in food the Lord made up to me in the goodly degree of His Spirit which He bestowed upon me. What I had to eat was a matter of indifference to me. I was happy, and I rejoiced as I never had before. Dreams, visions and revelations were given to me, and the communion of the Spirit was most sweet and delicious.

I learned a lesson then, which I trust will never be forgotten: that there is a happiness which the servants and Saints of God can have that is not of earth, and that is not in the least dependent for its existence upon the possession of food, raiment or any earthly thing.

CHAPTER X

A NEW native house having been completed by Mr. Napela's men, it was offered to me as a meeting house. On Sunday the neighbors collected together, and we had two meetings, one in the forenoon and one in the afternoon, at which I spoke upon the principles of the gospel and their restoration to man upon the earth, with the authority to teach them. My testimony and words were favorably received by the people, and they were desirous that I should continue to hold meetings.

It was a busy time, and I was only able to hold one meeting during the week. But on the next Sunday I had a most excellent time. Five were baptized and confirmed, and the spirit was powerfully poured out upon all present; many were stirred up to repentance, their hearts were touched and the tears coursed down their cheeks. Brother James Keeler, who had been stopping in Lahaina, was with me that day, he having reached there the previous day. Our joy was very great, and I thought it one of the best days in my life.

We held meetings during the week, and on Sunday I baptized and confirmed six persons.

It was in much weakness that I labored in the ministry; but I began to taste a joy that I had never before known, and my heart was filled with praise and gratitude to the Lord for deeming me worthy to receive the Priesthood, and to go forth on a mission.

Nineteen persons had joined the Church at Kula, and I felt impressed by the Spirit to go elsewhere and open other places in which to minister the word to the people.

The news of what was being done at Kula—the new religion as it was called—the new method of baptism—for up to that time the people had been sprinkled—and the doctrine, so strange to them, that God had spoken again to man, and sent His holy angels to minister unto him, was noised about, and there began to be a great curiosity felt by many of the people to hear.

Although the natives of the Sandwich Islands had been taught to read, and the Bible had been placed in their hands, and they had been trained to look upon the sectarian missionaries as their spiritual teachers, yet the religion of these missionaries did not generally satisfy them. There was not the power about the God which the missionaries worshiped that they believed there was about the gods of their fathers. The missionaries taught them that God no longer revealed Himself to men, that prophecy, miracles and the gifts mentioned in the Bible, had ceased.

But we taught the very opposite of all this. We told them God had not changed. He was the same today that He was when the Bible was written. His gifts and blessings were for men now, as much as they were eighteen hundred years ago. Men had lost faith, and they did not obey God's laws, therefore, they had lost favor with the heavens, and the gifts and blessings were withheld.

The Bible upheld us in our teachings, and there was a consistency in our doctrines which pleased the honest.

The most of the natives of the islands supposed the Bible meant what it said; they had not learned to think that it meant one thing when it said another. But after our arrival the sectarian missionaries tried hard to teach them that the word of God had a hidden meaning, and that it was not like other language — a task, however, which, with a plain, simple people like the natives, they found very difficult.

The missionaries had great influence with the chiefs and the government. Their religion was, in fact, the State religion, though not so declared by law; it was popular to be a member of their church, while it was unpopular not to be connected with it.

It looked like a formidable and hopeless task to attempt to preach the gospel to a people and in a government over whom sectarian priests had such complete control. But we knew God could break down every barrier, and remove every obstacle. We put our trust in Him, and we were not disappointed.

I was led, as I have said, to prepare to go to some other place to labor, so as to extend the knowledge of the gospel. I had arranged to start on a certain day, but was detained. My detention was providential, for that day Brother James Keeler arrived, accompanied by a native, by the name of Namakaiona. Brother Keeler, after leaving Kula, had traveled around the island until he reached a place called Keanae, where he stopped. He had read the scriptures to the people of that place, and quite an interest had been awakened among them; many were anxious to hear preaching, and to be baptized. He wished me to come over there; they had furnished him with a horse to come over after me and bring me.

The road over which we traveled part of the distance to reach Keanae, passed through a most romantic country. The vegetation was of the most luxuriant description, the trees being a kind new to me, and very grand. Such a wealth of vegetation I had read of, but never before beheld; and is not seen in any land outside of the tropics. The shrubs and ferns were in great variety, and grew in almost endless profusion. Many of the trees were masses of living green from the root upward, being covered with a multitude of vines and creepers of various kinds.

The road was impassable for carriages or wagons; in fact, horsemen had to dismount and lead their horses in many places up and down the hills, they were so steep. Whatever the people who lived in the villages on that side of the island needed, they either carried in, on their backs, or brought around in boats. To me the journey was most romantic, and I enjoyed it, the more so as I now understood the language, and was able to obtain many interesting items from the natives with whom we traveled and met, concerning the country, and their history and traditions.

Our arrival at Keanae created great excitement. The people had been watching for us, and seeing us approach from a long distance, had gathered to meet us. Had we been princes they could not have treated us with greater consideration and honor. We obtained the Calvinistic meeting-house the afternoon of our arrival, and there was a large attendance to hear the preaching.

This was on Wednesday, and from that time until Monday we were constantly speaking, baptizing, confirming and counseling the people. During that time there were upwards of one hundred and thirty baptized. The Spirit of the Lord was powerfully poured out, and all rejoiced; I never enjoyed myself so well before in my life.

When I started back to Kula, which I did on Tuesday morning, I felt very tired, with the amount of labor that I had performed. My object in returning then, was to organize the Saints who had been baptized into a branch, so that I could return again to Keanae.

In organizing the branch at Kula, I ordained two teachers whose names were Kaleohano and Maiola, and three deacons, Pake, Kahiki, and Mahoe.

After two weeks' absence, I returned to Keanae, and we organized four branches of the Church in that region. We only ordained teachers and deacons as officers, thinking it better to let them gain experience in the duties of these callings, before ordaining them to the Melchizedek Priesthood.

CHAPTER XI

WHILE at Keanae, we were gladdened with the news of the arrival of other missionaries from Utah; and, after the conference, Brother Keeler and I repaired to Lahaina to meet them. They were Elders Philip B. Lewis, Francis A. Hammond and John S. Woodbury; the two former had their wives with them; the latter, for want of means, had left his wife in California, and she came down shortly afterwards. Brother Lewis had been appointed by Elder Parley P. Pratt to preside over the islands.

I had become so accustomed to talking in the Sandwich Islands language that it was hard for me to speak in my mother tongue. I well remember how difficult it was for me to pray in English, when called upon to do so, in the family circle, the evening after I got to Lahaina.

I had been so anxious to learn the language that I would not read any book in English excepting the Book of Mormon and the Doctrine and Covenants, and had even trained myself to think in that language. I did this so that I might be thoroughly familiar with it, for I was anxious to preach the gospel in exceeding plainness unto the people.

Of course, it required an effort on my part to thus train myself; but I was paid for it all, in the fluency with which I used the language. I was able to speak and write it with greater ease and correctness than my mother tongue.

The adversary was not idle at Keanae. We had been very successful in baptizing the people. The Spirit had been poured out, and much good had been accomplished; but, no sooner had we gone to Lahaina, to meet the newly arrived Elders, than the enemy began his operations.

After spending a few days in Lahaina, I returned to Kula and remained a short time there. I felt impressed to go from there to Keanae. Some of the native brethren wished me to stop till the end of the week, and they would accompany me; but I could not stop, I felt that I was needed for some cause at Keanae.

My impressions were correct. The people of Keanae were in great trouble. They had been assailed by enemies from every side, and those who were weak in the faith were in perplexity. Some had turned away, not being able to withstand the pressure. The Presbyterian missionary of that district had been there, and had done all in his power to blacken our characters, to deride our doctrines and to persuade the people to forsake the Church. Two Frenchmen, Catholic priests, had also been there, and they had done all in their power to frighten the people from the truth. Another Presbyterian missionary had sent one of his native preachers there for the same purpose.

It seemed as if the devil had set all his agencies into operation to destroy the work of God, and they told all the lies that could be brought to bear against us. The French priest had said that we ought to be driven out of the place and off the island, and had circulated many false reports about us. The Presbyterian missionary had visited the houses of the people, and had brought all his influence to bear upon them.

Brother Keeler had been there part of the time; but his want of the language troubled him greatly, as he had not acquired it sufficiently at the time to enable him to counteract these lies or to make full explanations concerning them.

I learned that many of the Saints were doubting, and

they had been praying to the Lord for me to return. This was the cause of my anxiety to get back. The Lord hears the prayers of those who pray to Him in faith, and hundreds of instances like this have occurred within my knowledge.

It is frequently the case that when Elders have been successful in baptizing the people, the devil exerts himself with increased power and cunning among them to destroy them. There are but few who have joined the Church who have escaped temptations of this character; and no man knows the power of the devil as those who have embraced the truth. It seems that those who are ignorant of the gospel and the power of God, never experience the opposite power like those who have been blessed of the Lord. Still they should not yield to the temptations of Satan, nor be entrapped by his snares.

The people who had been baptized at Keanae had known but little about the two influences of which we speak; but no sooner had they joined the Church, than they were assailed and tempted in a way that they never had been previously. As a consequence of this, some fell away from the truth; but others became stronger in the faith, so long as I remained on the island.

We had many excellent times at Keanae. While I was there, at the time of which I write, I went with the natives, men and women, to a creek about two miles distant, where fish were very plentiful. The fishers gathered a quantity of plants, a shrub which is called by them *auhuhu,* and made two piles of them in the bed of the creek. The men and women surrounded these piles, each of them having a stick about five or six feet long. At a given signal from one of the party, they commenced thrashing the brush. They were very dextrous in the use of this flail, turning the piles over and over and pounding them well, and never hitting each other. The pounding of the bush had the effect to stain the water all around, and to kill the fish, which soon floated on the surface in great numbers.

Fish so caught are excellent eating. This shrub, though it kills the fish, is not injurious to man. It was one of the liveliest sights that I had ever seen, and was very picturesque. The women were adorned with garlands of green leaves, and had flowers entwined in their hair and around their bodies. Many of the men were stripped to the waist and also had garlands entwined around them. The swimming and diving of some of the women surprised me; they appeared to be almost amphibious.

CHAPTER XII

NOT satisfied with bringing religious influences to bear against us, the missionaries (of whom mention was made in the last chapter) stirred up the owners of the land and the officer having it in charge to stop the meetings and to threaten the people with punishment if they persisted in holding them. This officer assembled the people, and called them out individually, and tried to make them promise that they would not attend any of our meetings again. To accomplish his design, he used both persuasion and threats; he said that if they met again, he would have them bound and either carried to the capital of that island —Lahaina—or to the seat of government—Honolulu.

In consequence of these interruptions and persecutions, of which Elder Keeler brought me word, at Kula, where I then was, it was deemed best for me to go to Honolulu, and, if possible, see the king, or some officers of the government.

Elder Philip B. Lewis, who was then living at Honolulu, and was president of the mission, and I saw several of the king's ministers. The American Commissioner espoused our cause very warmly, and demanded of the government all the rights for us which were extended to any preachers. We did not see the king, his health being very poor; but afterwards, at Lahaina, I had an interview with the two princes, who have since been kings, and from them received assurances of protection. The visit, altogether, was satisfactory and resulted in good.

I have found that nothing is ever lost by Elders standing up for their rights. People respect others who are spirited in claiming the privileges which belong to them; and no Elder should ever forget that he is the ambassador of the King of heaven, and that he should maintain his calling. If he be firm and respectful, he will be respected.

We succeeded in building a fine meeting-house at Keanae, and in all that region faithfully preached to the people.

I told you in a previous chapter about the manner in which I had been treated by the missionary at Wailuku, the place where Napela lived. His persecution had been so strong that I thought it wise to withdraw from that place for a while; but the time had now come for me to return; I felt impressed to do so; and, in company with Elder Francis A. Hammond, I reached there one evening. We did not know where to go to obtain quarters for the night; for the missionary who lived there had used every means in his power to frighten the people against entertaining us. Even Napela, who had previously afforded me a home, was under heavy condemnation for his kindness towards me. I felt delicate about going to his house again, thinking, probably, he might be reluctant to entertain us in view of the opposition which would be sure to follow.

When we got to the edge of the town in the hills, one of us went and prayed for the Lord to open our way and raise us up friends while the other watched to prevent interruption. We felt led to go to Napela's house, thinking that if he received us kindly we would stop with him, but if he appeared cold and distant, we would go elsewhere. We found him in conversation with four or five intelligent natives, most of whom had been classmates of his in the high-school. One of them, Kamakau, which translated means the *fish-hook*, was a preacher, a very well-educated man, and said to be the best native orator in their church. They were questioning Napela about our principles, arguing with him upon them, he defending them to the best of his ability.

Our arrival seemed most opportune; he was glad to see us, gave us a warm welcome, and soon transferred the conversation to us. At this time, Brother Hammond's knowledge of the language was very limited, so I found myself the principal spokesman. We sat up until the roosters crowed in the morning, conversing upon our principles and reasoning from the Bible. For some time they were disposed to combat our views, but finally were silenced and sat and listened to what I said, occasionally asking questions.

This was the commencement of a great work in that region. The preaching of the gospel created a great excitement; the people came by hundreds to hear the testimony, and I had the satisfaction of seeing the missionary who had treated me so badly and who had so bitterly opposed and lied about the work, almost deserted by his congregation; they having left his church to hear us preach, and see us baptize.

[*168*]

I confess that to see him thus treated pleased me; I did not wish him to receive any bodily injury, but I had hoped and prayed the day would come when he would see his followers desert his church, embrace the truth and leave him to himself.

We baptized a large number of people at Wailuku and the adjacent towns, erected a large meeting-house at that place and smaller ones at the other villages, and organized large and flourishing branches of the Church.

When Elder Hammond and his wife came to the island they had one child. Several children were born to them on the mission before they returned. After we had been successful in organizing branches at Wailuku, Waiehu and other places around there, Elder Hammond brought his family from Lahaina, where they had been living, to Waiehu. There they lived for some time. Afterwards, through his labors, a branch was raised up in Lahaina, and they moved there. All the Elders who labored in that field have reason to remember their kindness to them. Under their roof we always found a warm welcome, and it was home—a home which men who were constantly speaking the native language, living in the native houses and having to conform, to some extent at least, to their modes of eating, could appreciate. Sister Hammond's unvarying kindness, her patience and cheerfulness in the midst of privation, and her unsparing labors in our behalf, to sew and do other work for us, which, among such a people we had need to have done, as well as his constant efforts for our comfort, will never be forgotten by those who enjoyed their hospitality.

The contrast between my position then and what it had been when formerly at Wailuku, was to me a constant cause of gratitude to the Lord. He had revealed unto me that it was my duty to remain on the islands, acquire the language, and bear testimony of His great work to the people. He had given me many promises connected therewith. And now I began to feel how true His words had been. Many and many a time, when I sat in the meetings and heard the people speak in the demonstration of the Spirit of the Lord, filled with its power and its holy influence, bearing testimony to the truth of the gospel, to its restoration and to the gifts which had been bestowed, my joy was so great that I could scarcely contain myself. I felt that, however devotedly I might labor, I could not show the gratitude to the Lord which I felt, at being permitted to receive the Priesthood and to exercise it for the salvation of the children of men. Surely, never were men happier than we who labored in the ministry among that people in those days; we had a fullness of joy, and it seemed as if there were no room for more.

The people, too, with all their faults and weaknesses, were greatly blessed. The power of God rested mightily upon them, and many a time their faces would glisten and appear almost white under the influence of the Spirit. They knew that Jesus was the Son of God and the Savior of the world, and that Joseph Smith and Brigham Young were Prophets and servants of God. This knowledge had come to them through obedience to the commandments.

The report of what was being done went through all the islands. The natives frequently went from one island to another. They are a talkative, gossipy people, and exceedingly fond of telling news, which never loses anything after its first recital. I afterwards traveled all over the group, and I found myself well known by name to all the people. This was frequently embarrassing to me, because I felt that I could not meet the expectations which had been created respecting my skill in the language, etc., etc.

The king and his nobles all heard of us, and of what we were doing, and though we were often misrepresented, we could not blame the Hawaiians for much of this. If left to themselves, they had but little of the spirit of slander and persecution so common to the white race. They were naturally kind and hospitable. Had there been no priestcraft among them, misleading them and poisoning their minds against the truth, and tempting them with worldly advantages and popularity, the entire nation, I am convinced, could have been readily brought to receive and believe in the principles of the gospel. But everything was done to have them shun us, to inspire them with suspicion, to make us unpopular. These influences with those vicious and destructive practices which are fast hurrying the nation to extinction, were against us. But for all this, we had wonderful success among them.

Like our Indian race, the Sandwich Islander is being destroyed and blotted from the face of the earth, by too much of what is called in Babylon, civilization.

There is one remarkable feature of the Hawaiian character which I will here note. Among all the races of white men of which I have yet heard where the gospel is preached, the practice of sin, and especially with the other sex, is attended with the loss of the Spirit; and unless there is deep and heartfelt repentance, such sinners are apt to become enemies of the truth, and are frequently bitter in their opposition to the work of God and His servants. Not so with the Hawaiians, so far as my observation extended. It is true that by indulging in sin they would lose the Spirit; that could be plainly seen; but I never saw that bitter apostate feeling among them which is so common among white men who apostatize. They were not given over to the spirit of unbelief as other races are.

This difference struck me, and I account for it in two ways; first, because of their ignorance the Lord does not hold them to so strict an accountability as He does us; and second, they are of the seed of Israel, and to them peculiar promises have been made. I believe the same characteristics will be found among the Lamanites; but that can be better told by those who have had experience in laboring among them.

CHAPTER XIII

AT THE Fall Conference, 1852, held at Salt Lake City, nine Elders were appointed on missions to the islands. They reached Honolulu in the month of February, 1853. Their names were: Benjamin F. Johnson, William McBride, Nathan Tanner, Reddin A. Allred, Redick N. Allred, Thomas Karren, Ephraim Green, James Lawson and Egerton Snider. These Elders were a great help to the mission. Nearly all of them were men of experience. Their presence brought additional life and energy, the effect of which soon became visible everywhere. The most of them took hold of the work with zeal.

They brought with them the copy of the revelation on celestial marriage, which was first published at the conference at which they were called to go to the islands. They also brought the spirit of the conference with them, and we all felt the benefit of it.

After their arrival, the work received a great impulse on the Island of Oahu, and especially in Honolulu. That town was made alive with excitement, and large numbers were baptized. A branch of the white members was organized, over which Elder B. F. Johnson was appointed to preside. Elders Tanner and Karren were chosen as counselors to Elder Philip B. Lewis, the president of the mission. Upon the Islands of Hawaii and Kauai, also, the work made great strides, and hundreds were added to the Church.

I omitted to mention that Elder William Perkins, who had been appointed on a mission to the islands, reached there, accompanied by his wife and Sister John S. Woodbury, about the last of November, 1851. They remained for some time, laboring to the best of their ability. Brother Perkins was released to return home because of his wife's failing health.

For the purpose of visiting the Saints and people on the Island of Hawaii (the Owyhee of Captain Cook), I had occasion to sail to that island in April, 1854.

In those days, money was very scarce with the Elders, and we had not the means to transport us from island to island on the regular vessels which sailed in those seas. I, therefore, in company with several of the brethren, traveled, preaching by the way, through the hilly and rough country that lay between Lahaina and Kawaipapa on eastern Maui, a point considered the best to embark at to cross the channel to Hawaii.

Our company consisted of Elder R. N. Allred, who was at that time president on the Island of Maui; Elder J. H. Napela, and four native Elders belonging to Maui, who had been appointed to labor in the ministry on the Island of Hawaii. Their names were Kaelepulu, Kapono, Hoopiiaina and Peleleu.

The channel which we had to cross was at times very rough and dangerous, and many lives had been lost in it; but we had faith to believe that the Lord would preserve us in crossing, although our vessel was one that very few white men would care to venture out to sea in. It was a canoe hollowed out of a tree. Both ends of the canoe had boards fitted in as a sort of a deck, which was covered with mats. These mats were lashed to the canoe and made the top of the deck as round as a log and perfectly water-tight. You would think this deck a curious place to go to sea on, yet the native islanders were perched on both ends of the canoe on this deck with their paddles to row the canoe when the wind did not blow. In the center of the canoe a certain space was left for us to sit in, and sides were formed by lashing mats to some poles that were raised above the edge of the canoe. In this place the natives had fixed plenty of mats, so that we could sit or recline, as suited us, very comfortably. Lashed across the canoe, were two poles, each a little distance from the end of the canoe. These poles extended six or eight feet into the water, and fastened to their ends was a board, which ran parallel with the canoe. This we call an outrigger; it was for the purpose of keeping the canoe balanced when the sail was hoisted. On these poles, when the wind commenced to blow, the islanders sat, easing up and bearing down, according to the strength of the wind, so as to keep the canoe from capsizing. The greater part of the time some portion of their bodies was in the water. But the sea has no terrors for the Sandwich Islanders. They can swim in the water for hours without being at all fatigued.

When I looked at these men perched on the deck of the canoe, it looked like going to sea on a log; and had I not been familiar with the skill of the natives in managing their canoe, and had some confidence in my own powers as a swimmer, with them to aid me in the water, I should scarcely have ventured in such a craft as this was.

We prayed to the Lord, before we started, to give us a pleasant and favorable voyage, and the natives said they had never had a more favorable time.

We reached Upolu on the island of Hawaii between three and four o'clock, having started from Maui about eight o'clock in the morning.

While upon this subject I may say that we returned to Upolu after our visit had ended, and again crossed the channel, back to Maui, but this time we did not have a single canoe. One of the native Saints and his son had procured two new canoes and had lashed them together as was the fashion in former days, for their chiefs, by fastening pieces of timber across both canoes, the latter being from four to six feet apart. This was called in their language *kaulua.*

Our place to sit or recline was arranged between the canoes, by laying down boards and covering them with mats, making quite a comfortable floor for us to sit upon, and in the center of this the mast was raised and fastened.

As in the case of the single canoe, boards were fastened at the ends, with mats lying over them to keep out the water, making a deck to the canoe, while a small place was left in the center of both canoes for some of the natives to sit, and, if necessary, bail out water.

We left the four native Elders on the island, and brought away one with us, who was released from his mission to return to Maui. His name was Kailihune.

Our return passage was rough a good part of the distance, as we had a good stiff breeze about two-thirds of the way across. Then the wind died out; but we prayed to the Lord for more wind, and our prayers were answered. We were between six and seven hours in making the passage.

We traveled around the island, and visited the famous volcano, the largest in the world. Its name is Kilauea.

Our party had swelled, including whites and natives, to about twenty in number. In addition to Brother Allred, there were of our party Elder Thomas Karren, who lived at Lehi, Utah Co., but who is now deceased; Elder James Keeler, who has lately returned from another mission to the islands, and who now resides on the Sevier; and Elder Egerton Snider, who has since died.

Brother James Lawson, of this city, was also with our party, but having seen the volcano, he did not ascend with us. We had to go on foot, as we had no money to hire animals.

The Sandwich Islanders entertained a singular idea about the manner in which their islands came into being. Their belief was that the islands were brought forth, and that Papa, a woman whom they worshiped as a goddess, was the mother of them. The first-born, they think, was Hawaii, the nearest island to this continent, and the last born Kauai and Niihau. This Papa had a sister, they say, whose name was Pele. They worshiped her as a goddess, and even when we were there many still believed in her. They say she first lived at Kauai and from there removed from one island to another until she took up her residence at Hawaii. They believed that her place of residence was the pit of the active volcano, and that there, all the spirits of good chiefs and men went to dwell. The bad ones went, they believed, to a place of darkness in the center of the earth, over which a god called Milu reigned.

In former days the people threw the bones of some of their dead relatives into the volcano. They had the idea that if Pele was pleased with the sacrifice, she would consume the bones, and the spirit of the dead person would be permitted to return and be a familiar spirit to them, and be as one of the family. If the sacrifice was not acceptable, the bones were thrown out of the volcano.

The pit of the volcano is probably three miles across. There have been times when the whole bottom of the pit was one mass of lurid, seething fire. This must have been an awfully grand sight, but when we visited it, we found an immense field of lava which extended all around the pit, and which resembled, in many respects, the sea in its wave-like appearance. It might also have been compared to a field of shore-ice, from which the water had receded, leaving it shattered and cracked; in fact, it looked like a frozen sea. except that it was black as coal. In cooling it had cracked, leaving large seams, from which steam and heat issued.

We found the pit in which the fire was raging to be about fifty or sixty feet deep; it was nearly round, and about one hundred yards across. The sides were perpendicular; the strongest heat seemed to be around the sides. On one side there were two large holes very close together, which looked more like the mouths of two very large furnaces than anything else I ever saw. Here the melted lava was in constant motion, surging and heaving like the waves of the sea. The sound which it made was somewhat similar to the paddles of a steam vessel in the ocean, only it was far greater. We heard this sound before we reached the mouth of the volcano, and it resembled, to our ears, the booming of heavy artillery at a distance.

The lava kept flowing in the direction of these two holes of which I spoke, and rocks thrown down upon the surface of the lava would melt when near these holes like sealing wax held in a candle. It was surprising to see with what ease the fire would melt this stony mass of lava, which in some parts of the pit would cool on the surface, and convert it again into a fluid.

Sometimes showers of hot lava would be thrown up in the air, and descend on the edges of the pit where we stood. When this occurred the bystanders would have to scamper off as fast as they could, or be severely burned.

The sight of this pit surpassed in sublimity and grandeur anything I had ever witnessed or imagined. It far exceeded what I had read in written descriptions, or even what I expected to see. Language fails to convey to the mind a correct idea of its appearance.

We were told that a party of natives had just been there, throwing the bones of one of their relatives into the volcano with hogs, fowls, etc., sacrifices with which to gain the favor of Madame Pele, the goddess.

For some years there had not been any eruptions from this crater which we visited; but others had broken out in the same neighborhood, the fire and smoke of which had been seen for a long distance, and ashes from which, it is said, had fallen on the decks of vessels hundreds of miles at sea. From these eruptions the lava had run down to the sea, sweeping everything before it, and heating the sea for several miles in such a manner as to kill large quantities of fish.

The Island of Hawaii is very frequently shaken by earthquakes, the effects of the hidden fires.

CHAPTER XIV

RETURNING from the volcano towards Upolu, we had a meeting house to dedicate at a place called Pololu, and the Saints there had prepared a feast on the occasion.

An account of a Hawaiian feast may be interesting to my readers and I will describe this one. The vegetable portion of the feast consisted of *poi*. This I have before described to you. It is not kept in dishes of earthenware but in calabashes, some of which are very large and will hold several gallons of the food. On this occasion the people sat on the ground on mats. For tablecloths there were large green leaves of the plant called *ki*. On these were placed packages of beef, pork, fowl, dog, and goat, done up in the leaves in which they had been cooked. Fish also was served up in this manner.

As soon as the blessing was asked, everyone dipped his or her forefingers into the *poi*, and, lifting as much as the fingers would hold, they passed them into their mouths, throwing their heads back as they did so, to get a good mouthful. The hogs, chickens and little dogs were speedily dissected, the fingers being the only knives, forks and spoons used among them. The scene was one of true enjoyment.

The Sandwich Islander is never so happy, so musical, so full of pleasant talk, as when seated at a good meal; and the quantity one eats on such occasions would astonish an American who had never seen them. Usually they are particular about having their hands clean, and eating with due respect to each other's rights. One waits for the other to put his fingers in the *poi*, and their ideas of decorum and manners, such as they are, are as strict as ours.

We Elders who ate with them were also seated on mats and ate the same kind of food that they did, only in place of using our fingers we either used spoons or small paddles which we whittled out of wood, to convey the food to our mouths, thinking it would be better to set them an example in this respect.

CHAPTER XV

ONE incident, I will relate, which occurred a few months after we went to Wailuku, to show how the Lord hears and answers prayer.

We were very much in need of some means to buy stuff for garments, etc. The natives were very poor, and we felt delicate about asking them for anything; but we knew that the Lord would hear and answer our prayers; so we prayed to Him. Brother Hammond had brought his wife and child over from Lahaina, and they were living, as I have told you, in the village close to Wailuku. He and I had to make a visit to a town about twelve or fifteen miles distant, and before starting, we had prayed to the Lord to open the way so that we might obtain what we wanted.

We had traveled from the house about three miles, when, in passing some houses which were on the beach, we met a man by the name of Freeman, an American, who accosted us and inquired if we had authority to marry. Upon our informing him that we had, he asked us if we could spare the time to stop at his house and marry him. We told him as it was on our way we would stop. I performed the ceremony, and at his request addressed the people who had assembled at the house. He gave us a five-dollar gold piece.

We had married many before that, but this was the first money which had ever been given to us. His five dollars supplied our necessities, for in those days we were content with very little.

I have always looked upon this as a direct answer to our prayers, for when we met the man he was evidently on his way to Wailuku, with his intended wife, to be married by the missionary there. The missionary missed the fee, but as he knew nothing respecting it, he was no poorer. I do not suppose he needed it as badly as we did.

It is always more pleasant for an Elder, when he is in need of anything, on a mission, to apply to the Lord for it than to ask the people; at least, I have always found it so.

The Lord blessed the natives who joined the Church in many ways, and they rejoiced exceedingly in the gifts of the Spirit. One day a young man made application to be baptized who had been so sick that he was not expected to live. His elder brother was in the Church, and the evening previous to his baptism the Elders had been called to administer to him. He was so much restored by morning that he was able to arise and afterwards attend the meeting, and was baptized.

The same day Brother Napela and some of the other native Saints had visited a woman who believed in the gospel, who wished to be baptized; she had been unable to walk upright for five years, but she was anxious for them to administer to her, that she might be restored. They laid their hands upon her and commanded her in the name of the Lord Jesus Christ, to arise and walk. She immediately stood up and walked, and went and was baptized.

This created quite an excitement in the neighborhood, for she was well known, and the people were much astonished at her restoration. The attention of numbers were turned to the gospel by this occurrence.

Another instance which happened about the same time was that of a woman who was a member of the Presbyterian church. She was afflicted with dropsy, or something very like that disease. She had tried various remedies, but obtained no relief. She had heard about the gifts in the

Church, and she called upon Brothers Napela and Uaua to administer to her, saying she was willing to covenant and foresake her sins. They administered to her and she was healed; all the swelling left her and she was baptized. On Sunday she attended meeting, and afterwards made some remarks derogatory to the work, indulging in a spirit of apostasy; her disease returned immediately, and she was as bad as ever.

Another instance was that of a woman, one of whose limbs was withered, and who was afflicted with palsy. She was baptized, and was speedily restored to health.

A niece of hers was afterwards afflicted similarly; she requested us to administer to her, and when we did so, she was restored to health.

The same day that this latter person had hands laid upon her, we had a meeting at a place called Waiehu. After the meeting was over, three persons requested to be administered to, one of whom was a blind man. He had been blind for upwards of thirty years, but his sight was restored to him. He began to amend from the time hands were laid upon him, and the next morning he was able to see. He was afterwards able to go about without any guide; and I have frequently seen him come into meeting, winding this way among the people, without any aid, to a seat which he was accustomed to occupy near the speaker. His restoration caused a great stir in the neighborhood, for his blindness was well known. He had a son, a mature man, who could barely recollect when his father was able to see and go about without aid.

I will relate another instance of which I was not an eye witness; but which I have every reason to believe occurred as I will relate it. I have mentioned an Elder whose name was Uaua. He was a man of considerable faith. His wife had been stricken down in his absence and had been, to all appearance, dead for some three hours before he had arrived at his house.

In that country when a person dies, the friends and relatives of the family assemble together and manifest their grief by wailing. They were indulging in these lamentations and outcries when he returned, every one supposing that she was dead. He was, of course, very much shocked; but the first thing he did was to anoint her and lay hands upon her; and, to the astonishment of all who had assembled, she instantly recovered.

I might multiply instances of this kind without number; but I write these, to show you that the same works and power of God, which were manifested anciently through the faith of the servants and Saints of God have been shown forth in our day and under the administration of the people of God, who now live.

The natives of the Sandwich Islands had great faith to lay hands on the sick, and also to have hands laid upon them when they were sick. It was not contrary to their traditions for them to believe in this ordinance, for their old native priests, before the missionaries came, had considerable power which they exercised, and in which the people had confidence.

Many Elders desire, when they are called as missionaries, to go to enlightened and cultivated nations. They think their experience among such people would be profitable to them, and that they would become polished and learn many things which they could not obtain among a people, for instance, like the Sandwich Islanders or the Lamanites. Such Elders forget that the Lord sends His Elders out to teach and not to be taught. Missionaries should not have the idea of self-comfort and self-indulgence in their minds; but the salvation of souls.

The man who goes out expecting the people to whom he is sent, to teach, enlighten and benefit him commits a great blunder. He does not understand the nature of his Priesthood and calling.

I shall probably never forget the feelings expressed to me by John Hyde, Jr., on this point. He had been called, at a Conference (April, 1856) at Salt Lake City, to go on a mission to the Sandwich Islands. He came to San Francisco on his way. I was then publishing the *Western Standard* and presiding over the California mission. It was with a feeling akin to disgust that he spoke to me about his mission. If he had only been called to go to France, to England, or to any of the so-called enlightened nations, he said he would have gone willingly; but to go to a degraded, heathenish people was entirely beneath him. A man with his talent and acquirements would be thrown away upon them.

He apostatized while on the voyage to Honolulu; or, to state it more properly, he made up his mind while on the sea to dissolve his connection with the Church. He was an apostate in his heart and feelings before he left San Francisco. But can any one, who understands this work, wonder that a man who felt thus should lose the Spirit and apostatize? It would be a wonder if he did not.

The experience of the Elders who have been on missions to the Sandwich Islands is encouraging to all who are called to go on missions to the Lamanites. They may have privations to endure, but they will be swallowed up in the joy of the Lord. I am sure the Lord makes up for any lack of temporal comforts by an additional outpouring of His Spirit.

The soul of a Sandwich Islander or a Lamanite is as precious in the sight of the Lord as the soul of a white man, whether born in America or Europe. Jesus died for one as much as the other, and to the men of red skins the Lord's promises are very great and precious. Those who administer ordinances of salvation to them will have fully as great joy over them in the day of the Lord Jesus as if they had been more enlightened.

Blessed shall be the faithful men who have labored, who now labor, and who may hereafter labor among the Lamanites for their salvation. In such labor the Elders will enjoy the power of the Priesthood, the gifts of the Spirit, and pure, heavenly happiness to their hearts' content, and that is all they could enjoy among the races which they may think more favored.

I say this because my own experience has proved it to be true, and because of the great blessings and promises which are made to those who shall labor for the salvation of the seed of Israel and the covenant people of the Lord.

In what position could the sons of King Mosiah have learned as much concerning the power of God as they did during their missions among the Lamanites? Among what people could they have saved more souls? And will they not have joy with them in the kingdom of the Father?

Thousands of Elders will yet have to labor among the red men for their salvation. They should not look upon this as a hardship, but as a great and inestimable privilege —a work in which angels delight to engage.

CHAPTER XVI

SOME of my readers may be placed in circumstances similar to those which surrounded me a part of the time on the Sandwich Islands; and it may be profitable to tell them how I kept from losing courage and becoming homesick. My love for home is naturally very strong. For the first year after I left home I could scarcely think about it without my feelings getting the better of me. But here I was in a distant land, among a people whose language and habits were strange to me. Their very food was foreign to me, and unlike anything I had ever before seen or tasted. I was much of the time separated from my companions, the Elders. Until I mastered the language and commenced preaching and baptizing the people, I was indeed a stranger among them.

Before I commenced holding regular meetings, I had plenty of time for meditation, and to review all the events of my short life, and to think of the beloved home from which I was so far separated. It was then that I found the value of the Book of Mormon. It was a book which I always loved. But I learned there to appreciate it as I had never done before. If I felt inclined to be lonely, to be low spirited, or homesick, I had only to turn to its sacred pages to receive consolation, new strength and a rich outpouring of the Spirit. Scarcely a page that did not contain encouragement for such as I was. The salvation of man was the great theme upon which its writers dwelt, and for this they were willing to undergo every privation and make every sacrifice.

What were my petty difficulties compared with those afflictions which they had to endure? If I expected to share the glory for which they contended, I could see that

I must labor in the same Spirit. If the sons of King Mosiah could relinquish their high estate, and go forth among the degraded Lamanites to labor as they did, should not I labor with patience and devoted zeal for the salvation of these poor red men, heirs of the same promise?

Let me recommend this book, therefore, to young and old, if they need comfort and encouragement. Especially can I recommend it to those who are away from home on missions. No man can read it, partake of its spirit and obey its teachings, without being filled with a deep love for the souls of men and a burning zeal to do all in his power to save them. Every Latter-day Saint should read it, as well as the other records which the Lord has given to us.

The conversations, which I had with the natives concerning the Book of Mormon and the origin of the red men, made them anxious to see it. After branches had been built up at Wailuku, at Waiehu and other places around, by Elder F. A. Hammond and myself, I was led to commence the translation of the Book of Mormon into the language of the Islands—the Hawaiian language, as it is called.

My place of residence was at Brother J. H. Napela's, in Wailuku. He was an educated, intelligent Hawaiian, who thoroughly understood his own language, and could give me the exact meaning of words. The meaning attached to many words depended upon the context. It was important, therefore, in translating, to know that the words used conveyed the correct idea. Unless the language used carried to the Hawaiian mind the same meaning precisely which the words in our translation gave to us, it would not be correct.

Probably but few in the nation were as well qualified as Brother Napela, to help me in this respect. He was a descendant of the old chiefs of the Island of Maui, in whose families the language was preserved and spoken in the greatest purity, and he had advantages which no other equally well educated man, at that time, possessed. He had studied the principles of the gospel very thoroughly, he had a comprehensive mind to grasp the truth, and he had been greatly favored by the Spirit. As I progressed with the translation, his comprehension of the work increased. He got the spirit of the book, and was able to seize the points presented to him very quickly.

In the last days of the month of January, 1851, I commenced the work of translation. My fellow-laborers, the Elders, encouraged me, and from the First Presidency at home— Presidents Young, Kimball and Richards—came words of cheer, approving of what I was doing, and counseling me to persevere.

The labor of preaching, baptizing, confirming, organizing branches, administering to the sick and traveling around visiting branches, and over other islands, pressed upon me and claimed the greater portion of my time. Those were busy seasons for all who would labor, and they were exceedingly delightful. The Lord seemed very near to us upon those islands in those days.

The time occupied by me in translation, were the days and hours which were not claimed by other duties. In the beginning my method was to translate a few pages, and then, when opportunity offered, explain to Brother Napela the ideas, whether historical or doctrinal, in great fullness. By this means he would get a pretty thorough comprehension of the part I was translating. I would then read the translation to him, going carefully over every word and sentence, and learning from him the impression the language used conveyed to his mind. In this way I was able to correct any obscure expression which might be used, and secure the Hawaiian idiom.

The Spirit of translation rested upon me; it even became a very easy labor for me. I obtained great facility of expression in the language, and before I got through with the book I had a range of words at my command, superior to the great bulk of the people.

This was a very natural result. Doctrines, principles and ideas were in the Book of Mormon which were outside the ordinary thoughts of the people. The translation of these called forth the full powers of the language, and really required—that which I felt I had while engaged in this work—the assistance of the Spirit of inspiration.

At some times in revising the translation, I had other intelligent men present with Brother Napela.

In this way I went through the whole book, carefully reading and explaining every word and sentence to him and to them; and if there was an obscure expression, not leaving it till it was made plain. When it had been thus revised I copied it into a book. The copying, however, into the book, for the want of time, was never quite finished. But, excepting that it was written in very fine writing, because of the scarcity of paper, it really did not need copying.

The translation was finished on July 22nd, 1853—about two years and a half from the time I commenced it. But it was not until the 27th of the succeeding September that we completed the revision.

My labors in the ministry have always been to me exceedingly joyful; but no part of them ever furnished me such pleasure as did my work at translating that precious record. After I commenced it, I had, in preaching, an increased flow of the Spirit, in testimony I had greater power, and in the administration of all the ordinances of the gospel I felt that I had greater faith. I felt very happy. In truth, my happiness was beyond description. Thankfulness constantly filled my heart, because of my being permitted to do this work.

In December, 1853, I visited Kauai, the extreme westerly island, which is inhabited, of the group. I had a double purpose in visiting this island—to visit the Saints and bear testimony to all the people concerning the work, and to again revise the translation of the Book of Mormon. There was a native Elder laboring in the ministry with Elder William Farrer at that time on the island, by the name of Kauwahi, a man of acute intellect and talent and good education, and who was called the most eloquent and best reasoner in the Hawaiian nation. I was desirous to have him and Brother Farrer go through the translation with me, to see that no word had been omitted, and to correct any inaccuracies which might have escaped my previous reading.

We commenced this revision at the town of Waimea, the farthest inhabited point west on the Sandwich Islands, on the 24th of December, 1853, and finished it on the last day of January, 1854.

While attending to this we did not neglect our other duties among the Saints and people. During this revision, I read the book through twice, with the exception of a few pages: once to Brother Farrer, who looked at the English version, to see there were no words or sentences omitted; afterwards to Brother Kauwahi, who also looked at the English book, he being a little acquainted with English, to correct any inaccuracies in the translation or the idiom.

Where there was an expression that was not very plain, or that was out of the ordinary line of the Hawaiian thought—and there were many such—I took pains to explain it fully to Brother Kauwahi, as I had done before to Brother Napela, so as to be sure that I had used the most simple and clear language to convey the idea.

In my journal I find that I say it was more free from mistakes than I could expect it to be under the circumstances in which I was placed at the time of translating—there were calls to preach, frequent interruptions to go and administer to the sick, and often conversations which distracted my attention; but in the midst of which I had to translate and copy.

At a conference of the Elders, held at Wailuku, October 6th, 1853, the question was discussed, whether it would be better to employ some printing firm to print the Book of Mormon, or to purchase a press and printing materials for the mission, with which to print that and other works necessary for the instruction of the Saints. It was decided that the better course would be to buy a press, etc. A committee of three—Elders Philip B. Lewis, Benjamin F. Johnson and myself—was selected to take such measures as might be necessary to raise the funds.

At that conference I was released from the charge of the Island of Maui, and appointed to travel all through the islands, to collect means for the publication of the Book of Mormon. And here it may be proper to say that those who subscribed for one copy or more of the work, were afterwards furnished therewith when it was published.

Brother Edward Dennis, a white man who had been baptized at Honolulu, loaned the committee, on their note, one thousand dollars towards the purchase of the press, type, paper, etc. These funds we sent to Brother John M. Horner, California, for him to use for the purchase of what we wanted. The press, type and paper were purchased in New York, were shipped around Cape Horn to Honolulu, and, as I had returned home to Salt Lake Valley, they were sent to Elder Parley P. Pratt, by his request, at San Francisco, California. He thought at that time of publishing a paper there, and wrote to the First Presidency for me to be appointed to a mission to assist him.

I had barely reached home after an absence of five years. I remained there about five months and a half. At the April Conference, 1855, I was called to go on a mission to California, to publish the Book of Mormon in the Hawaiian language, and to assist Elder Pratt in the publication of a paper. Elders Joseph Bull and Matthew F. Wilkie were selected to go with me. When we reached San Francisco, Elder Pratt had started for home. I succeeded in reaching him at Brother John C. Naile's ranch, where he was completing his preparations for the journey. He set me apart to preside, in his place, over Northern California and Oregon, and we separated, he to go home, and I to return to San Francisco.

Our first business was to secure a suitable office, set up the press, and go to work. Brothers Bull and Wilkie knew nothing about the Hawaiian language; but the copy, to begin with, was good, and they soon became so familiar with the words that they could set it in type nearly as well as they could English, and made but very few mistakes.

President Young counseled me to take my wife with me upon this mission. My method of reading the proof was to get her to read the English book while I looked at the proofs of the translation. By this means I was able to detect any omission of words or sentences. After going through the proofs in this way, I read them again, to see if any errors in spelling, etc., had escaped me. This was my only way of reading by copy; for I had no one with me who could read the Hawaiian. When we had the edition struck off and bound they were sent to the Elders upon the islands.

Thus was the Book of Mormon first translated and published in the language of a race of red men—a part of the race for whom its promises are most abundant. The Elders who have since labored upon those islands, know the good the book has accomplished. Its circulation can ñever fail to benefit all who will read it.

The language of the Sandwich Islanders is a dialect of the Polynesian language, spoken by the Islanders with red skins all through the Pacific. Should the day ever come, as I trust it will, when the natives of other groups shall be visited and brought to the knowledge of the gospel, it will take but little trouble to adapt the Hawaiian translation to their language. But whether or not, the book has been published to the Hawaiian nation. The Lord plainly manifested that it was His will that this work should be done, and for its accomplishment He opened the way most marvelously.

The publication of the book was not a part of my first mission; but as the sketch of the translation would not be complete without the addition of these few particulars respecting its publication, I insert them. In addition, I may also say that, after the publication of the Book of Mormon, the press and type were used for the publication of the *Western Standard,* a paper which many of my adult readers may remember.

CHAPTER XVII

THE time had arrived for the five Elders, who had remained out of the first ten who were sent to the islands —to return home. It had been a matter of some thought how we would be able to obtain means to return. The Islanders had but little money. A dollar with them was a very large sum; a ten cent piece was a much larger sum with them generally, and more difficult to procure, than a dollar was to Americans. But when they learned we were soon to be released, they manifested a very kind and liberal spirit. Still, with all they had done, when our passages were engaged, we did not have near enough money to pay for them. But we had faith that the necessary means would come from some quarter. And it did. Through the kindness of Elders Lewis, Johnson and Hammond and some white brethren whom we had baptized, we had enough, and some money to take with us, to help us when we reached San Francisco.

Elder James Keeler, one of the five, failed to reach Honolulu in time to sail on the vessel on which we had engaged our passages. This was a great disappointment.

Elders Henry W. Bigler, James Hawkins, William Farrer and myself bade farewell to the Elders and Saints at Honolulu on Saturday, July 29th, 1854, and sailed for San Francisco, homeward bound. The wharf at Honolulu was crowded with native Saints and others, to see us embark. We had quite an ovation. There also were the Elders from home and Sister Hammond—Sister Lewis was not able to be out—to bid us farewell.

When the signal was made for all to go on board, we had considerable difficulty in making our way to the vessel, through the throng of people who crowded around to shake hands. My feelings were indescribable. My dear white friends I had been associated with on terms of the closest intimacy for several years. Ties of blood could not, it seemed to me, have caused us to be more attached to each other than we were. We had endured privation and toil together; we had counseled and prayed together; we had had seasons of joy and happiness together, such as those only know who have been engaged in similar labors.

My feelings were so acute at the thought of parting with these beloved companions and Saints, that, long as the years had been during which I had been absent from home, and much as I had yearned for that home and its loved associations, I could not control my emotions.

How great the contrast between our landing and our departure! We had landed there friendless and unknown —so far as man was concerned. Now there were thousands who loved us, who rejoiced in the truth of the gospel and in the testimony of Jesus.

More than twenty-five years have elapsed since my departure from the Sandwich Islands. During that period my life has been a happy one. I have filled many missions, have seen great varieties of life, and have had exceedingly agreeable and delightful associations; but, after making allowance for growth and increased capacity to enjoy, I can truthfully say that, destitute as we were of many things which people brought up as we are think necessary to comfort, at no time, or under no circumstances, have I enjoyed more sweet, pure and soul-filling joy than I did on MY FIRST MISSION.

JACOB HAMBLIN

By JAMES A. LITTLE

JACOB HAMBLIN

JACOB HAMBLIN

was born April 2, 1819, at Salem, Ashtabula
County, Ohio. In his youth he moved to Wisconsin,
where he was baptized and became a member of
the L. D. S. Church on March 2, 1842. The same
year he moved to Nauvoo, and from that time on
all his activities were inseparably connected with
the Mormon people. In 1850 he made the journey
across the plains to Utah, and located in Tooele.
It was here that he became interested in the Indians. He believed that by talking with them he
could appeal to their better judgment, and avoid
open conflict between them and the white settlers.
This policy was the key to his life's success in
dealing with the Indians. In 1854 he moved to the
Santa Clara in Washington County and became an
Indian missicnary. In 1858 he visited the Moqui
villages in northern Arizona and did missionary
work among them. He also worked with the Navajo tribes and endeavored to persuade them to live
peaceably with the white men. In this work he had
many thrilling adventures which are set forth in
this volume. Between 1870 and 1878, while living
at Kanab, Jacob Hamblin dictated the story of his
life and his activities among the Indians to his
friend and neighbor, James A. Little. Mr. Little
wrote the story in longhand, and it was published
in 1881 as the fifth volume of the Faith Promoting Series. In 1878 Jacob Hamblin moved to Arizona and located in the town of Amity. From there
he moved in 1882 to Pleasanton, New Mexico,
where he died on August 31, 1886. On his monument he is eulogized as having been "A peacemaker
in the camp of the Lamanites."

CHAPTER I

I WAS born in Salem, Ashtabula Co., Ohio, on the 6th of April, 1819. When I was three months old, my father removed to Geauga Co., in the same State. That country was then a wilderness, covered with a heavy growth of timber. In my early life I assisted my father in chopping timber and clearing land.

It required twenty faithful days' work to clear one acre, and render it fit for the harrow and a crop of wheat. In about three years the roots of the trees would decay, so that the soil could be worked with a plow.

In 1836, I removed, with my father, to Wisconsin Territory. I remember passing through Chicago, then a mere hamlet, but now a large and wealthy city.

Seventy miles north-west of Chicago, my father, in company with two friends, Messrs. Pratt and Harvey, located at a place called Spring Prairie. It was the most delightful country I had ever seen. It was beautiful with rolling prairies, groves of timber, numerous springs of pure water, and an occasional lake abounding with fish.

My father and I each made a claim on eighty acres of government land which was expected soon to come into the market. I was not yet of age, and my father, wishing to return to Ohio for his family, proffered to give me the remainder of my time, during the summer, if I would take care of the crop already sown.

During his absence, I had the misfortune to cut one of my knees. I took cold in it, and it became much inflamed and swollen. The family with whom I was living did not think I could get well. The swelling had reached my body, and as soon as it extended a little farther, the people expected me to die. I quite despaired of ever seeing my parents again.

In my childhood, I had imbibed a belief that there was a God who would hear my prayers when I was in trouble. I managed to drag myself a short distance into a hazel thicket, where I besought the Lord to have mercy upon me, and not let me die.

That evening, a Mrs. Campbell called at the house. She said she was passing by and felt impressed to call in, but did not know for what purpose. After explaining to her my situation, she said "I now know why I came in here, for I can bring that swelling all out."

This was accomplished by steaming, and I soon got about, and again had the privilege of meeting my parents and other relatives.

The second season after this occurrence my father told me that, as I had been a faithful boy, I might go and do something for myself. I took a bundle of clothing, and travelled westward 118 miles to the Galena lead mines. I worked there nearly a year.

Twice during that time I barely escaped being buried about 100 feet under ground, by the caving in of the earth. At one time, when 200 feet below the surface of the ground, a rock fell on a man who was working with me, and killed him instantly. While dragging his mangled body along the drift, and arranging a rope by which to raise it up the shaft, such an aversion to mining came over me, that I did not go back to my labor again. I returned with the money I had earned, and paid for my land.

In the autumn of 1839 I married Lucinda Taylor. She, as well as myself, had a numerous circle of relatives. I enclosed my land with a good fence, built a comfortable house, and made up my mind to live and die on the place.

I believed the Bible, but was without faith in any of the religious sects of the day, and had given up all hope of finding a religion that I could believe to be true.

In February, 1842, a neighbor called at my house and told me that he had heard a "Mormon" Elder preach. He asserted that he preached more Bible doctrine than any other man he had ever listened to, and that he knew what he preached was true. He claimed that the gospel had been restored to the earth, and that it was the privilege of all who heard it to know and understand it for themselves.

What this neighbor told me so influenced my mind, that I could scarcely attend to my ordinary business.

The Elder had left an appointment to preach again at the same place, and I went to hear him. When I entered the house he had already commenced his discourse. I shall never forget the feeling that came over me when I saw his face and heard his voice. He preached that which I had long been seeking for; I felt that it was indeed the gospel.

The principles he taught appeared so plain and natural, that I thought it would be easy to convince any one of their truth. In closing his remarks, the Elder bore testimony to the truth of the gospel.

The query came to my mind: How shall I know whether or not these things are so, and be satisfied? As if the Spirit prompted him to answer my inquiry, he again arose to his feet and said: "If there is anyone in the congregation who wishes to know how he can satisfy himself of the truth of these things, I can assure him that if he will be baptized, and have hands laid upon him for the gift of the Holy Ghost, he shall have an assurance of their truth."

This so fired up my mind, that I at once determined to be baptized, and that too, if necessary, at the sacrifice of the friendship of my kindred and of every earthly tie.

I immediately went home and informed my wife of my intentions.

She told me that if I was baptized into the "Mormon" Church, I need not expect her to live with me any more.

The evening after the Elder had preached I went in search of him, and found him quite late at night. I told him my purpose, and requested him to give me a "Mormon Bible." He handed me the Old and New Testament.

I said, "I thought you had a new Bible." He then explained about the coming forth of the Book of Mormon, and handed me a copy of it.

The impressions I received at the time cannot be forgotten. The spirit rested upon me and bore testimony of its truth, and I felt like opening my mouth and declaring it to be a revelation from God.

On the 3rd of March, 1842, as soon as it was light in the morning, I started for a pool of water where I had arranged to meet with the Elder, to attend to the ordinance of baptism. On the way, the thought of the sacrifice I was making of wife, of father, mother, brothers, sister and numerous other connections, caused my resolution to waver.

As my pace slackened, some person appeared to come from above, who, I thought, was my grandfather. He seemed to say to me, "Go on, my son; your heart cannot conceive, neither has it entered into your mind to imagine the blessings that are in store for you, if you go on and continue in this work."

I lagged no more, but hurried to the pool, where I was baptized by Elder Lyman Stoddard.

It was said in my confirmation, that the spirits in prison greatly rejoiced over what I had done. I told Elder Stoddard my experience on my way to the water.

He then explained to me the work there was for me to do for my fathers, if I was faithful, all of which I believed and greatly rejoiced in.

On my way home, I called at the house of one of my neighbors. The family asked me if I had not been baptized by the "Mormon" Elder. I replied that I had. They stated that they believed what he preached to be the truth, and hoped they might have the opportunity of being baptized.

The following day Elder Stoddard came to my house, and told me that he had intended to leave the country, but could not go without coming to see me. For what purpose he had come, he knew not.

I related to him what my neighbors had said. He held more meetings in the place, and organized a branch before leaving.

When my father learned that I had joined the "Mormons," he said he thought he had brought up his children so that none of them would ever be deceived by priestcraft; at the same time he turned from my gate, and refused to enter my house.

Other relatives said that my father knew better than to be deceived as I had been. I answered them by predicting that, much as he knew, I would baptize him into the Church before I was two years older.

All my relatives, except one brother, turned against me, and seemed to take pleasure in speaking all manner of evil against me. I felt that I was hated by all my former acquaintances. This was a great mystery to me.

I prayed to the Lord and was comforted. I knew that I had found the valuable treasure spoken of by our Savior, and I was willing to sacrifice all things for it.

My wife's father took great pains to abuse and insult

me with his tongue. Without having any conception how my prediction would be fulfilled, I said to him one day, "You will not have the privilege of abusing me much more." A few days after he was taken sick, and died.

Soon after the death of her father, my wife asked me, good-naturedly, why I did not pray in the house or with her. I replied, that I felt better to pray by myself than I did before unbelievers. She said that she was a believer; that her father had appeared to her in a dream, and told her not to oppose me any more as she had done; and that he was in trouble on account of the way he had used me. Soon after this she was baptized, which was a great comfort to me.

In the autumn of 1842, Elder Stoddard returned to the country where I lived, to labor in the ministry, and ordained me an Elder.

About the same time my wife was taken very sick. By her request, I administered to her, and she was immediately healed. I visited my father and told him that signs followed the believer, as in the days of the apostles; that I was a believer, and had been ordained an Elder in the Church of Jesus Christ of Latter-day Saints, and that the signs followed my ministrations.

He ordered me out of his house for believing such nonsense. I went out, reflecting as to whether or not I had done wrong in predicting that I would baptize him in less than two years.

Some time after this he was taken sick, and I went to see him. My mother told me he had the spotted fever, and that there was no hope of his recovery. She believed he was dying, and so it appeared to me; but I thought that God could and would save him if I prayed for him.

I retired to a private place, and prayed to the God of Abraham to have mercy on my father and heal him, that he might have an opportunity of obeying the gospel.

It was a moonlight night, and when I returned to the house my mother stood at the door. She spoke to me very kindly, and said:

"Jacob, the fever has left your father; he has spoken and wants to see you."

As I approached him he said, "The fever has left me, and your mother says that you came to me and went away again. What has made such a sudden change? Do you know?"

I answered that I had prayed for him, that I was a believer in the gospel of the Son of God, and in the signs following those that believe.

"Well," said he, "if it is the gospel, I would like to know it; but if it is priestcraft, I want nothing to do with it."

Soon after the sickness of my father, I sold my home, gathered up my effects and started for Nauvoo, Hancock Co., Illinois.

In passing my father's house I found him quite well, and he desired me to remain over night. He showed much interest in the principles of the gospel, and, when I left his house in the morning, the Spirit manifested to me that my father and his household would yet accept the truth.

CHAPTER II

I TRAVELED westward about 100 miles to the Mississippi river, where I took passage on a steamer to Nauvoo. I landed in the night. In the morning, I asked a young man where the Prophet lived. He pointed out the way to the residence of Joseph Smith, Jr., and said, "If you are going to see the Prophet, do not take any money with you. If you do, he will get it."

I asked the youth if he was a "Mormon." He replied that he was, and that his father was a High Priest. I thought it strange that he should talk as he did.

As I passed along one of the streets of the town, I saw a tall, noble-looking man talking with another. An impression came over me that he was the person I was looking for. Inquiring of a bystander, I learned that my impression was correct.

One of the company asked the Prophet for some money he had loaned him. He replied that he would try and get it during the day. I offered him the money, but he said: "Keep your money. I will not borrow until I try to get what is owing me. If you have just come in and wish to pay your tithing, you can pay it to Brother Hyrum; he sees to that."

I soon learned to discriminate between the different kinds of people who had gathered to Nauvoo. Some were living the lives of Saints; others were full of deceit and were stumbling-blocks in the way of those who were striving to do right.

The following winter I chopped wood on an island in the Mississippi River, twenty miles above Nauvoo.

The Prophet Joseph had told the people that the time had come which was spoken of by the Prophet Malachi, when the hearts of the fathers must turn to the children, and the hearts of the children to the fathers; the Saints must seek for the spirit of this great latter-day work, and that they must pray for it until they received it.

I had made a practice for several days, of retiring to a private place early each morning, to pray for this Spirit and blessing, when an influence came over me that made manifest to me my nothingness before the Lord. This so affected me for a time, that I was almost led to wish that I had never been born. When thus humbled, it was shown to me how a man could obtain salvation, and what he might attain to. With this I felt satisfied. What was then shown me has been of great worth to me since. I then comprehended that the most implicit obedience to the will of God was necessary in order to attain to eternal life.

In February, 1844, Joseph Smith, the Prophet, published an address to the people of the United States, on the Powers and Policy of the General Government, and offered himself as a candidate for the office of President of the United States.

The same year, at the April Conference, Elders were called and sent forth, two by two, into each State of the Union, with the "Address to the People of the United States," in pamphlet form, for distribution, and to preach the gospel. I was sent with Brother John Myers, to the State of Maryland.

We took passage on the steamer Osprey, in company with seven of the quorum of the Twelve Apostles, and seventy-one of the Seventies. My companion and I went to Pittsburg, Penn., and from there we traveled on foot with our valises, without purse or scrip, through the State of Pennsylvania.

We were often hungry and weary, and, in some instances, were accused of being beggars and deceivers. This, coupled with my natural independence of character, seemed humiliating, and made our travels anything but agreeable.

We journeyed through Derrytown, Hagerstown, Sharpsburg and Antietam, and preached in the States of

Pennsylvania, Virginia and Maryland. We visited some places where branches of the Church had been previously organized.

The way appeared to be opening up for a good work to be done in that country, when, about the 4th of July, news reached me that the Prophet, about whom I had preached so much, had been shot by a mob when confined in jail. I did not believe the report until I offered to preach to those who were gathered around me in the small town of Mechanicsburg. They manifested a spirit of exultation, and a feeling of deep gloom passed over me. I felt more like weeping than preaching.

I concluded to hunt up my companion, from whom I was then separated. For this purpose I started for Hagerstown, where I hoped to find him, or learn of his whereabouts.

I had traveled about a mile when I came to a cross road, and the Spirit whispered to me, "Stop here, and Brother Myers will soon be along." I remained on the spot about ten minutes, when I saw him coming, with his hat in one hand and his valise in the other. He did not believe that the Prophet was killed.

We journeyed together to Lightersburg. After meeting and passing many people, the Spirit indicated to us that a man on the opposite side of the street was an Elder in Israel. It proved to be a Latter-day Saint Elder, who had reliable information of the murder of the Prophet Joseph and the Patriarch Hyrum Smith. He also informed us that the Elders who were abroad were all called home.

On the 15th of July, 1844, when taking leave of a small branch of the Church in Lightersburg, one of the sisters offered me some money that she had earned in the harvest field. I took one dollar, and told her that I could get home with that.

After starting, I began to reflect on my situation. I must travel on the river steamers from Pittsburg to Nauvoo, via Cincinnati and St. Louis, and I had only two dollars in my pocket. I had been often surprised, when traveling on foot at the pains people would take to invite me to ride or to step into a grocery and take a lunch, and I had considerable faith that the Lord would soften the heart of some one to assist me, when I was in need.

When I arrived in Pittsburg, I had one dollar left. There were two steamers at the landing about to start for St. Louis. They offered to take passengers very cheap. I told the captain of one of them, that I would give all the money I had for a passage to St. Louis. He took my money and gave me a ticket, but appeared rather cross.

I was soon on my way down the river, but still a long way from home, and without money or anything to eat. I began to feel the want of food.

Nothing special occurred with me until evening, when the lamps were lit in the passengers' cabin. I was then asked by a young married lady, if I was not a "Mormon" Elder. I replied that I was; and she told me that her little child was dying with the scarlet fever, and she wished me to lay hands on it and heal it.

I replied that I could administer to it, and I presumed that the Lord would heal it. I asked her if she believed in such things. She said that she did, and that she belonged to the Church, but her husband did not. I was puzzled in my mind to know what to do, for the boat was crowded with passengers, and all unbelievers excepting the mother of the sick child and myself. It seemed like a special providence that, just then, the lamp in the cabin should fall from its hangings, and leave us all in the dark.

Before another lamp could be lit, I had administered to the child, and rebuked the fever in the name of the Lord Jesus, unobserved by those around. The Lord blessed the administration, and the child was healed.

The mother called her husband, and said to him, "Little Mary is healed; now do not say anything against 'Mormonism.'" The man looked at his child, and said to me, "I am not a believer in any kind of religion, but I am on my way to Iowa, opposite to Nauvoo, where I presume you are going. You are welcome to board with me all the way, and if you want any money I will let you have it."

I arrived in Nauvoo on the 5th of August, 1844.

CHAPTER III

AT NAUVOO I found Sidney Rigdon busy among the Saints, trying to establish his claim to the presidency of the Church. He was first Counselor to the Prophet Joseph at the time of the latter's death. The Church was fourteen years old, and he claimed that it was its privilege and duty to appoint a guardian; and he wished the people to sanction his guardianship.

I was much dissatisfied with the course he was taking, and as I could not sustain him, I felt to leave Nauvoo for a season. I went into the country, where I had left my wife and two children with my sister Melissa. When I met my sister, she threw her arms around my neck and thanked the Lord that I had returned. She had seen an account of a man being drowned in the Ohio River, and, from the description, thought that it might have been me.

On the 8th of August, 1844, I attended a general meeting of the Saints. Elder Rigdon was there, urging his claims to the presidency of the Church. His voice did not sound like the voice of the true shepherd. When he was about to call a vote of the congregation to sustain him as President of the Church, Elders Brigham Young, Parley P. Pratt and Heber C. Kimball stepped into the stand.

Brigham Young remarked to the congregation: "I will manage this voting for Elder Rigdon. He does not preside here. This child" (meaning himself) "will manage this flock for a season." The voice and gestures of the man were those of the Prophet Joseph.

The people, with few exceptions, visibly saw that the mantle of the Prophet Joseph Smith had fallen upon Brigham Young. To some it seemed as though Joseph again stood before them.

I arose to my feet and said to a man sitting by me, "That is the voice of the true shepherd—the chief of the Apostles."

Our enemies, finding that the death of the Prophet did not break up "Mormonism," as they had expected, began their persecutions again, by burning the houses of the brethren in the outlying settlements.

I joined a company of minute men to assist in protecting the Saints. In one of our scouts we visited Carthage. I examined the jail in which Joseph and Hyrum were assassinated. I noticed that the latches on the two doors that the mob broke in, when they killed the Prophets, had been rendered useless by bending down the catches, so that the latches would clear them. All the entrances to the prison yard appeared to me to have been prepared beforehand for the easy admittance of the mob.

The blood on the floor where the Patriarch fell, had left a black spot about the size and shape of the body. The ball holes in the plastering about the window out of which Joseph leaped, and those in the door and in the wall above where Hyrum had lain, and also where John Taylor had been shot at, denoted that the assailants were desperadoes and well prepared for their work.

When the District Court sat in Hancock County, the judge allowed one of the leaders of the mob to act as an official. He also professed to try to have the murderers indicted, but as several of them were on the grand jury, there were no indictments found against them.

The following winter I assisted in guarding the Saints in and around the city of Nauvoo. My brother Obed lived about thirty miles out in the country. He was taken sick, and sent for me to come and see him.

On arriving at his house, I found that he had been sick nearly three months, and that doubts were entertained of his recovery. I anointed him with holy oil in the name of the Lord Jesus, laid on hands, and prayed for him, and told him that he should recover, which he did immediately.

This occurrence had much influence on my parents. They both attended the following April conference. At its close, my father asked me if I did not wish to baptize him and my mother. As they were both desirous that I should do so, I baptized them in the Mississippi river, on April 11th, 1845.

My father told me that it was not any man's preaching that had convinced him of the truth of the gospel, but the Lord had shown it to him in night visions. Said he, "It is your privilege to baptize your parents, for you have prayed for them in secret and in public; you never gave them up; you will be a Joseph to your father's house."

In 1845, I labored on the Nauvoo temple, doing any work that was required of me. In the autumn, the enemies of the Saints commenced to plunder in the country settlements. Teams were sent from Nauvoo to save and bring in what grain they could. It was necessary to send guards with the teams.

These afflictions, heaped upon the Saints by their enemies when they were struggling to complete the temple, in compliance with the word of the Lord, greatly added to their difficulties.

When winter came, they were instructed to unite their efforts to manufacture wagons, and make preparations for a long journey. I assisted in getting out timber for wagons.

The house of the Lord being far enough completed to give endowments and do other necessary work, I received my blessings in it just before crossing the Mississippi river, in February, 1846.

I labored with the company of pioneers to prepare the way for the Saints through Iowa, after which I had the privilege of returning to Nauvoo for my family, which consisted of my wife and three children. I moved them out into Iowa, 200 miles, where I left them, and returned 100 miles to settlements, in order to obtain food and other necessaries.

I was taken sick, and sent for my family to return to me. My wife and two children were taken sick the day after their arrival. We found shelter in a miserable hut, some distance from water.

One day I made an effort to get some water for my suffering family, but failed through weakness. Night came on and my family were burning with fever and calling for water.

These very trying circumstances called up some bitter feelings within me. It seemed as though in this, my terrible extremity, the Lord permitted the devil to try me, for just then a Methodist class leader came along, and remarked that I was in a very bad situation. He assured me that he had a comfortable house that I could move into, and that he had plenty of everything, and would assist me if I would renounce "Mormonism." I refused and he passed on.

I afterwards knelt down and asked the Lord to pity us in our miserable condition, and to soften the heart of some one to administer to us in our affliction.

About an hour after this, a man by the name of William Johnson came with a three gallon jug full of water, set it down and said: "I came home this evening, weary, having been working with a threshing machine during the day, but, when I lay down I could not sleep; something told me that you were suffering for water. I took this jug, went over to Custer's well and got this for you. I feel now as though I could go home and sleep. I have plenty of chickens and other things at my house, that are good for sick people. When you need anything I will let you have it." I knew this was from the Lord in answer to my prayer.

The following day the quails came out of the thickets, and were so easily caught that I picked up what I needed without difficulty. I afterwards learned that the camps of the Saints had been supplied with food in the same way.

The spring following these events my eldest brother came from Pottawatomie Co., Iowa, with a team to take me home with him. While preparing to leave, the team became frightened, ran along a steep side hill, capsized the wagon, and I was thrown down the hill and the load came on top of me.

The same Mr. Johnson who had before administered to my wants, took me into his house. This was in the morning, and I knew nothing until ten o'clock in the evening.

When I became conscious, I was lying on a mattress covered with blood. I looked around the room, and asked what it all meant. The lady of the house informed me what had happened, and told me that Mr. Johnson did not expect me to live. She further stated that he had called in some of the neighbors, that the doctor had been to see me and wished to bleed me, but I would not let him; that I told them that if they knew where there were any of the Elders of Israel, I wanted them sent for. She informed me that I said other things which displeased the doctor and the neighbors, and they went away.

I assured the family that I was not responsible for what I had said or done, for I knew nothing about it. Mrs. Johnson said that she did not hear or see anything wrong, but the neighbors believed that I was trying to palm off some great "Mormon" miracle on them. I denied trying to deceive any one, but all to no purpose.

The owner of the house I had rented hurried me out of it, saying I could not live in his house any longer. In the month of March I moved into the wagon, with my wife and four children, the youngest not two weeks old.

On the 11th of the following April, 1847, I arrived at my father's house, in Western Iowa. I had previously baptized four of my brothers, and all my father's family had embraced the gospel.

My mother had sunk under hardships, and died on the road from Nauvoo, yet I was thankful to find all my relatives rejoicing in the truth.

In the spring of 1850 I felt like making an effort to gather with the Saints in the mountains. This at first appeared impossible, as my animals had all strayed off, and I could not learn of their whereabouts.

I had concluded to remain another year, when I dreamed, for three nights in succession, where my oxen were, and went and got them. I found my other lost animals in the same manner.

These kind providences, with strict economy, enabled me to make a start for Utah with the company of Aaron Johnson, in the spring of 1850, as I had desired.

I joined the camp, to travel over a thousand miles of desert, with nine in family, one small wagon, one yoke of oxen and two cows.

While crossing the ferry over the Missouri river, with a boat load of cattle, they crowded to one side of the boat and capsized it. Some of the people on board saved themselves by getting on to the bottom of the boat, others by holding on to planks.

I made an effort to swim to the landing, below which was some three miles of perpendicular river bank, and the water along the bank was full of whirlpools and eddies. Despite my efforts, the current took me past the landing. As I was almost carried under by a strong eddy, I began to despair of saving myself. Fortunately, I discovered where a path had been cut through the bank to the water's edge. I succeeded in getting so near the top of the bank, that a woman who was near, and had discovered my situation, managed to get hold of my hand, and, with a great effort, I was saved from the surging waters.

In traveling up the Platte river on our way to the mountains, we found the road side, in places, strewn with human bones. The discovery of gold in California and the excitement it had created, had induced many of the Missouri mobocrats, the year previous, to leave their homes in search of the god of this world.

The cholera had raged among them to such an extent, that the dead were buried without coffins, and with but a slight covering of earth. The wolves had dug up and feasted upon their carcasses, and their bones lay bleaching on the desert. There were days of travel in which human skeletons were usually in sight.

We saw the literal fulfillment of the predictions of Joseph the Prophet, during the persecutions of the Saints in Missouri. He said that those who took an active part in driving them from their homes, should themselves die away from home without a decent burial; that their flesh should be devoured by wild beasts, and their bones should bleach on the plains. Boards had usually been placed at the heads of the graves, on which were the names of those who had been buried in them. Many of these names were those of well-known Missouri mobocrats.

The destroyer came into our company, and several persons died. I told my family that it was a plague from the Lord, that nothing but His power could save them from it, and that it would attack some of the family. My wife thought that I had done wrong in asserting that it would attack our family, as the children would be afraid and be more likely to have it. I told her that it would come, but when it did we must depend entirely upon the Lord and all would be right.

One evening, as I returned to my wagon from assisting to bury a Sister Hunt, Sister Hamblin was taken violently with the cholera, and she exclaimed, "O Lord, help, or I die!" I anointed her with consecrated oil in the name of the Lord Jesus, and she was instantly healed. The next day the cholera attacked me and I was healed under the hands of my father.

I was advised to get into the wagon and ride the remainder of the day. As my eldest son, a small lad, took the whip to drive the team, he fell forward to the ground and both wheels on the left side of the wagon ran over his body. It appeared to me that he never could breathe again. My father took him out of the road, administered to him, and he arose to his feet and said that he was not hurt.

My youngest son, Lyman, was taken with the cholera, and my father in administering to him, rebuked the destroyer, and commanded it to depart from him, from the family and from the company. To my knowledge no more cases of the cholera occurred after that in the company.

We arrived in Salt Lake Valley on the 1st of September, 1850.

CHAPTER IV

I SETTLED, with my father and brothers, in Tooele Valley, thirty-five miles west of Salt Lake City. The people built their houses in the form of a fort, to protect themselves from the Indians, who frequently stole their horses and cattle. Men were sent against them from Salt Lake City, but all to no purpose. The Indians would watch them during the day, and steal from them at night.

This kind of warfare was carried on for about three years, during which time there was no safety for our horses or cattle. We had a military company, of which I was first lieutenant. I went with the captain on several expeditions against the thieves, but without accomplishing much good. They would watch our movements in the canyons, and continually annoy us.

At one time, I took my wife three miles up a canyon, to gather wild fruit while I got down timber from the mountain. We had intended to remain over night, but while preparing a place to sleep, a feeling came over me that the Indians were watching with the intention of killing us during the night.

I at once yoked my oxen, put my wife and her babe on the wagon, and went home in the evening. My wife expressed surprise at my movements, and I told her that the Indians were watching us. She wished to know how I knew this, and asked if I had seen or heard them. I replied that I knew it on the same principle that I knew that the gospel was true.

The following day I returned to the canyon. Three Indians had come down on the road during the night, and robbed a wagon of a gun, ammunition and other valuables. One of them, from the size of the track, must have been an Indian known as "Old Big Foot." I thanked the Lord that He had warned me in time to save my wife and child, as well as myself.

The following winter I asked for a company of men to make another effort to hunt up the Indians. On this scout we traveled at night and watched during the day, until we discovered the location of a band of them.

One morning at daybreak, we surrounded their camp before they were aware of our presence. The chief among them sprang to his feet, and stepping towards me, said, "I never hurt you, and I do not want to. If you shoot, I will; if you do not, I will not." I was not familiar with their language, but I knew what he said. Such an influence came over me that I would not have killed one of them for all the cattle in Tooele Valley.

The running of the women and the crying of the children aroused my sympathies, and I felt inspired to do my best to prevent the company from shooting any of them. Some shots were fired, but no one was injured, except that the legs and feet of some of the Indians were bruised by jumping among the rocks.

I wished some of the men to go with us to the settlement. They were somewhat afraid, but confided in my assurance that they should not be injured.

On my arrival home, my superior officer ignored the promise of safety I had given the Indians, and decided to have them shot.

I told them I did not care to live after I had seen the Indians whose safety I had guaranteed, murdered, and as it made but little difference with me, if there were any shot I should be the first. At the same time I placed myself in front of the Indians. This ended the matter, and they were set at liberty.

From the feelings manifested by the Bishop and the people generally, I thought that I might possibly be mistaken in the whole affair. The people had long suffered from the depredations of these Indians, and they might be readily excused for their exasperated feelings, but, right or wrong, a different feeling actuated me.

After this affair, the presiding Elder directed me to take another company of men, go after the Indians, to shoot all we found, and bring no more into the settlement. Again we traveled at night and watched during the day. We found the trail of a small band who had come near the valley, and then turned back on account of a light fall of snow, which would make their trail too easily discovered for thieving operations.

We surprised them near a large mountain between Tooele and Skull Valleys. They scattered in the foot hills, and the company divided to the right and left to keep them from the mountains. I rode my horse as far as he could go on account of the difficulties of the ground, then left him, and secreted myself behind a rock in a narrow pass, through which I presumed some of the Indians would attempt to escape. I had not been there long before an Indian came within a few paces of me.

I leveled my rifle on him, and it missed fire. He sent an arrow at me, and it struck my gun as I was in the act of re-capping it; he sent the second, and it passed through my hat; the third barely missed my head; the fourth passed through my coat and vest. As I could not discharge my gun, I defended myself as well as I could with stones. The Indian soon left the ground to me.

I afterwards learned that as he went on, he met two others of our company and passed them safely, as their guns also missed fire. When the company gathered back to the place from which they scattered, we learned that not one was able to discharge his gun when within range of an Indian. One of the company received a slight arrow wound, which was the only injury inflicted.

In my subsequent reflections, it appeared evident to me that a special providence had been over us, in this and the two previous expeditions, to prevent us from shedding the blood of the Indians. The Holy Spirit forcibly impressed me that it was not my calling to shed the blood of the scattered remnant of Israel, but to be a messenger of peace to them. It was also made manifest to me that if I would not thirst for their blood, I should never fall by their hands. The most of the men who went on this last expedition, also received an impression that it was wrong to kill these Indians.

On a fourth expedition against them, we again surprised their camp. When I saw the women and children fleeing for their lives, barefooted over the rocks and through the snow, leaving a trail of blood, I fully made up my mind, that if I had anything more to do with the Indians, it would be in a different way.

I did not wish to injure these women and children, but, learning that "Old Big Foot" was there, and feeling that he deserved killing, I soon found his trail and followed it. There being snow on the ground, his trail was easily seen. It passed along the highest ridges. As I approached a cedar tree with low, thick foliage, a feeling came over me not to go near it. I passed it under the brow of a steep hill. When beyond it, I saw that no trail had passed on. I circled around in sight of the Indian, but he in some way slipped off unobserved.

Afterwards, when trying to make peace with these Indians, "Big Foot" told me, that himself and party had laid their plans to kill me and my wife and child, the summer before when in Pine Canyon, had we remained there over night. During the same interview he said, placing his finger on his arrow, "If, when you followed me in the cedar hills, you had come three steps nearer the tree where I was, I would have put an arrow into you up to the feather."

I thanked the Lord, as I often felt to do, for the revelations of His Spirit.

After returning home from the expedition, in which I had followed the trail of "Old Big Foot," I dreamed, three nights in succession, of being out west, alone, with the Indians that we had been trying about three years to destroy. I saw myself walk with them in a friendly manner, and, while doing so, pick up a lump of shining substance, some of which stuck to my fingers, and the more I endeavored to brush it off the brighter it became.

This dream made such an impression on my mind, that I took my blankets, gun and ammunition, and went alone into their country. I remained with them several days, hunting deer and duck, occasionally loaning them my rifle, and assisting to bring in their game. I also did all I could to induce them to be at peace with us.

One day, in my rambles, I came to a lodge where there was a squaw, and a boy about ten years old. As soon as I saw the boy, the Spirit said to me, "Take that lad home with you; that is part of your mission here, and here is the bright substance which you dreamed of picking up." I talked with him and asked him if he would not go with me. He at once replied that he would.

The mother, naturally enough, in a deprecating tone, asked me if I wanted to take her boy away from her. But after some further conversation she consented to the arrangement. At this time I had not learned much of the language of these Indians, but I seemed to have the gift of making myself understood.

When I left, the boy took his bows and arrows and accompanied me. The woman appeared to feel so bad, and made so much ado, that I told the lad he had better go back to his mother; but he would not do so. We went to the side of the mountain where I agreed to meet the Indians. His mother, still anxious about her boy, came to our camp in the evening.

The following morning, she told me that she heard I had a good heart, for the Indians told her that I had been true to what I said, and the boy could go with me if I would always be his father and own him as my son.

This boy became very much attached to me, and was very particular to do as he was told. I asked him why he was so willing to come with me the first time we met. He replied that I was the first white man he ever saw; that he knew a man would come to his mother's lodge to see him, on the day of my arrival, for he was told so the night before, and that when the man came he must go with him; that he knew I was the man when he saw me a long way off, and built a smoke so that I would come there.

CHAPTER V

AT THE April conference of 1854, I was called, with a number of others, on a mission to the Indians in Southern Utah. Taking a horse, cow, garden seeds and some farming tools, I joined in with Brother Robert Ritchie, and was soon on my way.

We commenced operations at a place we called Harmony, twenty miles south of Cedar City, in Iron County. I made it my principal business to learn the Indian language, and become familiar with their character.

About the end of May of that year, President Brigham Young, Heber C. Kimball, Parley P. Pratt and others to the number of twenty persons, came to visit us. President Young gave much instruction about conducting the mission and building up the settlement we had commenced. He said if the Elders wanted influence with the Indians, they must associate with them in their expeditions.

Brother Kimball prophesied that, if the brethren were united, they would be prospered and blessed, but if they permitted the spirit of strife and contention to come into their midst, the place would come to an end in a scene of bloodshed.

Previous to this meeting, President Young asked some brethren who had been into the country south of Harmony if they thought a wagon road could be made down to the Rio Virgen.

Their replies were very discouraging, but, in the face of this report, Brother Kimball prophesied in this meeting, that a road would be made from Harmony over the Black Ridge; and a temple would be built on the Rio Virgen, and the Lamanites would come from the east side of the Colorado river and get their endowments in it. All these prophecies have since been fulfilled.

On the 1st of June, 1854, I went with Elder R. C. Allen and others, to visit the Indians on the Rio Virgen and Santa Clara, two streams now well known as forming a junction south of the city of St. George.

On the 9th of June, we camped on ground now enclosed in the Washington field. There we saw many Indian women gathering a red, sweet berry, called "opie." The Indians were also harvesting their wheat. Their manner of doing so was very primitive. One would loosen the roots of the wheat with a stick, another would pull up the plant, beat the dirt off from the roots and set it up in bunches. I loaned them a long sharp knife, which greatly assisted them in their labors.

The company returned to Harmony with the exception of Brother William Hennefer and myself, who were left to visit the Indians on the upper Santa Clara. We found a few lodges, and with them a very sick woman. The medicine man of the tribe was going through a round of ceremonies in order to heal her.

He stuck arrows into the ground at the entrance of the lodge, placed his medicine bow in a conspicuous place, adorned his head with eagle's feathers, and then walked back and forth in an austere manner, making strange gestures with his hands, and hideous noises at the top of his voice. He would then enter the lodge, and place his mouth to the woman's, in order to drive away the evil spirits, and charm away the pain. Some one told the sick woman that the "Mormons" believed in "poogi," which, in their language, means administering to the sick. She wished us to wait, and if the Piute charm did not work, to try if we could do her any good.

The medicine man howled and kept up his performances the most of the night. The sick woman's friends then carried her some distance away from the lodge, and left her to die.

Some of her relatives asked us to go and administer to her. We could not feel to refuse, so we laid on hands and prayed for her.

When we returned to our camp, she arose and followed us, and said she was hungry. We sent her to her own lodge. Some of the inmates were frightened at seeing her, as they had considered her a dead woman.

We returned to Harmony about the last of June. On the 3rd of July, I accompanied a hunting party of Indians into the mountains east of Harmony. While with them, I spared no labor in learning their language, and getting an insight into their character.

I had ever felt an aversion to white men shedding the blood of these ignorant barbarians. When the white man has settled on their lands, and his cattle have destroyed much of their scanty living, there has always appeared in them a disposition to make all reasonable allowances for these wrongs. Ever since I was old enough to understand, and more especially after being with them around their camp fires, where I learned their simple and child-like ways, and heard them talk over their wrongs, I fully made up my mind to do all I could to alleviate their condition.

From time to time, when the Saints have had any trouble with them, and I have had anything to do with settling the difficulty, I have made it a specialty to go among them, regardless of their numbers or anger. Through the blessing of the Lord, I have never yet failed in accomplishing my object, where no other persons have interfered in a matter they did not understand.

Returning from this hunting expedition, I made my way, in September, to Tooele Valley, to visit my family, and found them well. I remained with them but a short time, and returned to my missionary labors in Southern Utah.

Our crops had done well. After assisting to gather them, I labored for a season on the fort we were building, the better to defend ourselves in case of trouble with the Indians.

In November, I was sent alone among the Indians on the Santa Clara, to use my influence to keep them from disturbing the travelers on the southern route to California.

When there, without a white companion, a dispute arose between some of the Indians about a squaw. As was their custom, they decided that the claimant should do battle for her in the following manner:

The warriors of the band were to form in two files, and a claimant should pass between the files leading the squaw, and prepared to fight anyone that opposed his claim. The affair had made considerable progress, when one of the parties who had been roughly handled, claimed kinship with me by calling me brother, and asked me to help him.

Not wishing to take part in any of their barbarous customs, I objected. The Indians then taunted me with being a coward, called me a squaw, etc.

I soon took in the situation, and saw that it would not be well to lose caste among them. I accepted the challenge under the promise that they would not be angry with me if I should hurt some of them. I had but little anxiety about the result, for they were not adept in the art of self-defense.

The Indians, numbering about one hundred and twenty, formed in two lines, and I took the squaw by the hand, and commenced my passage between them.

Only one Indian disputed my progress. With one blow I stretched him on the ground. All would probably have passed off well enough, had I not kicked him as he fell. This was contrary to their code of honor, and I paid a fine for this breach of custom.

I was acknowledged the victor, and it was decided that the squaw was mine. I immediately turned her over to the Indian that she desired for a husband.

This was my first and last fight for a squaw. It gave me a prestige among them that greatly added to my subsequent influence.

This short and lonely mission was brought to a close by my return to Harmony.

In the beginning of winter, I went down to the Santa Clara in company with Brothers Ira Hatch, Samuel Knight, Thales Haskell and A. P. Hardy.

We worked with the Indians, and gained much influence over them. We built a log cabin, and a dam to take out the waters of the Santa Clara Creek to irrigate the bottom land. Hard labor and exposure brought on me a severe attack of sickness. At the same time there came a heavy fall of snow, which made it impracticable to get any assistance from the nearest settlement, forty miles distant.

The brethren began to entertain some doubts about my recovery. However, after laying sick fourteen days, with nothing to nourish me but bread made of moldy, bitter corn meal, Brother Samuel Atwood arrived from Harmony with some good things to strengthen me.

After a few days, I started with Brother Atwood on horseback, for Harmony. I rode to Cottonwood Creek, where the town of Harrisburg now stands. I felt exhausted, and could go no farther. I was assisted off my horse and lay on the ground, where I fainted. Brother Atwood brought some water in the leather holster of his pistol, and put some of it in my mouth and on my head, which revived me.

With slow and careful traveling I was able to reach Harmony; but I was so reduced in flesh that my friends did not recognize me.

As soon as my health would permit, I returned to the Santa Clara.

I have before referred to a custom among the Piutes of taking women from each other. Sometimes two claimants decided who should be the possessor of the woman, by single combat; but more generally, each claimant would gather to his assistance all the friends he could, and the fighting would be kept up until one side was conquered, when the claimant who had led the victorious party, would take possession of the woman.

I have seen such engagements last all day and a part of the night. In one of these, in which over one hundred men took a part, some of the combatants became angry, and fought in good earnest.

At the close of the day, it was still undecided who was the victor. At night large fires were lighted, arranged in a circle, and some forty of the combatants came in to decide the matter.

They pulled each other's hair and fought desperately, regardless of the rules usually governing such affairs.

The unoffending woman seemed to fare quite as hard, or worse than the combatants. She was finally trampled under foot, and the women who looked on became excited. Some ran with their willow trays filled with coals from the fire, which they threw over the men and burnt them out, as each one found employment in running and brushing the coals from his hair and back.

In the meantime, the woman lay on the ground with her mouth filled with blood and dirt.

At this stage of the affair we used our persuasive powers, and succeeded in inducing the men to let the woman go with the man she wanted.

In the summer of 1855, we cultivated a few acres of land on the Santa Clara. We raised melons, and had the privilege of disposing of them ourselves. I do not think that the Indians ever took any without leave. We raised a small amount of cotton, which was probably the first grown in Utah Territory.

In the autumn of 1855, I returned to Tooele Valley, and removed my family to the Santa Clara. My brother Oscar, also Brother Dudley Leavitt, and their families, accompanied me.

In the winter of 1855-6 we were instructed to build a fort for our protection. There were at that time on the Santa Clara, ten missionaries, and four stonemasons from Cedar City. We enjoyed Indian help, and everything we put our hands to prospered, so that in less than ten days we built a fort one hundred feet square, of hammer-faced rock, the wall two feet thick and twelve feet high. It was afterwards said by President Young to be the best fort then in the Territory.

We invited the Indians to assist us to construct a strong, high dam to take the water out of the Santa Clara to a choice piece of land.

For this purpose they gathered into the settlement to the number of about thirty lodges, but rather reluctantly, for they believed that the *Tonaquint,* their name for the Santa Clara, would dry up the coming season, as there was but little snow in the mountains.

With much hard labor we completed our dam, and watered our crops once in the spring of 1856. The water then failed, and our growing crops began to wither.

The Indians then came to me and said, " You promised us water if we would help build a dam and plant corn. What about the promise, now the creek is dry? What will we do for something to eat next winter?"

The chief saw that I was troubled in my mind over the matter, and said, "We have one medicine man; I will send him to the great mountain to make rain medicine, and you do the best you can, and maybe the rain will come; but it will take strong medicine, as I never knew it to rain this moon." I went up the creek, and found it dry for twelve miles.

The following morning at daylight, I saw the smoke of the medicine man ascending from the side of the Big Mountain, as the Indians called what is now known as the Pine Valley Mountain.

Being among some Indians, I went aside by myself, and prayed to the God of Abraham to forgive me if I had been unwise in promising the Indians water for their crops if they would plant; and that the heavens might give rain, that we might not lose the influence we had over them.

It was a clear, cloudless morning, but, while still on my knees, heavy drops of rain fell on my back for about three seconds. I knew it to be a sign that my prayers were answered. I told the Indians that the rain would come. When

I returned to the settlement, I told the brethren that we would have all the water we wanted.

The next morning, a gentle rain commenced falling. The water arose to its ordinary stage in the creek, and, what was unusual, it was clear. We watered our crops all that we wished, and both whites and Indians acknowledged the event to be a special providence.

I think more corn and squash were grown that year, by us, than I ever saw before or since, on the same number of acres. The Indians gathered and stored up a large amount of corn, beans and dried squash.

From that time they began to look upon us as having great influence with the clouds. They also believed that we could cause sickness to come upon any of them if we wished. We labored to have them understand these things in their true light, but this was difficult on account of their ignorance and superstitions.

About this time an Indian came in from another small band east of the Santa Clara. The Indians who worked with us told him how matters were going with them.

He ridiculed them for their faith in us and what we taught them, and told them that they were fools for living without meat, when there were plenty of cattle in sight. To more fully exemplify his views and set an example of self-assurance, he killed one of our oxen.

Four or five of the brethren went to him, armed. I felt impressed that a peaceful policy would be the best, and, for that reason, I requested them to let me manage the matter. I went into his lodge and sat down by him. I told him that he had done a great wrong, for we were working to do the Indians good.

He talked insultingly, and wanted to know if I wished to kill him, or if I could make medicine strong enough to kill him. I told him that he had made his own medicine, and that some evil would befall him before he got home.

About this time, the President of the mission received a letter from President Brigham Young, requiring us to say to the Indians that if they would live cleanly and observe certain things pertaining to the gospel, they should grow and increase in the land. Also, that we should require them to wash the sick before we administered to them.

An Indian wished us to administer to his sick boy. We required him to wash his child; he refused to do so, and the boy died. The man burnt his lodge, went to the mountains, and called on others to follow him. Some did so, and before leaving, burned a log store house which they had filled with supplies.

The angry man's name was Ag-ara-poots.

The chief of the band came to me and said, "Old Ag-ara-poots will never be satisfied until he has killed you or some one who is with you. You know that he has killed two Piutes since you came here. The Piutes are all afraid of him. I am going away."

I asked him if he would not go to Ag-ara-poots with me.

"No"; he replied, "he thinks that you let his boy die, and he will never be satisfied until he has blood. There are many with him, and you must not go where he is."

As I felt like seeing him, I invited all the missionary brethren, one by one, to go with me, but they all refused except Brother Thales Haskell. One of the brethren remarked that he would as soon go into a den of grizzly bears.

When I went to the house of Brother Haskell and opened the door, he said, "I know what you want. You wish me to go with you to see Ag-ara-poots. I am just the man you want."

The difference between me and my brethren in this instance did not arise from superior personal courage in myself, but in the fact that I have mentioned before: that I had received from the Lord an assurance that I should never fall by the hands of the Indians, if I did not thirst for their blood. That assurance has been, and is still with me, in all my intercourse with them.

Brother Haskell seemed inspired to go with me on this occasion. We started in the morning, and followed the trail of Ag-ara-poots until afternoon, when we found him and his band.

His face was blackened, and he sat with his head down, apparently in rather a surly mood. I told him that I had heard that he intended to kill me the first opportunity.

Said he: "Who told you that I wanted to kill you?"

I answered that the Piutes had told me so.

He declared that it was a lie; but he had been mad and was mad then, because I had let his boy die.

I told him that *he* had let his boy die, because he did not think enough of him to wash him so that the Lord would heal him, and now he was mad at someone else.

I told him we were hungry, and were going to eat with a man who was not mad, and that he had better go with us. As we left his lodge, he arose to go with us, but trembled, staggered and sat down in the sand.

All the Indians but Ag-ara-poots gathered around us. We told them they had been foolish in burning up their food, going into the mountains, and leaving their friends; that the women and children had better go back to the settlement where there was something to eat, and let the men who wished to hunt, remain. The most of them started for the settlement the same night.

The following day Titse-gavats, the chief, came to me and said, "The band have all come on to the Clara except Ag-ara-poots, and he came on to the bluff in sight of it, and his heart hardened. You cannot soften his heart again. He has gone off alone. You had better pray for him to die, then there will be no bloodshed. Do not tell him what I have said to you."

I did ask the Lord that, if it would be for the glory of His name, Ag-ara-poots might not have strength to shed the blood of any of us. In a few days the Piutes told me that he was not able to walk nor help himself to a drink of water. He lingered until spring and died.

CHAPTER VI

A PETTY chief, living west of the settlement on the Santa Clara, and on the California road, came to me and said that he had stolen from some "Mormons" as they passed by; that there could not be medicine made to kill him, for he was a hard one to kill, and he would steal from the "Mormons" again the first opportunity.

Some two weeks after this conversation, the Indians told me that this chief was dead. In going home from the Santa Clara settlement, he stole an animal from a "Mormon" traveler, and hid it up until he had gone by; then drove it to his lodge, killed it, and when it was about half skinned he was taken sick, went to his lodge and died.

An Indian living near us said he had killed an animal, and wished to pay for it. I took some pay from him that he might be satisfied, and told him to go his way and steal no more.

He was afterwards caught stealing another ox, after

which I chanced to meet him alone. He asked me what I was going to do about it. I replied, "Nothing."

He talked in an excited manner, and said in an angry tone, "If you are going to do anything, do it now; do it here." I explained to him that if evil came upon people they brought it upon themselves by their mean acts.

He talked and acted in such a rascally manner that I was disgusted. I told him that he was in the hands of the Lord; if He would forgive him, I would, but I did not believe that He would. This man died in a few days after this conversation.

The Lord had sent the gospel of their fathers to these Indians, and with it the testimony of many special manifestations, so evident to them, even in their ignorance, that they might be without excuse.

In addition to the destruction of the wilfully wicked and perverse, many promises to them were fulfilled, their sick were healed, etc.

These testimonies more fully established the influence of the Elders among this people, and they looked to us for counsel, and endeavored to do as they were instructed. The men ceased to abuse their families, and they did as well as could be expected of people in their low condition.

They would wash the sick, and ask the Elders to lay hands on and pray for them. The Lord had great regard for our administrations, for I do not recollect administering to one that did not recover. We were careful not to say or do anything wrong, and I feel that a good spirit governed us in all our intercourse with this people. They soon learned to regard our words as law.

At length the Santa Clara and Muddy Indians got into a quarrel, and began to kill each other whenever they could get an advantage. We endeavored to make peace between them, but blood had been spilled, and nothing but blood would satisfy them.

One morning, a Muddy Creek Indian killed one of the Santa Clara band in the wood near our fort. The Santa Clara Indians farther up the stream, hearing of it, took a Moapats woman, fastened her to a small tree and burned her.

When they first tied her, a young Indian came in haste to let me know what was going on. I hurried towards the spot, but before I arrived there another boy met me, and said that it was of no use for me to go on, for matters had gone too far to save the woman. I think they had hurried to consummate the terrible deed before I could get there.

When I talked with the perpetrators they cried, and said that they could not have done less than they did. That is, they were so bound up in their traditions and customs, that what they had done was a necessary duty.

They appeared so child-like, and so anxious to have me think that what they had done was all right, that I said nothing, but felt that I would be truly thankful if I should ever be so fortunate as to be called to labor among a higher class of people.

These things took place in the summer and autumn of 1856. Soon after the burning of the Indian woman, Brother Ira Hatch and I started for Cedar City, by way of the Mountain Meadows. At night we camped near another trail which crossed the one on which we were traveling.

When we arose in the morning, I told my companion that the Cedar Indians had been to the Muddy to attack the Indians living there, and had got the worst of it; that on their return they had stolen the horses from the Santa Clara.

We had never traveled the trail they were on, but I told Brother Hatch that if he would take it, he would find the thieves camped at a certain spring, and when they saw him they would be so surprised that they would let him have the horses without any difficulty.

Brother Hatch found matters as I had predicted, and the Indians got up the horses for him, and appeared anxious to have him take them away.

We afterwards learned that the Cedar Indians had gone to the Muddy, and stolen two squaws from the band that lived on that creek. The Muddy Indians had pursued the robbers, and retaliated by killing a chief of the Cedar Indians, and wounding two more of their party. They also recovered the captive squaws.

It was by the dictation of the Holy Spirit that I sent Brother Hatch to recover the horses. It was the same Spirit that had influenced me to take my wife and child out of Pine Canyon the evening before I had intended to, and thereby saved their lives and my own. It was the same also that had saved me from being killed by "Old Big Foot," when I lived in Tooele Valley.

At this time we had established as good a form of government among the Santa Clara Indians as their circumstances would permit.

They worked for a living, and promised to be honest. If anyone stole, he either paid a price for what he had taken, or was stripped, tied to a tree and whipped, according to the magnitude of the offense. The Indians did the whipping, while I generally dictated the number and severity of the lashes.

In the winter of 1856-7, after the Indians had been trying for some time to follow our counsels, they said to me, "We cannot be good; we must be Piutes. We want you to be kind to us. It may be that some of our children will be good, but we want to follow our old customs."

They again began to paint themselves, and to abuse their women, as they had done before we went among them.

Up to this time, Elder R. C. Allen had been president of the Southern Indian Mission, and had generally resided at Harmony. He had given me charge of the settlement on the Santa Clara Creek.

The following letter shows his release, and my appointment to take his place, and exhibits the Indian policy of President Brigham Young:

"PRESIDENT'S OFFICE,
Great Salt Lake City,
August 4, 1857.

"ELDER JACOB HAMBLIN:—You are hereby appointed to succeed Elder R. C. Allen (whom I have released) as president of the Santa Clara Indian Mission. I wish you to enter upon the duties of your office immediately.

"Continue the conciliatory policy towards the Indians which I have ever commended, and seek by works of righteousness to obtain their love and confidence. Omit promises where you are not sure you can fill them; and seek to unite the hearts of the brethren on that mission, and let all under your direction be united together in holy bonds of love and unity.

"All is peace here, and the Lord is eminently blessing our labors; grain is abundant, and our cities are alive with the busy hum of industry.

"Do not permit the brethren to part with their guns and ammunition, but save them against the hour of need.

"Seek the spirit of the Lord to direct you, and that

He may qualify you for every duty, is the prayer of your
fellow-laborer in the gospel of salvation,

BRIGHAM YOUNG."

Early in the autumn of 1857, Apostle George A.
Smith visited the settlements in Southern Utah. He informed the Saints that a United States army was on the
way to Utah. What the result would be, he said he did
not know. He advised the people to be saving their grain,
and not sell any to travelers to feed their teams; for they
could live on grass better than our women and children.
He thought that all we could afford to do, under the circumstances, was to furnish travelers with bread. That if
we would not deny the gospel, we might yet suffer much
persecution, and be compelled to hide up in the mountains.
"At all events," said he, "bread is good to have."

When President Smith returned to Salt Lake City,
Brother Thales Haskell and I accompanied him. On our
way we camped over night on Corn Creek, twelve miles
south of Fillmore, with a party of emigrants from Arkansas, traveling on what was then known as the southern
route to California. They inquired of me about the road,
and wrote the information down that I gave them.

They expressed a wish to lay by at some suitable place
to recruit their teams before crossing the desert. I recommended to them, for this purpose, the south end of the
Mountain Meadows, three miles from where my family
resided.

After our arrival in Salt Lake City, news reached us
that this company of emigrants, on their way south, had
behaved badly, that they had robbed hen-roosts, and been
guilty of other irregularities, and had used abusive lang-

uage to those who had remonstrated with them. It was also reported that they threatened, when the army came into the north end of the Territory, to get a good outfit from the weaker settlements in the south.

A messenger came to President Young, informing him of these things, and asking advice.

In reply, Brigham Young sent general instructions to the settlements, advising the people to let the emigrants pass as quietly as possible; and stating that there was an army on our borders, and we could not tell what we might be obliged to do before the troubles were over. He said we might be under the necessity of going into the mountains, and that he wished all supplies of food to be in a shape to be readily available in such an emergency; and we would do the best we could.

Brother Haskell and I remained in Salt Lake City one week, and then started for our homes in Southern Utah. On the way, we heard that the Arkansas company of emigrants had been destroyed at the Mountain Meadows, by the Indians.

We met John D. Lee at Fillmore. He told us that the Indians attacked the company, and that he and some other white men joined them in the perpetration of the deed. This deplorable affair caused a sensation of horror and deep regret throughout the entire community, by whom it was unqualifiedly condemned.

In Cove Creek Valley we met others from the south, who told us that the Indians were gathering to attack another company of emigrants. I procured a horse, left the wagons, and rode on day and night. At Cedar City I found Brothers Samuel Knight and Dudley Leavitt.

As I was weary with hard riding and want of sleep, I hurried them on after the emigrants, while I traveled more slowly. I instructed these men to make every possible effort to save the company and their effects, and to save their lives at all hazards.

They overtook the company one hundred and fifty-six miles from Cedar City, on Muddy Creek, in the heart of the Indian country. They found a large body of excited Indians preparing to attack and destroy them.

Finding it altogether impossible to control the Indians, they compromised the matter. The Indians agreed to only take the loose stock of the company, and not meddle with the teams and wagons, and not make any effort to take their lives.

The Indians took the loose stock, amounting to four hundred and eighty head, on the fifty-mile desert beyond the Muddy.

The brethren remained with the company, determined to assist in its defense, should the Indians attempt anything more than they had agreed.

The company continued their journey safely to California. Brothers Knight and Leavitt returned to the Santa Clara.

As soon as possible, I talked with the principal Indians engaged in this affair, and they agreed that the stock not killed should be given up. I wrote to the owners in California, and they sent their agent, Mr. Lane, with whom I went to the Muddy, and the stock was delivered to him as the Indians had agreed.

CHAPTER VII

IN THE winter season, my family usually lived at the Santa Clara settlement, thirty miles south of the Mountain Meadows, to which place they moved in the spring, to keep stock during the summer.

Late in the autumn of 1857, a company came along on their way to California. They brought a letter from President Brigham Young, directing me to see this company and their effects safely through to California. They were mostly merchants who had been doing business in Salt Lake City, and, anticipating difficulty between the people of Utah and the United States army, were fleeing to the Eastern States by way of California and the Isthmus of Panama.

When the company arrived in Cedar City, they sent a messenger ahead of them with the letter to me. Having occasion to go to Cedar City about the same time, I met the messenger. I directed him to return to the company and tell them to come on, and I would be with them in time.

I returned to Santa Clara to make some preparations for the journey, and then started to meet the company on the creek, twelve miles from the settlement.

When I reached the California road, the company had passed, and was some distance ahead of me. While traveling to overtake it, I found a man who had been traveling alone, also in pursuit of the company, with a view of getting through with it to California.

When I found him he was already in the hands of the Indians, and stripped of his clothing. They were making calculations to have a good time with him, as they expressed it, that is, they intended to take him to their camp and torture him.

The stranger, seeing I had influence with the Indians, begged me to save his life, and said if I would do so he would serve me as long as he lived.

I replied that I did not wish any reward for saving him.

In answer to his inquiry, I informed him that I was a "Mormon."

"Well," said he, "I am not a Mormon, but I wish you would save my life."

I assured him that it made no difference to me whether he was a "Mormon" or not. I told the Indians to bring back his clothing, which they did, except his shoes, and I took him along with me to the company.

I found a few Indians around the company, and there appeared to be some excitement. One of the merchants asked me if I could save the ship. I replied that I could see nothing to hinder me. He said: "You can take the helm, but do not run it too near the rocks or shoals; we have plenty of presents for the Indians."

He wished to know what they should do with their animals. I told him I knew where there was good grass, and I would send two Indians to take care of them; to let the two Indians have their suppers, and a shirt each when they brought in the animals in the morning.

At first they refused to let the animals go. I assured them that if I was to direct matters, I should do it in my own way.

After some consultation, they concluded to let me have my own way. The animals were sent out to feed in charge of the Indians, but I presume that some of the company did not sleep much during the night.

The animals were all brought safely into camp in the morning.

After that the company appeared to feel quite safe, and took much pains to have things move as I directed.

When we had traveled about sixty miles towards Muddy Creek, a Moapat Indian told me that the Indians on that stream were preparing to attack the company. I started at daydawn the following morning, and arrived at the crossing of the Muddy about two hours in advance of the company. The Indians had collected in the vicinity of the crossing, with the view of attacking the company when in camp. They believed they could easily kill the men, and obtain a large amount of spoil.

I called them together, and sat down and smoked a little tobacco with them, which I had brought along for that purpose. I then said: "You have listened to my talk in times past; you believe that it is good to hear and do what I say." They all answered, "Yes."

I then told them I was going through to California with some friends, Americans and merchants; and that we had brought along many blankets, shirts and other useful articles. I hoped they would see that none of the animals were stolen, and if any strayed, they would bring them into camp. Some of the Indians did not readily consent to let the company pass in peace.

For further security, I sent for their women and children to come out of their hiding place, where they had been sent for safety, as is the custom of the Indians when preparing for battle.

I had matters in a much better shape on the arrival of the company, when I found them. I was careful to listen to all the talk of the Indians, and spent the evening and also the night with the largest collection of them, so that they could not make any general move without my knowledge.

We continued our journey across the fifty-six mile desert to Las Vegas springs. There we met Brothers Ira Hatch and Dudley Leavitt, on their return from a mission to the Mohave Indians.

Those Indians, on the arrival of these brethren among them, took their horses, and then held a council to decide whether they should kill the brethren or not. The chief called a vote of his people, and it was decided that the brethren should die.

A Piute friend who had accompanied the Elders from Las Vegas, began to mourn over their fate, and said to them, "I told you that the Mohaves would kill you if you came here, and now they are going to do it."

Brother Hatch told their Piute friend, who acted as interpreter, to tell the Mohave chief, Chanawanse, to let him pray before he was killed.

The chief consented, and Brother Hatch knelt down among the bloodthirsty savages, and asked the Lord to soften their hearts, that they might not shed their blood. He also said more that was appropriate to the occasion.

The prayer was repeated in measured sentences by the interpreter.

It had the desired effect. The heart of the chief was softened. He took the brethren to his lodge, and put them at the farther end of it, in a secure place. There he guarded them until nearly morning, then told them to go as fast as they could to Las Vegas, eighty miles distant.

They traveled this distance on foot, and with but little food. When I met them they were living on muskeet bread. This is an article of food manufactured from a pod resembling that of a bean, which grows on the muskeet tree. These circumstances were related to me by the Elders when we met.

At Las Vegas I learned that the Indians there expected that the company would have been massacred at the Muddy Creek.

After we left this watering place, three Indians followed us and made an effort to steal. They were brought into camp and guarded until morning. The remainder of the journey we had no more trouble with the Indians.

We met companies of our people on their way from San Bernardino to Utah.

I was engaged the remainder of the autumn and the winter of 1857-8, on the road between the Santa Clara and Las Vegas springs, in assisting the Saints who were moving to Utah.

On the return of spring I removed my family, as was my custom, to the Mountain Meadows, to take care of our stock.

CHAPTER VIII

THE following letter from President Brigham Young so well illustrates his peaceable and civilizing policy towards the Indians, that I think it should find a place in this narrative:

"PRESIDENT'S OFFICE,

Great Salt Lake City,

March 5, 1858.

"DEAR BROTHER:—Your note of the 19th of last month came to hand on the 3rd inst. I was happy to learn of the success and the general prosperity of the mission, and trust that the genial and salutary influences now so rapidly extending to the various tribes in that region, may continue to spread abroad until it shall pervade every son and daughter of Abraham in their fallen condition.

"The hour of their redemption draws nigh, and the time is not far distant when they will receive knowledge, and begin to rise and increase in the land, and become a people whom the Lord will bless.

"The Indians should be encouraged in keeping and taking care of stock. I highly approve of your designs in doing your farming through the natives; it teaches them to obtain a subsistence by their own industry, and leaves you more at liberty to visit others, and extend your missionary labors among them. A few missionaries to show and instruct them how to raise stock and grain, and then not eat it up for them, is most judicious. You should always be careful to impress upon them that they should not infringe upon the rights of others; and our brethren should be very careful not to infringe upon their rights in any particular, thus cultivating honor and good principles in their midst by example as well as precept.

"As ever, I remain your brother in the gospel of salvation,

BRIGHAM YOUNG."

The sending of an army by the general government to look after the affairs of the Saints, occasioned some excitement and much talk among the people. The terrible wrongs and persecutions of Missouri and Illinois came up vividly in the minds of those who had suffered in them, and greatly intensified the public feeling concerning the wrongs which the general government evidently intended to inflict upon the Saints in Utah.

Elders coming in from the European missions, by way of California, thought the government would send a force into Southern Utah by that route.

It being expected that I would visit the Indians and look after matters a little in that direction, in the spring of 1858 I took five men and went by way of Las Vegas springs to the River Colorado, at the foot of the Cottonwood Islands, 170 miles from the Santa Clara settlement.

As was my policy at all times, I cultivated the good feelings of the Indians in that country.

A small steamer lay at the head of the islands, and a company of men, with animals, were making their way up the river, on the opposite side from us. I requested Brother Thales Haskell to hail the boat's crew from a thicket of willows, while the rest of the company remained secreted. If a boat were sent to take him over, he was to pass as a renegade from Utah, and learn who they were and their intentions. Brother Haskell was soon taken on board of the steamer.

I prayed for him that night, for my mind was filled with gloomy forebodings. I dreamed that the officer in charge of the boat offered the Indians a large reward for my scalp.

At daydawn I sent two men back on our trail to see if there was any one on it, with instructions if they saw anything wrong to not return, but go on their way homeward.

Soon afterwards we saw the yawl from the steamer land Brother Haskell. He informed us that the company was of a military character, and exhibited very hostile feelings against our people; that the expedition had been sent out by the government to examine the river, and learn if a force could be taken into Southern Utah from that direction, should it be needed, to subjugate the "Mormons."

We were soon on our way homeward.

The first night out from the river, a Las Vegas Indian overtook us, and informed us that soon after we left the river, the steamer came down below the Cottonwood Islands, brought a large amount of blankets and other goods ashore, made some presents to the Mohaves and Piutes, and offered to pay well for the capture of any "Mormon" they found in their country.

When we overtook the brethren sent out early in the morning, they told us that they met two of the boat's crew examining the trail we traveled on to the river. The two men started for the steamer, and the brethren traveled the other way.

At this time there were three or four brethren at Las Vegas Springs, laboring to make a settlement. We counseled together, and it was thought advisable to vacate the place. Some of them started for home. My brother, Oscar Hamblin, remained to assist the Indians in putting in their crops.

Brother Dudley Leavitt and I went thirty-five miles west, on the road to California, to a lead mine, to obtain a load of lead.

As I had some knowledge of smelting the ore, our efforts were a success.

The evening after completing our load, I started up the mountain on the side of which the mine was located, to look at it before leaving. I stepped back, and calling Brother Leavitt, I told him that an Indian was watching our horses, and if he did not bring them in and tie them up, they would be run off as soon as it was dark.

He replied that he would see to it. Being strongly impressed with the danger of losing our horses, I warned him a second time, to which he made an indifferent reply.

When I returned it was nearly dark and Brother Leavitt had just started for the horses.

All we ever saw of them afterwards was their tracks, and the trail of the Indian that had driven them off.

The Indians in that section of the country did not keep horses, and therefore were not accustomed to the use of them, but stole them for food.

Brother Leavitt was under the necessity of going to

Las Vegas, thirty-five miles distant, to get my brother to come with his team to take our wagon home.

As he did not return as soon as expected, I started to meet him. Not meeting him the first day, I stopped in a small cave for the night.

I had nothing to eat, and gathered some cactus leaves, or pods, to roast for supper.

They were a new variety to me, and had scarlet spots on them. (I afterwards learned from the Indians that they were poisonous.)

After cooking them in the embers, I ate a little, but they did not taste right. They produced a burning sensation in my stomach and pain in the glands of my mouth and throat. I soon became satisfied that I was poisoned.

My misery increased, and I became dizzy-headed. With no help near, I felt that my earthly career was nearly terminated, unless the God of Israel saved me, as I knew He had done many times before. I knelt down and earnestly asked Him to be merciful to me in my extremity, and save my life.

I then became very sick at the stomach, and vomited freely. Great thirst succeeded, and I soon exhausted the small supply of water in my canteen. This I soon ejected, when I became easy and lay down and slept until morning.

Not knowing whether my brother would come or not, I continued on my way to Las Vegas.

I was lank and hungry, and if I ever felt the want of food it was then.

About noon I saw my brother coming to my relief. It was a welcome sight.

Still farther west from the lead mine, there were two roads for about thirty miles. One of them was not usually traveled, but came into the main road. Some time before we were there, a company that had taken this by-road, had left wagons on it, and we were desirous of obtaining some of the iron.

When my brother Oscar and I arrived at the lead mine, we concluded to leave the lead where it was, and go west on this unfrequented road, to a spring, twenty-five miles from the lead mine, and get the iron that was left there.

On arriving at the spring we did not find as much iron as we expected, but we put what there was into the wagon.

Before I went on this trip to Las Vegas and the Colorado River, my team, driven by my Indian boy, Albert, had gone with Brother Calvin Read to Lower California. They had been gone nearly three months.

The morning after our arrival at the spring, when at prayer, the Spirit showed to me a company of our people, a few miles still farther west, on the by-road. I told my brother this, and that my team was with them, and my Indian boy was herding the animals on one side of the wagons near the spring.

I proposed that we unload the iron and drive in that direction.

My brother objected and said he had never heard of water in that direction short of twenty miles.

After much persuasion, my brother consented to unload the iron, but he drove on very reluctantly, telling me that I was a visionary man, and always seeing something.

We traveled about three miles, and came in sight of a camp. I found my boy Albert watching the horses; there was a good spring of water and plenty of grass. Just beyond were the wagons.

The brethren said they never rejoiced more to see any-one than they did us. They were unacquainted with the country, and needed our help to get into Las Vegas.

CHAPTER IX

AFTER my return from the Colorado River, I had oc-casion to go to Salt Lake City. I arrived there soon after the United States army had entered Salt Lake Val-ley. The people north of Utah County had vacated their homes and moved south.

Through the instrumentality of Colonel Thomas L. Kane, a peaceable solution of our difficulties with the gen-eral government had been arrived at, and the Saints were returning to their vacated homes.

It is generally known that the enemies of the Latter-day Saints have accused them of shielding from justice the white men, who, it was supposed, joined with the In-dians in the Mountain Meadow massacre. Mr. Cumming succeeded President Brigham Young as governor of Utah Territory in the early spring, before the arrival of the United States army in Salt Lake Valley.

President Brigham Young requested Elder George A. Smith to have an interview with the new governor, and learn his views concerning the Mountain Meadow massa-cre, and assure him that all possible assistance would be rendered the United States courts to have it thoroughly investigated.

Brother Smith took me with him, and introduced me as a man who was well informed regarding Indian matters in Southern Utah, and would impart to him any informa-tion required that I might be in possession of. He also urged upon Governor Cumming the propriety of an investigation of this horrid affair, that, if there were any white men engaged in it, they might be justly punished for their crimes.

Governor Cumming replied that President Buchanan had issued a proclamation of amnesty and pardon to the "Mormon" people, and he did not wish to go behind it to search out crime.

Brother Smith urged that the crime was exclusively personal in its character, and had nothing to do with the "Mormons" as a people, or with the general officers of the Territory, and, therefore, was a fit subject for an investigation before the United States courts.

Mr. Cumming still objected to interfering, on account of the President's proclamation.

Brother Smith replied substantially as follows: "If the business had not been taken out of our hands by a change of officers in the Territory, the Mountain Meadow affair is one of the first things we should have attended to when a United States court sat in Southern Utah. We would see whether or not white men were concerned in the affair, with the Indians."

At Salt Lake City, I was appointed sub-Indian agent.

During the summer of 1858, when I was at my home on the Santa Clara, one morning about 9 o'clock, while engaged in cutting some of the large branches from a cottonwood tree, I fell a distance of twenty or thirty feet to the ground. I was badly bruised and was carried to my house for dead, or nearly so.

I came to my senses about 8 o'clock in the evening, and threw off from my stomach quite a quantity of blood. I requested the brethren who were standing around to administer to me, and they did so. From the time I fell from the tree until then was lost to me, so far as earthly matters were concerned.

During the time my body lay in this condition, it seemed to me that I went up from the earth and looked down upon it, and it appeared like a dark ball. The place where I was seemed very desirable to remain in. It was divided into compartments by walls, from which appeared to grow out vines and flowers, displaying an endless variety of colors.

I thought I saw my father there, but separated from me. I wished him to let me into his compartment, but he replied that it was not time for me to come to him.

I then asked why I could not come.

He answered, "Your work is not yet done."

I attempted to speak about it again, but he motioned me away with his hand, and, in a moment I was back to this earth. I saw the brethren carrying my body along, and it was loathsome to me in appearance.

A day or two after my fall from the tree, I was carried to the Mountain Meadows, where I was fed on goat's milk and soon recovered.

In the autumn of this year, 1858, I received instructions from President Brigham Young to take a company of men and visit the Moquis, or Town Indians, on the east side of the Colorado River.

The object of this visit was to learn something of the character and condition of this people, and to take advantage of any opening there might be to preach the gospel to them and do them good.

My companions for this trip were Brothers Dudley and Thomas Leavitt, two of my brothers, Frederick and William Hamblin, Samuel Knight, Ira Hatch, Andrew Gibbons, Benjamin Knell, Ammon M. Tenney (Spanish

interpreter), James Davis (Welsh interpreter), and Nar-
aguts, an Indian. guide.

A Spanish interpreter was thought advisable, from the
fact that the Spanish language was spoken and understood
by many of the Indians in that region of country. A
Welsh interpreter was taken along, thinking it possible
that there might be some truth in a report which had been
circulated that there were evidences of Welsh descent
among these Indians. An Indian guide was requisite, from
the fact that none of the brethren had traveled the route.
This was the first of a series of journeys to this people.

The company, consisting of twelve men, including myself, left the Santa Clara settlement on the 28th of October. Our general course of travel was a little south of
east. The third night we camped at Pipe Springs, a place
now occupied by a stone fort, and known as Winsor
Castle.

While there, two or three Piutes came to our camp.
One of them asked me to go with him to some large rocks,
which lay under the high cliffs near by. As we approached
them he showed me a human skeleton. "There," said he,
"are the bones of Nahguts, who killed your ox on the
Clara. He came as far as here, was taken blind, could not
find the spring and died."

The following evening we camped at the foot of the
Kibab, or Buckskin Mountains, with the chief and nearly
all the tribe of Kibab Indians. They provided supper by
cooking a large number of rabbits.

They put these in a pile, and covered them with hot
ashes and coals. When sufficiently cooked, the chief performed the ceremony of thanking the Father for the success of their hunt, and asked for a continuation of His
blessings in obtaining food. He then divided the rabbits

among the company. We all joined in the feast. They gave us meat and we gave them bread.

I noticed an Indian sitting moodily, alone, and eating nothing. I sat down by him, and asked what he was thinking about.

Said he, "I am thinking of my brother, whom you killed with bad medicine."

I told him that his brother had made his own medicine, that he came to the Clara, killed an ox, and had brought a curse upon himself. I advised the Indian to eat with the company, and not make any bad medicine and kill himself.

This very prevalent idea of good and bad medicine, among these Indians, gives evidence of a very general belief in witchcraft.

The Indian took a piece of bread, saying he did not wish to die. I was told by our guide that this Indian had said, that in the night, when I was asleep, he intended to chop an axe into my head, but being afraid it would make bad medicine for him, he did not do it.

After climbing dangerous cliffs and crossing extensive fissures in the rocks, the tenth day out from home we crossed the Colorado River, at the Ute Ford, known in Spanish history as "The Crossing of the Fathers." The trail beyond the river was not only difficult, but sometimes very dangerous.

While traveling in the night, one of the animals that carried our provisions, ran off. Two men went in pursuit of it, while the company went on.

The third day after losing our provisions, having had but little to eat, we came to a place where sheep had been herded, then to a garden under a cliff of rocks. It was watered from a small spring and occupied fine terraces, walled up on three sides.

As we passed, we saw that onions, pepper and other vegetables, such as we raised in our own gardens at home, had been grown there. On arriving at the summit of the cliff, we discovered a squash, which evidently had been left when the crop had been gathered.

We appropriated it to our use. It tasted delicious, and we supposed it to be a better variety than we had before known, but we afterwards found that hunger had made it taste sweet.

Four miles farther on we came to an Oriba village, of about three hundred dwellings. The buildings were of rock, laid in clay mortar. The village stands on a cliff with perpendicular sides, and juts out into the plain like a promontory into the sea. The promontory is narrow where it joins the table land back of it.

Across this the houses were joined together. The entrance to the town on the east side, was narrow and difficult. The town was evidently located and constructed for defense from the marauding tribes around.

The houses are usually three stories high. The second and third stories are set back from the front the width of the one below, so that the roofs of the lower stories have the appearance of terraces.

For security, the first story can only be entered by ascending to the roof, and then going down a ladder into the room below.

After our arrival in the village, the leading men counseled together a few minutes, when we were separated and invited to dine with different families.

A man beckoned me to follow him. After traversing several streets, and climbing a ladder to the roof of the first story of a house, I was ushered into a room furnished with sheepskins, blankets, earthen cooking utensils, water urns, and other useful articles.

It seemed to me strangely furnished, yet it had an air of comfort; perhaps the more so, for the reason that the previous few days had been spent in very laborious traveling, on rather low diet.

The hostess made a comfortable seat with blankets, and motioned me to occupy it.

A liberal repast was provided. It consisted of stewed meat, beans, peaches and a basket of corn bread which they called *peke*. It was about the thickness of brown paper, dry and crumbling, yet quite palatable.

The hostess, apparently surmising that I would not know how to partake of the bean soup without a spoon, dexterously thrust her fingers, closed tightly together, into the dish containing it, and, with a very rapid motion carried the soup to her mouth. Then she motioned me to eat. Hunger was pressing, and a hint was sufficient.

The day following, the two brethren we had left behind came in with the runaway mule, and a part of our supplies.

We visited seven of these towns, all similarly located and constructed.

The people generally used burros for packing all their supplies, except water, up the cliffs to their dwellings. The water was usually brought up by the women, in jugs, flattened on one side to fit the neck and shoulders of the carrier, and this was fastened with a strap which passed around in front of the body.

Most of the families owned a flock of sheep. These might be seen in all directions going out in the morning to feed, and returning in the evening. They were driven

into or near the towns at night, and coralled and guarded
to keep them from being stolen by the thieving Navajos.

We found a few persons in all the villages who could
speak the Ute language. They told us some of their traditions, which indicate that their fathers knew the Mexi-
cans, and something about Montezumas.

A very aged man said that when he was a young man,
his father told him that he would live to see white men
come among them, who would bring them great blessings,
such as their fathers had enjoyed, and that these men
would come from the west. He believed that he had lived
to see the prediction fulfilled in us.

We thought it advisable for some of the brethren to
remain with this people for a season, to study their language, get acquainted with them, and, as they are of the
blood of Israel, offer them the gospel. Elders Wm. M.
Hamblin, Andrew Gibbons, Thomas Leavitt and Benjamin Knell were selected for this purpose.

Bidding adieu to our Moqui friends, and to our brethren who were to remain with them, we started for home.
Sixteen days of hard travel would be necessary to accomplish the journey.

We expected to obtain supplies at the Oriba village,
but failed on account of scarcity. We had nothing for our
animals but the dry grass, and they were somewhat jaded.
The cold north wind blew in our faces, and we lit no fires
at night, as they would have revealed our position to the
roving Indians.

The journey home was very laborious and disagreeable. With provisions scarcely sufficient for our journey,
we again lost some of them by a runaway, and, failing to
get meat from the Indians as we expected, we were reduced to very short rations.

At Pipe Spring the snow was knee deep, and falling fast. We made only eight miles to Cedar Ridge the first day, from that place. As night came on we counseled together over our situation.

Taking into consideration our empty stomachs and the difficulty of traveling in the snow, it appeared quite impossible to get home without killing one of our horses for food. We lived on this rather objectionable kind of food for two days.

On arriving home it was very pleasant to find a change of diet, and our families and friends all well.

During our absence, the brethren had some difficulty with the Santa Clara Indians, and the management of it seemed leading to bad results. I visited the natives, and found that there were no bad intentions on their part, and they were all much pleased to have the matter understood and settled.

The brethren whom we left with the Moquis returned home the same winter.

A division arose among the people as to whether we were the men prophesied of by their fathers, who would come among them with the knowledge that their fathers possessed.

This dispute ran so high that the brethren felt that but little or no good could result from remaining longer. Besides, the chief men among the Moquis advised their return.

The brethren suffered much privation and hardship in this effort to preach the gospel to this people. The Indians said that they did not want to cross the Colorado River to live with the "Mormons," for they had a tradition from their fathers that they must not cross that river until the three prophets who took them into the country they now occupy, should visit them again.

Their chief men also prophesied that the "Mormons" would settle in the country south of them, and that their route of travel would be up the Little Colorado. This looked very improbable to us at that time, but all has since been fulfilled.

CHAPTER X

EARLY in the autumn of 1859, I again visited Salt Lake City, when President Brigham Young called upon me to make another visit to the Moquis, and take with me Brother Marion J. Shelton, whom we had called to labor with that people, to learn their language and teach them.

He directed me to leave with him one of the brethren who had been with me for some time among the Indians. President Young also put in my charge sixty dollars worth of goods, consisting of wool-cards, spades, shovels and other articles which would be of value to the Indians, with instructions to dispense them in the best manner to create a good influence among them.

I returned home, and immediately made arrangements to carry out these instructions.

Our company consisted of Marion J. Shelton, Thales Haskell, Taylor Crosby, Benjamin Knell, Ira Hatch, John W. Young and myself.

We left the Santa Clara settlement on the 20th of October. Nothing of special interest occurred on our journey, except that at one time we did not find water where we expected, and were suffering with thirst, when some Piutes saw our fire and came to us. They informed us where water was located and in the morning piloted us to it.

We arrived among the Moquis on the 6th of November. We visited and talked with them three days.

I was at a loss to know who to leave with Brother Shelton, and was desirous that it might be made manifest to me. My mind rested upon Brother Thales Haskell. I went to him and told him that he was the only one I could think of to remain with Brother Shelton, but he had been out so much that I disliked to mention the subject to him.

He replied that he was the man, for it had been made known to him that he would be asked to remain before leaving home, but he had said nothing about it.

We left our Moqui friends and Brothers Shelton and Haskell on the 10th of November, and arrived home on the 25th. Brothers Shelton and Haskell remained on their mission until early spring, when they returned home and reported that the Moquis were kind to them, but they could not make much progress in the object of their mission. The fathers of the people told them, very emphatically, that they still believed that the "Mormons" who had visited them were the men prophesied of by their fathers, that would come among them from the west to do them good. But they could make no move until the re-appearance of the three prophets who led their fathers to that land, and told them to remain on those rocks until they should come again and tell them what to do.

Under these circumstances the brethren thought best to return home.

In the fall of 1860, I was directed to make another effort to establish a mission in some of the Moqui towns, and take with me George A. Smith, Jr., son of the late President George A. Smith.

I left the Santa Clara in October with a company of nine men: Thales Haskell, George A. Smith, Jr., Jehiel McConnell, Ira Hatch, Isaac Riddle, Amos Thornton, Francis M. Hamblin, James Pierce, and an Indian we called Enos. We took sufficient to sustain us in the Moqui country for one year.

In speaking at a public meeting the day before leaving, I said I felt different from what I had ever previously done on leaving home; that something unusual would happen. What it would be I did not know. Whether we should ever see home again or not I did not know, but I knew we were told to go among the Moquis and stay for one year, and that I should do so if I could get there.

When we arrived at the crossing of the Colorado River, I again felt the same gloomy forebodings I spoke of before leaving home.

On the morning before crossing, the brethren said I had spoken discouragingly several times, and they wished to know if there was any one in the company that I did not wish to go on.

I assured them that there was no one that I did not wish to go along, but I knew there would be something happen that would be very unpleasant, and that there would be very hard times for some of us.

Young George A. Smith said: "You will see one thing, that is, I will stick to it to the last. That is what I came for."

We all crossed the Colorado River with a firm determination to do the best we could to fill our mission.

The second day's travel from the river we found no water, as we had expected, and what little we had brought with us was exhausted.

About two o'clock in the afternoon, four Navajos

came to us, and told us that if we went on to the next watering place we would all be killed. They invited us to go with them to Spaneshanks' camp, where they assured us we would find protection.

We counseled about the matter, and concluded that the animals were too nearly famished for want of water to reach Spaneshanks' camp. If what the four Navajos told us about danger ahead was true, we were in danger from enemies if we went on to water and of perishing with thirst if we attempted to reach Spaneshanks' camp.

As the water was but a short distance ahead on our route, we concluded to push on to it and risk the consequences.

I requested Brother Thales Haskell to go on with the company and water the animals, he having been there before, and being, for this reason, acquainted with the ground. I directed him, for security, to take our animals on to the top of a table rock where there were about forty acres of grass, and which could be reached only through a narrow pass in the rocks, which would enable us to easily defend ourselves in case of attack.

The Navajos were gathering around us from different directions, and the Indian interpreter we had brought with us informed me that they were evidently bent on mischief. I determined to remain behind with them for awhile, and learn what I could by the interpreter and by observation. The interpreter learned from their conversation, that they were determined we should not go on to the Moqui towns, but they appeared undecided whether to kill us or let us go home.

We had taken two Indian women with us, thinking that they might be a great help in introducing something like cleanliness in cooking, among the people we were going to visit. The Navajos said we might go home if we would leave them.

I directed the interpreter to tell them that one of the women was Brother Hatch's wife, and the other was mine. They replied that they would not kill the men who had married them.

Two of the Navajos then hurried on to our camp, which was by the narrow pass, on to the table rock. There the Navajos made a treaty with us that if we would trade them the goods we had brought along, and especially the ammunition, we might go home.

As it seemed impossible to fill our mission, we felt justified in concluding to return.

The following morning we commenced to exchange articles of trade for blankets. While thus engaged, our animals were taken off the rock to water. When returning from the water, Brother George A. Smith's horse turned back on a trail, which, in a short distance, led over a hill and out of sight.

As he started after it, I told him that he had better not go alone, to which he made an indifferent reply. Something else immediately attracted my attention, and he was forgotten until the Navajos in our camp suddenly left, when I learned that he was after his horse, alone and out of sight. I sent two men after him.

They went about a mile, and found him lying by the trail, with three bullet wounds through the lower part of his body, and four arrow wounds between the shoulders.

I mounted a horse and rode to the spot, and learned that Brother George A. had found a mounted Indian leading off his horse, and that he took the Indian's horse by the bit, when the stolen horse was readily given up, with which the owner started for camp.

The Indian who had taken the horse and a companion then rode a short distance together, when one came up by the side of Brother George A., and asked him for his revolver. Not suspecting any treachery, he passed it to the Indian, who handed it to his companion a little in the rear. The latter then fired three shots into him, with the revolver only a few feet from his body.

Brother Smith was paralyzed, and soon fell from his horse. The two Indians then dismounted, and one threw his buckskin shirt over his head, and the other shot the arrows between his shoulders.

We took the dying man on a blanket near to the camp, when he earnestly requested us to lay him down and let him die in peace.

During this time about forty Navajos had gathered at a difficult place on the trail leading to the Moqui towns, probably anticipating that we would make an effort to go in that direction.

I sent our interpreter to ask them what they meant by shooting a man after they had agreed with us that if we would trade with them we might go in peace.

He returned with a message to the effect that three relatives of the Indians had been killed by pale faces like us, and, to avenge their death they had shot one of our men. They said: "Tell Jacob that he need not bury him, for we will eat him, and the women and children will help do it. We want to kill two more; and if Jacob will give them up or let us quietly kill them, the rest of the company may go in peace."

The question was asked me, "What are you going to do?"

Under the trying circumstances, it was a serious question; and the query was an earnest one with us all, "What can we do?" The heavens seemed like brass over our heads, and the earth as iron beneath our feet. It seemed utterly impossible to reach the Moqui towns, which were almost in sight, and like certain death to attempt to escape in the night with our jaded animals.

Our interpreter thought it would be better for two of the company to die, than for all to be killed.

I told him to go and tell the Navajos that there were only a few of us, but we were well armed, and should fight as long as there was one left.

He turned to go, rather reluctantly, saying again that he thought it better for only two to die than all.

I replied that I did not think so; that I would not give a cent to live after I had given up two men to be murdered; that I would rather die like a man than live like a dog.

As the interpreter turned to go, the two Indian women we had brought with us wept aloud, and accused me of bringing them along to be murdered. I went a little way off by myself and asked the Lord to be merciful, and pity us in our miserable and apparently helpless condition, and to make known to me what to do and say to extricate us from our difficulties.

I returned to camp and told the company that we would leave as soon as possible.

Some thought it was certain death whether we went or remained where we were.

I told them, however, that there would not be another one of us injured.

Our four Navajo friends who had come to us the day before, had remained, and now helped to gather our animals and pack up.

We were soon on our way.

[270]

I told Brother George A. that we must return home to save our lives, for we could not go any farther, as the Navajos were guarding the pass.

"Well," said he, "leave me; it will make but very little difference with me; it may make much with you. You cannot go very fast if you take me."

We put him in a saddle upon a mule, with Brother Jehiel McConnell behind him, to hold him on.

We left our camp kettles over the fire containing our breakfast, untouched, and all our camp outfit that we could possibly do without.

The Navajos who had been guarding our trail beyond the camp, started after us, coming down like a whirlwind.

Some of our party predicted that in ten minutes there would not be one of us left, but there was no flinching, no wilting in the emergency.

I again predicted that there would not be one of us hurt, for so the Spirit whispered to me.

The Navajos came almost within range of our rifles, and then turned suddenly to the right.

As they passed, the mule that carried our supplies went after them; but, to our surprise, it was brought back to us by a friendly Navajo.

We traveled as fast as possible, while the four old gray-headed Navajo friends guarded our front and rear. They often asked us to leave the dying man, as he was no longer of any use; that the one who shot him would follow to obtain his scalp, and that if we stopped to bury him they would leave, for our enemies would have his scalp if they had to dig his body up.

About sun-down George A. asked me to stop, and said that everything looked dark to him, and he was dying.

Our Navajo friends again said if we stopped they would go on. I said to Brother George A., "It will not do to stop now."

He asked, "Why?"

When I told him, he said, "Oh, well, go on then; but I wish I could die in peace." These were the last words that he said.

A few minutes afterwards, the Navajo friends said, "The man is dead. If you will leave him, we will take you to Spaneshanks' camp, where you will have friends."

Our last ray of hope for getting the body of George A. where we could lay it safely away in the rocks, was now gone. I said to the company, "What shall we do?" The answer was, "What can we do, only lay the body on the ground and leave it?"

I replied that such was my mind, for we would only risk our lives by making an effort to bury the dead, in which we would probably be unsuccessful.

We wrapped the body in a blanket, and laid it in a hollow place by the side of the trail, and then rode on as fast as our jaded animals could well carry us, until late in the night.

We halted on a patch of grass, held our animals by the lariats, and also put out a guard.

I sat down and leaned over on my saddle, but could not sleep. The scenes of the past two days were before me in vivid reality. The thought of carrying the wounded man with his life's blood dripping out of him along the trail, without his having the privilege of dying in peace, combined with the leaving of his body to be devoured by wolves and vultures, seemed almost too much to bear.

My imagination pictured another scene. South of us, in the distance, we could see a large fire, around which we presumed the Navajos were having a war dance over the scalp of our brother.

Then the thought of conveying the sad news to his father and mother and affectionate sister, all old and valued acquaintances of mine, pierced me like barbed arrows, and caused me the most bitter reflections that I have ever experienced in my life.

CHAPTER XI

AT DAYDAWN a Navajo came to us, and asked me to give him something as a present. I did so, and, as he turned away, I recognized Brother George A. Smith's revolver in his belt.

We were soon on our way for Spaneshanks' camp, where we found water, grass and friends.

That evening our Indian messenger came, and had an interview with Spaneshanks.

Our interpreter informed me that the message sent to our Navajo friends was, that they ought to kill us that night; and that Spaneshanks replied to the message that he was chief in that country and we should not be hurt.

We were further informed that the party that had done the mischief were from Fort Defiance.

We were warned that ahead of us was a narrow pass, where the Navajos had lately attacked the Utes, and killed their chief, Wahnonee, and that possibly they might attack us in the same place.

The following morning we left the friendly Spaneshanks, and, by making good use of our time, we watered our animals and got them on to a table rock before dark.

Deep cuts and fissures setting in from the north and east rendered our location unapproachable except by the way we had come. We placed one watch in the most difficult part of the trail, and felt safe for the first time in six days. In the morning we discovered a gun barrel with the stock shivered to pieces, shreds of blankets and clothing, and other signs which indicated that the place had been recently occupied. We concluded it was the spot where the Navajos had taken advantage of the Utes.

The second day from Spaneshanks' camp we crossed to the north side of the Colorado River. Four days afterwards on the Buckskin Mountain, the Piutes brought us an abundance of pine nuts.

The supply was very acceptable, as edibles were scarce in camp.

Five days subsequently we arrived home on the Santa Clara, jaded and worn with hard travel and much anxiety of mind.

Our relatives and friends had been much troubled in their minds concerning us in our absence. Some had unfavorable dreams, and they were filled with gloomy forebodings. A young lad, a nephew of mine, told his mother that there was something the matter with me, for he saw me walking along and weeping bitterly. He asked me what was the matter, and I replied, "Do not ask me, for it is too bad to tell."

I wrote quite a full account of this trip to President George A. Smith, after which he came to my house on the Santa Clara.

In conversing with him about the affair, he remarked, "I was much shocked on hearing of the death of my boy; but upon reflection, we all, in the Historian's Office, came to the conclusion that the Lord wanted the young man just in the way He took him."

President Young also looked upon the matter in the same light.

After this conversation, Brother Smith gave me a note from President Brigham Young, in which was a written request to raise a company of twenty men, and bring in what we could find of the remains of Brother George A. Smith, Jr. Winter having set in, I considered this a difficult task.

It was necessary to go to Parowan for men and supplies, a distance of some seventy miles. This accomplished, we were soon on our way.

Our route was a difficult one to travel in the winter season. The ford of the Colorado was deep and dangerous at any time, but especially when the ice was running. Sometimes there were steep rocks to climb, at other times the trail ran along the almost perpendicular sides of deep rock fissures, narrow, with frequent short turns, where a misstep might plunge us or our animals hundreds of feet below. Sometimes the precipitous rocks were covered with ice, which had to be hacked with our hatchets before we could feel any surety of a foothold.

At one time we waited until nearly midday for the sun to melt the frost and ice on a steep rock, that we might be able to get our animals out of a gulch on to the plain above. On this occasion my pack mule slipped and fell, then rolled and slid down to within about a yard of the edge of a chasm below. We fastened a long lariat to the animal, and saved it and the pack.

On arriving at the place where we had left the body of young Brother Smith, we found the head and some of the larger bones. We prepared them for carrying as well as we could.

At our last camp in going out, the chief who had led the hostile Navajos on our previous trip, came to us, accompanied by his wife, and said if he had known what he afterwards learned about us, he would have protected instead of injuring us.

Nothing of special interest took place in returning home. I went with the remains of George A. Smith, Jr., to Salt Lake City, and delivered them to his friends.

This completed one of the most trying series of circumstances of my life. That the misfortune was no greater is due to the kindly Providence of our Heavenly Father, and the faith in Him and confidence in each other, of the brethren involved in it.

President Young proffered to pay us for our trip. I replied that no one who went with me made any charge, and, as for myself, I was willing to wait for my pay until the resurrection of the just.

On my return to the Mountain Meadows, I found my family out of flour, and the roads blocked with snow, so that a team could not get in nor out of the Meadows. I had left my family with plenty of food, but they had lent· it to their neighbors. I was under the necessity of hauling both fuel and flour for them on a hand sled.

CHAPTER XII

IT WAS nearly two years before we made another trip to the Moqui towns. Many of the brethren appeared to think that no good could be accomplished in that direction. In the autumn of 1861, many Saints were called from the north to form settlements in Southern Utah. The city of St. George was founded, and settlements were extended, so as to occupy the fertile spots along the waters of the Rio Virgen and Santa Clara.

During the winter of 1861-2 there was an unusual amount of rain-fall. About the middle of February, it rained most of the time for a number of days, and the Santa Clara Creek rose so high that the water spread across the bottom from bluff to bluff, and became a turbulent muddy river.

Our little farms and the cottonwood trees that grew on the bottom lands were disappearing. The flood wood sometimes accumulated in a pile, and would throw the current of water on to ground which had apparently before been safe from its inroads.

Our fort, constructed of stone, and which was one hundred feet square, with walls twelve feet high and two feet thick, stood a considerable distance north of the original bed of the creek. Inside the walls were rooms occupied by families, and we had considered it safe from the flood.

One night, when most of the people were asleep, some one discovered that the water was washing away the bank on the south side of it, and also that the water was beginning to run around it, between it and the bluff. It was raining heavily at the same time.

The people were removed from the fort as soon as possible, and some temporary shelter was constructed of boards, blankets, etc.

While I was making an effort to save some property near the caving bank of the stream, the ground on which I stood suddenly slid into the water, about twenty feet below, and took me with it.

I still stood on the mass of dirt, but realized that it was being rapidly washed away from under me, and that I was liable at any moment to be precipitated into the raging torrent.

The thought flashed through my mind that there was not one chance in a thousand of my being saved. I heard someone say above me that I was gone; it was of no use to try to save me. I shouted at the top of my voice "It is of use to try to save me! Bring a rope and throw to me, and haul me out before the bank caves and I am gone!"

In a few moments I felt a rope drop over my head and shoulders. I lost no time in grasping it, and was pulled up just as I felt the last foothold giving way under me.

Again was my life preserved by that kindly providence which has so often saved me when in imminent peril.

What seems remarkable in the history of that gloomy night is, that in a few minutes after being rescued from death myself, I should be the means of saving another life.

A heavy and rapidly increasing current of water was now running between the fort and the bluff.

In some way or other a sick woman had been left in one of the rooms of the fort, and her husband was almost frantic with the idea that his wife was lost, as he did not think she could be got out. She had a young child, which was safe outside, while the mother was in peril.

I took the rope that had been the means of saving myself, tied one end of it to a tree, and holding on to it, got safely to the fort, where I fastened the other end. I entered the room, drew the woman from the bed on to my back, placed her arms over my shoulders and crossed them in front. I told her when I got to the running water that she must hold herself on my back, for I would be obliged to lay hold of the rope with both hands to get through the water.

When we arrived at the point of danger, her arms pressed so heavily on my throat that I was nearly strangled. It was a critical moment, for if I let go the rope we were sure to be lost, as the water was surging against me. I made the best possible use of time and strength, and reached the shore safely with my burden, to the great joy of the husband and children.

The flood swept away my grist mill and other improvements to the value of several thousand dollars. Most of the houses and the cultivated land of the settlement also disappeared.

In the autumn of 1862, it was thought best to again visit the Moqui villages. President Young recommended that we cross the Colorado River south of St. George, and explore the country in that direction, with the view of finding a more feasible route than the one we had before traveled.

A company of twenty men were set apart for this purpose, by Apostles Orson Pratt and Erastus Snow.

A team accompanied us to the river with a small boat, in which we conveyed our luggage across. Our animals swam the river.

Expecting to return the same way, after crossing the river we cached our boat and some of our supplies.

The first day we traveled south, up a "wash," for about thirty miles. We then traveled three days through a rough, bushy country, with some scrub cedar and pine timber. The fourth night from the river we camped at a small "seep" spring. The San Francisco Mountain lay a little to the southeast of us, and in sight.

In the morning our Indian guide refused to go farther with us, his reason being that we were going into a country destitute of water. We counseled together, and decided that we could reach the foothills of the San Francisco Mountain without perishing.

The first night from the "seep" spring, a light fall of snow came on. It melted and ran into the hollows of the rocks, and furnished an abundant supply of water. This seemed like a special providence in our favor.

The second night we made a dry camp. The third night we arrived at the foot of the San Francisco Mountain, where we again found snow.

The second day after leaving this mountain we reached the Little Colorado River, and then traveled a little northeast to the Moqui towns.

We spent two days in visiting among them. We left Brothers Jehiel McConnell, Thales Haskell and Ira Hatch to labor among them for a season.

The Moquis had been going through some religious ceremonies to induce the Great Spirit to send storms to wet their country, that they might raise an abundance of food the coming season. They assured us that their offerings and prayers were heard, for the storm would soon come, and advised us to delay starting for home until it should be over.

We had been talking with them about sending some of their chief men with us, to see our people and have a talk with our leaders. They objected on account of a tradition forbidding them to cross the great river, which has been referred to before.

We then started for home. The storm came the first night out and wet the country finely. We found shelter under a rock.

While there, three Moqui men came to us. They informed us that, after further consultation, their chief men had concluded to send them with us.

This storm, apparently in answer to the prayers of this simple people, and similar circumstances that have come under my observation among the Indians, have given me an assurance that the Lord is mindful of the wants of those barbarians, and that He answers their prayers with the blessings they need.

The snow fell sufficiently deep to cover up the grass, and our animals had to subsist principally on browse. The traveling was laborious, and when we arrived at the river by our old route, we had eight animals less than we left home with. This loss, and the poor condition of those that remained made traveling slow and tedious.

On arriving at the Ute crossing of the Colorado, we found the water deep and ice running. Fording was difficult and dangerous.

This, coupled with the traditions of the Moquis against crossing this river, visibly affected our Moqui friends. Anticipating that they might be entirely discouraged and not proceed farther, I forwarded their blankets and provisions by the first ones that crossed over.

When we desired them to cross, they expressed a wish to return home, but when I informed them that their things had been taken over, they concluded to follow. When the crossing was successfully accomplished, they returned thanks to the Father of all for their preservation.

On the north side, it occupied a day to bridge a muddy inlet and get on to the bench above. The crossing was accomplished the first day of the year 1863.

Brothers L. M. Fuller and James Andrus, whose animals were still in fair condition, were advised to push on as fast as practicable, and send us back some supplies, as we were very short of food.

The rest of the company traveled slowly to save the weak animals.

We lay by one day on the Pahreah, and killed and cooked crows to help out our rations.

Six days from the river we camped on Kanab Creek. That evening, Brother Lucius M. Fuller came into camp with a fat sheep, dressed, and some bread and flour, which were furnished by Brother Wm. B. Maxwell, from his ranch on Short Creek, forty miles beyond our camp.

When the Moquis saw this food they thanked the Great Father that He had pitied us and sent us food. Prayer and thanksgiving was the daily custom in our company—but to see these Indians, who are looked upon as barbarians, so humble and childlike in their reverence to the Great Father, seems worthy of special notice.

A man who came with Brother Fuller told me, after supper, that he had heard that one of my sons had been killed at Santa Clara, by the caving in of a bank of earth, and he thought it was Lyman. That night I had a dream or vision, in which I learned that it was Duane instead of Lyman, and I told the brethren so in the morning.

Three days afterwards we arrived at the settlements on the Rio Virgen. The brethren in these settlement furnished us with fresh animals and an abundant supply of food. We found a wide difference between feasting and fasting.

Soon after arriving home, Brother Wm. B. Maxwell and I took our three Moqui friends to Salt Lake City. The people on the way were very kind and hospitable. Arriving there, all possible pains were taken to instruct these men concerning our people, and to show them that which would gratify their curiosity, and increase their knowledge. They said they had been told that their forefathers had the arts of reading, writing, making books, etc.

We took them to a Welshman who understood the ancient Welsh language. He said he could not detect anything in their language that would warrant a belief that they were of Welsh descent.

As Lehi had promised his son Joseph that all his seed should not be destroyed, it was the mind of the brethren who reflected upon this subject, that in the Moqui people this promise was fulfilled.

CHAPTER XIII

WE LEFT St. George to take the Moqui visitors home on the 18th of March, 1863. The party consisted of six white men and our Moqui friends. As I was leaving home, my Indian boy, Albert, met me, and I remarked to him that the peach trees had begun to bloom, and it would be warmer than it had been.

He replied, "Yes, and I shall bloom in another place before you get back. I shall be on my mission!" (He doubtless referred by this to a vision which he had of preaching to a multitude of his people.)

Said I, "What do you mean by that?"

He replied, "That I shall be dead and buried when you get back."

We again took the route leading south from St. George. When we went out on this route the fall previous, we had expected to return the same way, and had cached our boat and some supplies on the south side of the river.

On arriving at the river we constructed a raft of dry timber, on which two men crossed over to obtain the boat. It was in good condition, but our supplies were ruined.

On the south side we looked around for a better crossing, as we had been requested to do, and found one five miles higher up the river, and also a good way of getting to and from the river. This is now called Pierce's Ferry.

We were here overtaken by Mr. Lewis Greeley, a nephew of Horace Greeley, of the New York *Tribune*. As he wished to accompany us, Brother Snow sent a man with him to the river.

We took our former trail as far as Seep Springs, the last water before crossing the three days' desert. The second and third days we found two camps, which, judging from the remains of camp kettles, pack saddles, etc., had doubtless been suddenly broken up, probably by the Apaches. We thought they were the camps of miners.

At the last camp there were five animals with Spanish brands. The Moquis desired to take them along, and, after some consultation, we consented for them to do so.

At Seep Springs we found a small band of Piutes, who had run off a party of Cohoneenes.

As we had intended to explore as much as practicable, after consulting with these Piutes and our Moqui friends, we concluded to take a trail to the left of our former route. This would take us down into Cataract Canyon, which heads near the foot of the San Francisco Peaks.

We followed down a side canyon all day, leading our animals most of the time, on account of the narrow and precipitous character of the trail. At night we camped without water.

About 10 o'clock the next day we came in sight of the Main, or Cataract Canyon. This was still far down in the earth below, and the stream running along its bottom appeared like a bright silver thread glittering in the sun.

In coming to this point we, at one time, traveled about three miles continuously on a trail made with considerable labor in the side of shale rock. I do not remember of a place in this distance where we could have turned our animals around to return, had we wished to do so. We afterwards learned that this part of the trail was considered by the people who lived in the canyon, as their strongest point of defense in that direction.

We traveled a very circuitous and still difficult trail, until four o'clock in the afternoon, before we arrived at the water we had seen six hours before. We found the stream to be about fifteen yards in width, with an average depth of over a foot.

It was rapid and clear, and skirted with cottonwood timber, growing on rich bottom land.

The bottom of Cataract Canyon, Lieut. Ives informs us, in his "Explorations of the Colorado," is 2,775 feet below the general level of the plateau above. We judged the sides of the canyon where we were, to be one-half of this distance in perpendicular height.

The first people that we met had been informed of our approach by one of our Moqui companions, whom we had sent ahead of us. While we were talking with them, others arrived from lower down the stream, who inquired rather sharply why we were there. They were soon satisfied with our explanations.

We were soon engaged in interesting conversation. They had heard of me and my travels, and appeared pleased to see me. They desired that I would not lead anyone into their hiding place, and particularly a stranger, without their consent.

They told us that the horses we had picked up belonged to the Walapies, and if we would leave them they would return them to the owners before we came back. We remained with this people one day. In going out we traveled up the main canyon.

Not long previously these people had been attacked in their stronghold by a band of Indians from the southeast.

They showed us a narrow pass where they had met them, and killed seven of their number.

About three miles above where we first struck the stream, it boils from the bottom of the canyon in a large, beautiful spring. We found no water above this. About nine miles up the canyon above the water, we turned into a left-hand side canyon, through which it was about two miles to the country above.

The trail up this canyon was very steep and difficult. The trail we came in on, and this one, are said to be the only means of getting in and out of the Cataract Canyon. From what we could learn from the Indians, we supposed the distance from the spring to where the creek empties into the Colorado to be about eighteen miles.

Through some misunderstanding, two of our Moqui friends had continued up the main canyon. We made a dry camp that night. The Moqui man who remained with us was a religious leader among his people. He became very anxious about his companions, for he said they would find no water. He went through some religious ceremonies for their safe return.

In the night they arrived in camp. They had discovered their mistake, and returned until they found our trail. We had a little water left to relieve their thirst.

I should have before stated that these Moquis never send out any of their people in the public interest, without sending one of their religious teachers with them. The position of these religious men is probably a traditionary remnant of the pure priesthood held by their fathers.

This man who was with us carried a small sack, in which were some consecrated meal, wool, cotton and eagle's feathers. To this sack was attached a stick, which he took out each morning, and, after looking at the sun, made a mark upon, thus keeping a memorandum of the number of days we had spent on the journey.

Our route was considerably to the north of the one we had traveled when on our former trip. The day after leaving Cataract Canyon, about 4 o'clock in the afternoon, we came to a cross trail made by wild animals. Following it a few hundred yards into the head of a canyon, we found a pool of good water.

This was the 7th of April. We traveled two days without water for our animals, and camped where we could see the water of the Little Colorado, but it was in a deep gulch, out of our reach. The next day we traveled thirteen miles up the river bank, and camped by the water.

The night of the 11th we were about twelve miles from a Moqui town. Our Moqui companions wished to go home; and did so, while we camped until morning.

They informed the three brethren who had remained in the Moqui towns during the winter, of our approach, and the following morning these brethren met us about two miles out. They rejoiced much in seeing us, and hearing from their families and friends at home. We remained two days with our Moqui friends.

Taking Brothers Haskell, Hatch and McConnell with us, on Tuesday, the 15th of April, we started for the San Francisco Mountain, which was about ninety miles to the southwest. We aimed to strike the Beal road, which runs on the south side of the mountain.

On the 20th of April we got into the foothills on the north side of the mountain, where we found plenty of timber, grass, and snow for water. Game was abundant, and we had no trouble to kill what we needed. The same day Mr. Greeley discovered a pond of clear, cold water, several acres in extent, in the crater of a volcanic peak.

Monday, the 21st of April, we spent in exploring in different directions. We discovered a wagon road, which proved to be the one laid out by Captain Beal. We had traveled around on the north side of the mountain, and struck this road six miles west of Lareox Spring.

On the 22nd we killed two antelopes, and dried the meat, preparatory for starting home.

On the 24th we started for home. We traveled west on the Beal road until the 28th, when we left it and traveled across the desert where Lieut. Ives and party suffered from thirst.

We directed our course for Seep Springs, spoken of in the account of our outward trip, as our last camp before going into Cataract Canyon.

I was fifty-six hours without any water. Brother Jehiel McConnell was so far gone that he could only whisper. Both men and animals suffered severely. From Seep Springs we directed our course for the crossing of the Colorado, south of St. George.

The third day from Seep Springs we traveled into the night, and got off our trail. We tied up some of our animals and hobbled others, to wait for daylight.

During the night, what we at first supposed to be the hooting of an owl, attracted our attention. After listening a little while we concluded that the hooting was counterfeit; that Indians were around us and we had better look after our animals.

I followed a trail a few hundred yards by moonlight, and discovered the tracks of two Indians. Suffice it to say, we lost ten animals out of eighteen.

Assisted by some Piutes, we made an effort the next day to recover them, but failing, on the 6th of May we continued our journey. Five of our animals we packed, which left but three to ride. As there were ten men in the company, we traveled mostly on foot.

We afterwards learned that the Cataract Canyon Indians had not returned the Walapies' horses as they had agreed to, and the Walapies made that an excuse for stealing ours.

When we arrived at the river our feet were badly blistered. We had learned to appreciate the value of the animals we had lost.

Between the ferry and St. George, one day, in the Grand Wash, our animals becoming dry, a mule smelt of the ground and pawed. We concluded that it smelt water under the ground. We dug down about three feet, and found plenty. There has been water there ever since, and it is called White Spring.

We arrived in St. George on the 13th of May, 1863. We had been absent fifty-six days. We had explored a practicable, though difficult route, for a wagon from St. George to the Little Colorado, had visited the Moqui towns, and explored some of the country around the San Francisco Mountain.

I found on my return home that my Indian boy, Albert, was dead and buried, as he had predicted he would be when I left home.

I supposed his age to be about ten years when he came to live with me; he had been with me twelve years, making him twenty-two years old when he died. For a number of years he had charge of my sheep, horses and cattle, and they had increased and prospered in his hands.

Some time before his death he had a vision, in which he saw himself preaching the gospel to a multitude of his people. He believed that this vision would be realized in the world of spirits. He referred to this when he said that he should die before my return home, and be on his mission .

He was a faithful Latter-day Saint; believed he had a great work to do among his people; had many dreams and visions, and had received his blessings in the house of the Lord.

CHAPTER XIV

A T THIS time a considerable change had taken place in the spirit and feelings of the Indians of Southern Utah, since the settlement of the country in 1861-62. Up to that time, our visits among them and our long talks around their camp fires, had kept up a friendly feeling in their hearts.

After the settlement of St. George, the labors of the Indian missionaries, from force of circumstances, became more extended and varied, and the feelings of the Indians towards the Saints became more indifferent, and their propensity to raid and steal returned.

The great numbers of animals brought into the country by the settlers, soon devoured most of the vegetation that had produced nutritious seeds, on which the Indians had been accustomed to subsist. When, at the proper season of the year, the natives resorted to these places to gather seeds, they found they had been destroyed by cattle. With, perhaps, their children crying for food, only the poor consolation was left them of gathering around their camp fires and talking over their grievances.

Those who have caused these troubles have not realized the situation. I have many times been sorely grieved to see the Indians with their little ones, glaring upon a table spread with food, and trying to get our people to understand their circumstances, without being able to do so. Lank hunger and other influences have caused them to commit many depredations.

When our people have retaliated, the unoffending have almost invariably been the ones to suffer. Generally those that have done the stealing have been on the alert, and have got out of the way, while those who have desired to be friends, from the want of understanding on the part of our people, have been the sufferers. This has driven those who were well disposed, to desperation.

The Navajos and other Indians east of the Colorado River have taken advantage of these circumstances to raid upon the settlements, and drive off many hundreds of cattle and valuable horses and mules.

In 1864 I visited the Indians east of St. George, accompanied by Brother George Adair. They had gathered between St. George and Harrisburg, for the purpose of carrying out their threat to destroy some of the settlements the first favorable opportunity.

I was asked how many men I wanted to go with me on my contemplated visit. I replied only one, and that I did not want any arms, not even a knife, in sight.

When we arrived in their camp I asked them to come together, and bring their women and children, and all hear what we had to say. They had prepared for hostilities by secreting their women and children, as is their custom.

By talking with them, a better influence came over them, and the spirit of peace triumphed over irritation and a sense of wrong.

About seventy-five miles west of St. George, a band of Piutes had confederated with a band of Indians that had been driven out of California, and they threatened the settlements of Meadow Creek, Clover Valley and Shoal

Creek. Brother Andrew Gibbons accompanied me on a visit to these Indians. It was summer, and they had left their corn fields to dry up, and gone to the mountains. Our people had manifested as much hostility as the Indians, having killed two of their number.

We sent out word for all to come in and see us. We made a feast by killing an ox, and, in a general talk, they told over their grievances. They said that they felt justified in what they had done, and also in what they intended to do.

I could not blame them, viewing matters from their standpoint. In the talk I rather justified them in what they expected to do, but told them that in the end it would be worse for them to carry out their plans than to drop them, and smoke the pipe of peace. That the grass upon which the seeds had grown which served them for food was all eaten up, and from that time would be; but if they would be friendly, they could get more food by gleaning our fields than they had before we came into their country.

The talk lasted for hours. The difficulty was settled and we returned home.

Early in 1865, the Navajos stole a few horses from Kanab. I was requested to go over the Colorado, and, if practicable, have a talk with them, and recover the stolen horses. I was also to have a talk with the Moquis, and invite them to move over into our country.

We did not succeed in recovering the stolen horses. We were informed by the Moquis that the old Navajo chief, the friendly Spaneshanks, had been discarded by his band, that his son had succeeded him as chief, and that he was disposed to raid at any favorable opportunity.

For these reasons we thought it would be useless and perhaps dangerous to go into their country. We had a meeting in the Oriba village, with the principal men of that place and one of the largest of the Moqui towns. It was an interesting interview.

We told them we did not expect to visit them much more where they were, and we wished them to move over the river into our country, live with us, and build cities and villages the same as other people.

They again told us that they could not leave their present locations until the three prophets who had led them into their country should appear among them again, and tell them what to do. They predicted that our people would yet move into the country south of them, and would travel with wagons up the Little Colorado.

Aside from their traditions against moving across the great river, they could not see the utility of going over to live with us when we would yet move into their country. They were quite anxious that we should not be angry with them, as they desired that we should be friends, and thought that we might sometimes visit them.

On our return home we were disappointed in not finding water in two places where we had always found a supply on former trips. At the second place we camped for the night. On account of thirst our animals were very uneasy, and we tied them up and guarded them until morning.

The nearest water to us was ten miles distant, over a sandy desert, and directly out of our way; that is, we would have to travel twenty miles to get water, and again reach our trail for home. It was nearly two days' travel on our way home to water, and both men and animals were already greatly distressed.

I ascended a hill near the camp, and earnestly asked the Lord in my heart what I should do under our difficult circumstances. While thus engaged I looked towards the Colorado, which was about forty miles distant, and saw a small cloud, apparently about the size of a man's hat. It rapidly increased, and it did not appear to me more than half an hour before we were enveloped in a heavy snow storm. The snow melted and ran into the cavities of the rocks, until there was an abundance of water.

When we started on our journey we found the ground dry in less than a mile and a half from our camp.

I thanked the Lord that He had sent us relief in our great need, but there were those in the company who did not appear to see the hand of the Lord in it.

In the autumn of 1865 Dr. Whitmore and I made a trip to Las Vegas Springs and the Colorado River. We visited the Cottonwood Island Indians and the Mohaves.

In the winter after our return, Dr. Whitmore and his herder, young McIntyre, were killed near Pipe Springs, about fifty-five miles east of St. George, by the Navajos, who also drove off their sheep and some cattle.

I started out after them with a company, was taken sick, and turned back to go home.

I stopped over night on the road in a deserted house, without food, bedding or fire. Having an opportunity, I sent word to my family about my condition. I got into the town of Washington, twelve miles east of Santa Clara, and could go no farther.

In a day or two my wife, Louise, arrived with a team and took me home. My health was very poor for about a year. At one time my friends thought that I was dying. At first I told them that I was willing that it should be so, for I had only been in their way for nearly a year; but my little children were crying around me, and the question came into my mind: What will they do if I am taken away? I could not bear the thought of leaving my family in so helpless a condition.

I then asked God, the Eternal Father, in the name of His Son, Jesus Christ, to spare my life long on the earth, and I would labor for the building up of His kingdom.

I afterwards felt a desire for food, and asked for something to eat. I was told that I had eaten nothing for two days. Some boiled beef and tea were brought me; I thought that I had never before eaten anything that tasted so good. From that time I slowly recovered.

CHAPTER XV

IN THE spring and summer of 1867 I was called upon to visit the bands of Indians to the east of the settlements on the Rio Virgen, and farther north. A number of settlements had been deserted on the Sevier River, and it was desirable that the temper of the Indians should be so modified that they could be re-established.

I went east seventy-five miles, to the present location of Kanab. After gathering around me some of the Indians, and planting some corn and vegetables, I crossed over the rim of the basin, north, and traveled down the valley of the Sevier.

I sought out places where the Indians were gathered in the largest numbers. I had many long talks with them, which seemed to have a good effect. Although some of the bands were considered quite hostile and dangerous to visit, I felt that I was laboring for good, and had nothing to fear.

In the fall of 1867, as soon as the water in the Colorado was low enough for the Navajos to ford it, I kept close watch of the eastern frontiers of Southern Utah. I met with quite a number of young Piutes when I first went into the country. They said they had dreamed that I was coming out into their country, and they proposed to assist me in watching the frontiers. They proved to be quite useful in watching the passes, and waylaid and shot several raiders.

The season of 1868 was spent in a similar manner to that of 1867, in visiting the Indians in southeastern Utah, and cultivating peace among them.

In October, 1869, I was requested to make another trip to the Moqui towns, to talk with the people, and learn, if possible, whether there were other Indians besides the Navajos raiding on our borders.

I started with a company of forty men, twenty of the brethren and twenty Piutes. We crossed the Colorado where Lee's Ferry now is. Our luggage went over on rafts made of floatwood, fastened together by withes.

On arriving at the Moqui towns, I thought some of the people received us rather coldly. My old acquaintances told me that the Navajos intended to make another raid on our people in a short time. I felt like returning to our settlements immediately.

When we left the towns, I felt much impressed to take the old Ute trail, and cross the river thirty miles above where we crossed going out. Some of the company objected to this and made much of the difficulties of the crossing.

When we came to where a trail led to each of the crossings, I told the company that I did not know why, but I was satisfied that it was our duty to go home by the old Ute trail. I was much surprised to find that more than half of the brethren had made up their minds not to go that way. I told them if I knew anything about the mind and will of the Lord, it was for us to go that way.

The Piutes, to a man, were willing to go the way I desired. The brethren took the lower trail, and on we went. I remarked to them that our trip to the Moquis was a failure. When we arrived home, we learned that the Navajos had been into the settlements north of where our people had guarded, and driven off twelve or fifteen hundred head of animals, among them many valuable horses and mules.

I afterwards learned from the Piutes, that if the company had taken the Ute trail, we would have met the raiders with all these valuable animals on the open plains, after they had crossed the river. I felt vexed that I did not take the Piutes with me and save this valuable lot of stock for our people.

I slept out many cold nights in the winter of 1869-70, watching and guarding with the Piutes. One Navajo was shot when two or three hundred yards ahead of his company, which was driving out a small band of horses. The raiders were much frightened, threw down their luggage and wanted the Piutes to let them go home. The Piutes consented to let the Navajos go if they would leave what they had. They gladly accepted the terms. This took place in the Pahreah Pass, about twenty miles east of Kanab.

The Navajo that was shot was only wounded. I followed his trail the next day, to see what had become of him. I found where he had been picked up by his friends and carried two or three miles. Near him was another camp of raiders, resting.

One of the Piutes who was with me at the time, and had been told in a dream to go with me, shot two of this company, scalped one of them, and said that the other had sandy hair, and he dare not scalp him, for he seemed too much like a white man.

At another time, when Captain James Andrus, with a company of men from St. George, was with us, a few animals passed us in the night. We supposed there were three Navajos with them.

We followed them one day. By taking a circuitous route we came within range of them unobserved. Some of the company fired before the others were ready. Two of the raiders fell; the others, quick as thought, drove the horses upon a sharp point of rocks, where they took shelter in such a way that they could guard their horses without exposing themselves.

We endeavored to approach them to advantage, but without success. I was fired at several times, as also were several of the other brethren. Once, as I was secreted behind a cedar tree, a Navajo crawled up behind a sand rift, fired at me, and the bullet just missed my head.

Finding that the Indians had the advantage of us, we left them, only getting one of the horses. The Navajos secured ten horses and lost three of their men.

Captain Andrus and company returned to St. George, and left Brothers John Mangum, Hyrum Judd, Jehiel McConnell, my son Lyman, myself and the Piutes to watch the frontiers, as we had done through the winter.

The winter of 1869-70 was one of great hardship for the few brethren who, with the Piutes, watched the frontier. They suffered with the cold, and passed many sleepless nights. We crossed the Buckskin, or Kibab Mountain several times, with the snow in some places waist deep.

This Navajo war caused me many serious reflections. I felt that there was a better way to settle matters, and I made up my mind to go and see the Navajos, and have a talk with them as soon as circumstances would permit.

In the spring of 1870, President Brigham Young, his counselor, George A. Smith, Apostle Erastus Snow and other leading men of the Church, came to Kanab, accompanied by twenty men as a guard.

As we had been notified of this visit, we had things in as good order as possible. The Piutes, seventy in number, washed off the dirt and paint which usually besmeared their persons, and put on a fair appearance for Indians.

President Young at first objected to sending out the animals of the company to feed under an Indian guard, but afterwards consented to do so. He expressed himself well satisfied with my labors and policy on the frontiers.

I told him that I desired to visit the Navajos, and have a talk with them; that there had been a number of raiders killed, and I never saw a Navajo's bones on the ground, the flesh having been eaten off by wolves and vultures, but what I felt sorrow for the necessity of such things; that I always abhorred the shedding of blood, and desired to obtain peace in some better way.

When President Young arrived at Toquerville, on his return journey, he sent me a letter of instructions, directing me to do all I could to prevent the shedding of blood; not to let the Indians have any firearms or ammunition if I thought they would use them for killing miners or other travelers; and, if it were possible, he wished the people to get along without the killing of any more Navajos.

CHAPTER XVI

I DETERMINED to do all I could in the summer of 1870 to establish good feelings among the Indians in the neighborhood of our people, on the west side of the Colorado, that they might be disposed to favor us instead of our enemies. I determined to neglect no opportunity of visiting the Navajos, and endeavoring to get a good understanding with them.

I visited the Red Lake Utes, spent some time at Fish Lake, east of Parowan, and visited the Indians along the Sevier. I had many long talks with them, and believe I accomplished much good, in inspiring them with the spirit of peace.

I met Professor J. W. Powell, who stated that he had descended the Colorado River the previous year, and that the Indians in the neighborhood of Mount Trumbull, southwest of Kanab, had killed three of his men. He wished to visit them, and prevent the repetition of a similar calamity the next season; for he desired to descend the river with a company to explore the Grand Canyon.

He wished to employ someone who understood Indian character, and spoke their dialect, to go with him, and President Young had recommended me as a suitable person. He offered me liberal terms, and, as I was desirous of seeing the same Indians myself, a satisfactory arrangement was soon made.

We left Kanab for Mount Trumbull in September, 1870, and took two Kanab Indians with us. We arrived at our destination the third day, and selected a good camp ground by a spring of water.

We found some natives gathering cactus fruits, which grew there in great abundance. I requested them to bring in some of the party who took a part in the killing of Mr. Powell's men the previous year.

Some twelve or fifteen Indians got together the following day, and we called a council to have a good peace talk.

I commenced by explaining to the Indians Professor Powell's business. I endeavored to get them to understand that he did not visit their country for any purpose that would work any evil to them; that he was not hunting gold, silver or other metals; that he would be along the river next season with a party of men, and if they found any of them away from the river in the hills, they must be their friends, and show them places where there was water, if necessary.

They answered that some of their friends from the other side of the river crossed on a raft and told them that Powell's men were miners, and that miners on their side of the river abused their women.

They advised them to kill the three white men who had gone back from the river, for if they found any mines in their country, it would bring great evil among them. The three men were then followed, and killed when asleep.

The Indians further stated that they believed what I told them, and, had they been correctly informed about the men, they would not have killed them.

They said Ka-pu-rats could travel and sleep in their country unmolested, and they would show him and his men the watering places.

Ka-pu-rats, in the Piute language, means one arm cut off. Major Powell had lost an arm in the late war between the Northern and Southern States.

I think that a part of Major Powell's description of this affair in his "Explorations of the Colorado River," would not be out of place here:

"This evening, the Shi-vwits, for whom we have sent, came in, and, after supper, we hold a long council. A blazing fire is built, and around this we sit—the Indians living here, the Shi-vwits, Jacob Hamblin and myself. This man, Hamblin, speaks their language well, and has a great influence over all the Indians in the region round about. He is a silent, reserved man, and when he speaks, it is in a slow, quiet way, that inspires great awe. His talk is so low that they must listen attentively to hear, and they sit around him in death-like silence. When he finishes a measured sentence, the chief repeats it, and they all give a solemn grunt. * * * *

"Mr. Hamblin fell into conversation with one of the men, and held him until the others had left, and then learned more of the particulars of the death of the three men. They came upon the Indian village almost starved, and exhausted with fatigue. They were supplied with food, and put on their way to the settlements. Shortly after they had left, an Indian from the east side of the Colorado arrived at their village, and told them about a number of miners having killed a squaw in a drunken brawl, and no doubt these were the men. No person had ever come down the canyon; that was impossible; they were trying to hide their guilt. In this way he worked them into a great rage. They followed, surrounded the men in ambush, and filled them full of arrows.

"That night I slept in peace, although these murderers of my men, and their friends, the U-in-ka-rets, were sleeping not five hundred yards away. While we were gone to the canyon, the pack-train and supplies, enough to make an Indian rich beyond his wildest dreams, were all left in their charge, and were safe; not even a lump of sugar was pilfered by the children."

After this council with the Indians, Major Powell gave me charge of the commissary stores and pack train, and directed me to explore the country east, north and south. This afforded me an excellent opportunity to carry out my mission to the Lamanites.

I had many interesting talks with them. I labored to have them understand that there was an overruling Providence that had much to do with the affairs of men; that God was not pleased with the shedding of blood, and they must stop killing men, women and children, and try to be at peace with all men.

These teachings did not appear to have much influence at the time, but afterwards they yielded much good fruit.

CHAPTER XVII

IN THE autumn of 1871, Major Powell concluded to go east, by way of Fort Defiance, and desired me to accompany him. As this appeared to be an opening for the much-desired peace talk with the Navajo Indians, I readily accepted the invitation.

We started for Fort Defiance in October. Three men who were strangers to me, accompanied us, and Brothers Ammon M. Tenney, Ashton Nebeker, Nathan Terry and Elijah Potter; also Frank, a Kibab Indian.

We packed lumber on mules over the Kibab, or Buckskin Mountain, to the crossing of the Colorado, now known as Lee's Ferry. With this we constructed a small boat, in which we conveyed our luggage across. Our animals crossed over by swimming.

We traveled at night most of the way, to preserve our animals from the Indians. We visited all the Moqui towns, seven in number, and had much interesting talk with the people. Professor Powell took much interest in their festivals, dances, religious ceremonies and manner of living.

Arriving at Fort Defiance, Major Powell rendered me much assistance in bringing about peace with the Navajos. About six thousand of them were gathered there to receive their annuities.

All the chiefs of the nation were requested to meet in council. All the principal chiefs but one, and all the subchiefs but two were there. Captain Bennett, Indian agent, his interpreter, and Brother Ammon M. Tenney were also there.

Major Powell led the way by introducing me to the council as a representative of the people who lived on the west side of the Colorado River, called "Mormons." He stated that he had lived and traveled with these people, and, by acquaintance, had formed a very favorable opinion of them. He said that they were an industrious people, who paid their quota in taxes in common with other citizens of the United States, from which the Navajos were paid their annuities.

At the close of his introductory remarks, I arose and spoke about an hour. I stated that the object of my visit was to have a talk with them, and endeavor to bring about a better understanding between them and my people the "Mormons," and establish peace and friendship.

I explained to them some of the evils of the war which had commenced by killing two men and driving off their stock; that while they had taken from us many horses and mules, they had lost twenty or thirty of their men. That our young men had wanted to come over into their country and kill and drive them, but had been told to stay at home until all other means for obtaining peace had been tried and had failed.

I told them I had been acquainted, more or less, with the Indians on their side of the great river for many years, and I found that the Moquis were obliged to watch their stock, or the Navajos would steal it; and the Navajos were under the same necessity. Neither party could trust their sheep out of sight, through fear that they would never see them again. They dare not send their flocks out into the mountains where grass was abundant, and the result was, that they ate poor meat, and many times not enough of that.

Continuing, I said: "If you will reflect on your affairs, you will see that this is very bad policy, and that it would be much better to be at peace with your neighbors and with all men. I see much grass and many watering places on each side of the river. If we would live at peace with each other, we could take advantage of all the land, grass and water, and become rich or have all we need. Our horses and sheep would be fat. We could sleep in peace, awake in the morning and find our property safe. You cannot but see that this would be the better way.

"I hope you will listen to this talk. What shall I tell my people, the 'Mormons,' when I return home? That we may expect to live in peace, live as friends, and trade with one another? Or shall we look for you to come prowling around our weak settlements, like wolves at night? I hope we may live in peace in time to come. I have now gray hairs on my head, and from my boyhood I have been on the frontiers, doing all I could to preserve peace between the white men and Indians.

"I despise this killing, this shedding of blood. I hope you will stop this, and come and visit, and trade with our people. We would like to hear what you have got to say before we go home."

As I took my seat, I noticed the tears start in the eyes of Barbenceta, the Spanish name of the principal chief of of the Navajos.

He slowly approached, and put his arms around me, saying, "My friend and brother, I will do all I can to bring about what you have advised. We will not give all our answer now. Many of the Navajos are here. We will talk to them tonight, and will see you on your way home."

The principal chiefs spent much of the night talking with their people. Captain Bennett, the agent, and a U. S. army officer, said that I could not have talked better to bring about peace with the Navajos. He manifested much good feeling, and furnished us liberally with supplies for our journey home.

This council was held on the 2nd of November, 1871, The blessings of the Lord were over us in our efforts for peace.

This was probably the first time that the chiefs of the Navajo nation ever heard a gospel discourse adapted to their circumstances; as well as the first time they had heard, from the lips of a white man, a speech that carried with it the spirit and power of a heartfelt friendship. The hearts of many of them were open to reciprocate it.

We spent three days at Fort Defiance, endeavoring to create a good influence, and in getting our supplies ready. Brother A. M. Tenney, being able to converse in Spanish, accomplished much good.

On our way home we called at a Moqui town. There we met the principal chief of the Navajos, those chiefs who were not at Fort Defiance, and some minor chiefs who did not consider themselves as belonging to the United States agency at Fort Defiance.

We met in a room belonging to the principal man of the village. The Navajos, through their chief, told us that they had not come to talk any different from what was said at Fort Defiance, but to confirm what was said there. They never had heard better talk. They had a great desire to have what was said, carried out.

They said, "We have some bad men among us, but, if some do wrong, the wise ones must not act foolishly, like children, but let it be settled according to the spirit of your talk at Fort Defiance.

"Here is Hastele (one of the principal chiefs) ; I wish you to take a good look at him, so you will not be mistaken in the man. He never lies or steals. He is a truthful man; we wish all difficult matters settled before him. He lives on the frontier, nearest to the river; you can find him by inquiry."

The peace treaty talk here closed by the Navajos saying, "We hope we may be able to eat at one table, warm by one fire, smoke one pipe, and sleep under one blanket."

One of them gave me a note from the United States agent, stating that the bearer wished me to try and recover some sheep that were stolen from him, and were in one of the Moqui towns; and that two attempts had been made to recover them, which had failed.

We lay down to sleep about midnight, and were on our way at early dawn to the town, a few miles distant, where the Navajos said we should find the sheep.

Arriving at the residence of the man having the sheep, I found him to be a former acquaintance of mine. He appeared in a surly mood. We talked to him for some time, but could get no answer.

I then said, "You are the first man I traded with twelve or thirteen years ago. You told me then that before your father died, he took you in his arms, and told you that you would live to see the white men come from the west—good men, men of peace; and that it would be but a short time after they came until you could sleep in peace, eat in peace, and have peace in all things. You told me that you believed we were the men your father meant, and I hope you will not prevent peace coming into your country for the sake of a few sheep."

"Well," said he, "I will not; I will give up the sheep."

They were counted out, and the Navajo offered us one or two to eat on our way home. We told him we could get along without taking any of his sheep; he had but few, and would want them.

CHAPTER XVIII

WE WERE told by the Moquis that when the Navajos were at war with the United States, they were taken advantage of in their scattered condition by the Moquis, who hunted out the worst of the thieves among them, and killed them off. For this purpose the Moquis were furnished with guns and ammunition.

One man told me that he had hunted up and killed eight Navajos single handed.

I was also informed that the Moquis decoyed thirty-five of them into one of their villages, by promising them protection, and then disarmed them, and threw them off a high rock between two of their towns. I went to the place indicated and found a number of skeletons and some remains of blankets. This was done during the winter previous to our visit.

The Navajos have evidently been the plunderers of the Moquis for generations, and the latter have retaliated whenever they have had an opportunity. Peace between these tribes would be a great blessing to both.

Wishing to do all I could to give strength to a peaceful policy, I invited Tuba, a man of good report among his people, to take with him his wife, Pulaskanimki, to go home with me; get acquainted with the spirit and policy of our people, and become a truthful representative of them among his people.

I promised to pay him for what labor he might perform, and bring him home the next autumn.

After counseling with their friends, he and his wife accepted my invitation.

When we arrived on the cliffs before crossing the Colorado, the Piutes living in the Navajo country, came to me and said as they had taken a part with the Navajos in raiding on our people, they desired to have a good peace talk. They were about thirty in number.

After an interesting council, we commenced to descend the difficult cliff to the crossing of the river. While doing so, Brother Nathan Terry said he had a dream the night before, and that it had been on his mind all day, and he believed it meant something. In the dream he saw the company riding along the trail, when he heard the report of a gun. He looked around and saw one of the company fall to the ground, and he thought he went and put the person on his horse, and they continued their journey.

After descending the cliff, I was some distance in the rear of the company, when suddenly, what appeared like a flash of lightning came over me. It was with great difficulty that I could breathe. Not being able to help myself, I partly fell to the ground.

I lay there some time, when one of the Kanab Indians

who was with us came along, saw my situation, and hurried on to camp.

Brother Terry came back to me after dark. He administered to me in the name of the Lord, when the death-like grip that seemed to have fastened on my lungs let go its hold, and I could again breathe naturally.

On coming to the bank of the river the following day, Tuba, the Oriba, looked rather sorrowful, and told me that his people once lived on the other side of this river, and their fathers had told them they never would go west of the river again to live. Said he, "I am now going on a visit to see my friends. I have worshiped the Father of us all in the way you believe to be right; now I wish you would do as the Hopees [their name for themselves] think is right before we cross."

I assented. He then took his medicine bag from under his shirt, and offered me a little of its contents. I offered my left hand to take it; he requested me to take it in my right. He then knelt with his face to the east, and asked the Great Father of all to preserve us in crossing the river. He said that he and his wife had left many friends at home, and if they never lived to return, their friends would weep much. He prayed for pity upon his friends, the "Mormons," that none of them might drown in crossing; and that all the animals we had with us might be spared, for we needed them all, and to preserve unto us all our food and clothing, that we need not suffer hunger nor cold on our journey.

He then arose to his feet. We scattered the ingredients from the medicine bag into the air, on to the land and into the water of the river.

To me, the whole ceremony seemed humble and reverential. I felt that the Father has regard to such petitions.

The scattering of the ingredients from the medicine bag I understood to be intended as a propitiary sacrifice.

After this ceremony we drove our animals into the river, and they all swam safely to the opposite shore. In a short time ourselves and effects were safely over. Tuba then thanked the Great Father that He had heard and answered our prayer.

Arriving at Kanab, we found all well. Everybody appeared to feel thankful for the success of our mission and the prospects of peace. The Kanab Indians also congratulated us on our success.

Some of the Piutes from the east side of the river accompanied us home. They spent much of the night in talking over events that had taken place during the previous three years. They said they had not visited each other much during that time.

Choog, the Kibab chief of the Piutes, after learning all the particulars from the Indians who went with us, came to me and said: "Now the Indians east of the river have all made peace, the evil spirits will have no place to stop over there. They have followed you here. The destroyer will enter into the wind, fire and water, and do you all the mischief he can. Wherever he can get a chance to work he will go."

At the close of his remarks I smiled. Noticing it, he said with considerable warmth, "You are a wise, good man, and know more than I do; but I know that what I have told you will come to pass."

The third night after this conversation with the Kibab chief, the night of the 14th of December, a house in Kanab, in which resided the family of Brother Levi Stewart, took fire, from some unknown cause. The room in which the fire originated had but one entrance, and in it were stored some combustible materials. The houses were of logs, built in fort form, and the people and their effects were much crowded together.

At the time the fire broke out, people were generally asleep, and six of the the family of Brother Stewart were asleep in the room where the fire originated.

Before they could be rescued, a can of oil took fire, and the room was in a moment enveloped in an intense flame, which burst out from the only entrance. The shrieks of those in the fire, and the odor of their roasting bodies; the lurid glare of the fire in the darkness of night; the intense anxiety and sorrow depicted on the countenances of the father and husband, brothers, sisters and neighbors, made up a scene that can never be forgotten by those who witnessed it.

There were several other fires and accidents in the settlements of Southern Utah, soon after the fire in Kanab, which indicated that the Indian chief was prompted by the spirit of prophecy.

Some people call the Indians superstitious. I admit the fact, but do not think that they are more so than many who call themselves civilized. There are few people who have not received superstitious traditions from their fathers. The more intelligent part of the Indians believe in one Great Father of all; also in evil influences, and in revelation and prophecy; and in many of their religious rites and ideas, I think they are quite as consistent as the Christian sects of the day.

CHAPTER XIX

A FEW days after I arrived home from Fort Defiance, I went on a visit to St. George, and other settlements. I took Tuba and his wife with me, that they might have an opportunity of seeing some of our farming and manufacturing industries.

After looking through the factory at Washington, where some three hundred spindles were in motion, Tuba said it spoiled him for being an Oriba. He could never think of spinning yarn again with his fingers, to make blankets.

His wife, after looking at the flouring mill, thought it was a pity that the Hopees (meaning the Oriba women) were obliged to work so hard to get a little meal to make their bread, when it could be made so easily.

Tuba and his wife gleaned cotton in the fields one week, on the Santa Clara, where the cotton had been gathered by our people, and President Young gave him a suit of clothes.

When we returned to Kanab, we found eighty Navajos who had come in there to trade. Most of them were on foot, and had brought blankets to trade. Some of their women accompanied them, which is their custom when going on a peaceable expedition.

Comiarrah, one of their leading men, introduced his wife to me. She took hold of my hand and said, "We have come a long way to trade with your people. We are poor and have brought all we could on our backs. We have not much, and we want to do the best we can with it. We came home to our country three years ago, and found it naked and destitute of anything to live on. We once had many sheep and horses, but lost them all in the war. We were taken prisoners and carried to a poor, desert country, where we suffered much with hunger and cold. Now we have the privilege of living in our own country. We want to get a start of horses and sheep, and would like you to tell your people to give us as good trade as they can."

They traded for fifty horses in Kanab, then went to St. George and other settlements, and traded all the blankets they had for horses, and went back to their own country quite satisfied.

In September, 1872, I went to take Tuba home, as I had promised I would do. Brothers I. C. Haight, George Adair and Joseph Mangum accompanied us. We went by the old Ute crossing, and left some supplies for Professor Powell's party, at a point which had before been designated.

On the east side of the river, we crossed some dangerous places, deep canyons and steep rocks. Some of our animals fell and bruised their legs; one was so badly injured that we were compelled to leave it. Another fell from a cliff into a canyon and was killed instantly.

We made a line long enough to reach the animal by tying together lariats and rope. A place was found where a man could descend to the pack, and the things were hauled up in parcels.

After five days' traveling, visiting some of the Navajo ranches, and talking with the people, we arrived at Tuba's house in the Oriba village.

After feasting a day or two on peaches and green corn, we started for the Navajo agency. We remained there over the Sabbath, and attended a meeting conducted by a Methodist minister, employed by the government to preach to the Navajos.

We were granted the privilege of speaking in the afternoon. I spoke on the coming forth of the Book of Mormon, and about the ancient inhabitants of the American continent.

On our way home we visited some of the principal Navajo ranches. Some Navajos came to us to trade for horses. We camped one night with a party at the rock where young Geo. A. Smith was killed.

One of them said he was there when young Smith was killed, and that some of the Navajos tried to get up a dance over his scalp, but the majority of the party were opposed to it, and the dance did not take place. Most of them contended that the "Mormons" were a good people. The party that thought it right to kill the "Mormon" said, if the man who killed him would go and overtake his friends, and they would give him a present, they would acknowledge the "Mormons" to be a good people. He said the Navajo went on after us, and returned with a gun that we gave him.

The fact that an Indian overtook us, and that we gave him a gun, and recognized the revolver of George A. Smith on his person, has been mentioned in the account of young Brother Smith's death.

We were told that the murderer soon died a miserable death, and the Navajos believed it was because he had killed a "Mormon."

The Navajos continued to come to our settlements to trade, and went about in small parties, or singly, as suited them. They placed all confidence in us as their friends.

In 1871-72, I explored many places between Lee's Ferry and Uinta Valley; assisted in locating a settlement on the Pahreah, in starting a ranch in House Rock Valley, and in building a small boat at Lee's Ferry.

In the winter of 1873-74, I was sent to look out a route for a wagon-road from Lee's Ferry to the San Francisco forest, or the head waters of the Little Colorado. I procured the assistance of a Piute who lived on the east side of the Colorado, and was somewhat acquainted with the country. We readily found the desired route.

In the spring of 1874, a company of about one hundred wagons crossed the Colorado, well fitted out, with instructions to form a settlement on the Little Colorado, or on some of the tributaries of the Gila. I was requested to pilot the first ten wagons as far as Moancoppy, and remain there for further instructions.

For a considerable distance beyond the Moancoppy, the country is barren and uninviting. After they left that place, the first company became discouraged and demoralized, and returned.

In the meantime, I occupied myself in putting in a crop. With some help, I planted twelve acres with corn, beans, potatoes and other vegetables.

The companies that followed the one that had returned from the Little Colorado, partook of the same demoralizing spirit. They could not be prevailed upon to believe that there was a good country with land, timber and water, a little beyond where the first company had turned back. They all returned to Utah, and the great effort to settle the country south of the Colorado was, for the time being, a failure.

The failure was evidently for want of faith in the mission they had been called upon to fill by the Lord, through His servants.

When this company was sent into Arizona, it was the opportune time for the Saints to occupy the country. Soon after, the best locations in the country were taken up by others, and our people have since been compelled to pay out many thousands of dollars to obtain suitable places for their homes.

The Navajos carried on a peaceful trade with our people until the winter of 1874-75, when a circumstance occurred which greatly endangered our peaceful relations with that people.

A party of four young Navajos went to the east fork of the Sevier River, to trade with some Utes in the neighborhood. In Grass Valley they encountered a severe snowstorm, which lasted for three days. They found shelter in a vacant house belonging to one McCarty. He did not belong to the Church, and had that animosity towards Indians, too common with white men, which leads them to slaughter the savages, as they are called, on the most trifling pretences.

The Navajos, becoming hungry during the delay, killed a small animal belonging to Mr. McCarty. In some way he learned of the presence of the party on his ranch, gathered up some men of like spirit with himself, came suddenly upon the Navajos, and, without giving them an opportunity of explaining their circumstances, killed three of them and wounded the fourth.

The wounded man, after enduring excessive hardships, made his way across the river, and arrived among his own people.

Telling the story of his wrongs, it aroused all the bitter spirit of retaliation, so characteristic of the Indians from tradition and custom. The affair taking place in the "Mormon" country, where the Navajos naturally supposed they were among friends, and not distinguishing McCarty as an outsider, the murder was laid to the "Mormons."

The outrage created considerable excitement among both whites and Indians. When President Young heard of it, he requested me to visit the Navajos, and satisfy them that our people were not concerned in it.

Feeling that the affair, without great care, might bring on a war, I started at once for their country to fill my mission.

I left Kanab alone. My son Joseph overtook me about fifteen miles out, with a note from Bishop Levi Stewart, advising my return, as he had learned from the Piutes that the Navajos were much exasperated and threatened to retaliate the first opportunity.

I had been appointed to a mission by the highest authority of God on the earth. My life was of but small moment compared with the lives of the Saints and the interests of the kingdom of God. I determined to trust in the Lord and go on. I directed my son to return to Kanab, and tell Bishop Stewart that I could not make up my mind to return.

Arriving at the settlement of Pahreah, I found Lehi Smithson and another man preparing to start for Mowabby. We remained over night to procure animals for the journey. That night, my son Joseph came to me again with a note from Bishop Stewart, advising my return, and stating that if I went on I would surely be killed by the Navajos.

When we arrived at the Mowabby, we found that the store house of two rooms which had been built there, had been fitted up in the best possible manner for defense. This had been done by three or four miners who had remained there, on account of the excitement, for which there appeared to be considerable reason.

I felt that I had no time to lose. It was important to get an interview with the Navajos before the outbreak.

My horse was jaded, and wishing to go to Moancoppy, ten or twelve miles farther, that night, two brothers by the name of Smith brought in three of their riding horses, offered me one, and they mounted the others to accompany me.

At Moancoppy I hoped to find some Oribas who could give me correct information about the temper of the Navajos. Arriving there, we found only a Piute family and one Oriba woman. From them I learned that the young relatives of the Navajos killed in Grass Valley were much exasperated, but the older men expressed a desire to see me before anything was done or anyone hurt.

This news was encouraging to me. It being now evening, we lay down and slept until morning.

Tuba had been living at Moancoppy, and had left on account of the excitement. Some of his effects were lying around in a way that indicated that he left in a hurry.

I was informed that Mush-ah, a Navajo with whom I was somewhat acquainted, and in whom I had some confidence, was camped at a watering place twelve miles east of Moancoppy. I hoped to be able to see and have a talk with him, and get up a conciliatory feeling without exposing myself too much to the ire of the Indians.

Arriving at the water where we expected to find Mush-ah, we were disappointed. The place was vacated. We met a Navajo messenger, riding fast on his way to Mowabby, to learn of affairs at that place. He appeared much pleased to see me.

After a little talk, he pointed in the distance to a high mesa, and said the Navajos were camped at that point, and wished to see me.

We arrived at the lodges after sun down; in the neighborhood were gathered a large number of horses, sheep and goats.

Two or three gray-headed men came out to meet us good-naturedly, but did not appear as friendly as they had formerly. I told them my business. Soon afterwards some young men put in an appearance, whose looks bespoke no good.

There being a good moon, a messenger was soon on his way to inform those at a distance of my arrival.

I inquired for Hastele, who had been shown to me by the principal chief in our final peace talk, three years before, and for whom I was directed to inquire in case of difficulty.

I got no answer, which indicated to me that they did not wish for his assistance. I communicated to the old men the circumstances connected with the killing of the Navajos in Grass Valley, as I understood them. They replied that they were not ready for a talk or council, and said, "When the relatives are all here we will talk."

My spirit was weighed down with gloomy forebodings, and I would gladly have left the place could I have felt justified in doing so. Unless the Lord was with us, what were we to do with all these against us?

CHAPTER XX

THE night passed, and a part of the forenoon of the following day, when the Navajos who had been sent for began to gather in.

About noon, they informed me they were ready for talk. A lodge had been emptied of its contents for a council room. It was about twenty feet long by twelve feet wide. It was constructed of logs, with one end set in the ground, and the top ends leaning to the centre of the lodge, and fitted together. The logs were covered with about six inches of dirt.

A fire occupied the centre of the lodge, the smoke escaping through a hole in the roof. There was but one entrance, and that was in the end.

Into this lodge were crowded some twenty-four Navajos, four of whom were councilors of the nation. A few Indians were gathered about the entrance.

The two Smiths and I were at the farther end from the entrance, with apparently not one chance in a hundred of reaching the outside, should it be necessary to make an effort to save our lives.

The council opened by the Navajo spokesman asserting that what I had said about the murder of their relatives was false. He stated that I had advised their people to cross the great river and trade with my people, and in doing so they had lost three good young men, who lay on our land for the wolves to eat. The fourth, he said, came home with a bullet hole through him, and without a blanket, and he had been thirteen days in that situation, cold and hungry.

He also stated that I need not think of going home, but my American friends might if they would start immediately.

I informed the two Smiths of the intention of the Navajos concerning the disposal of myself. I told them they had been obliging to me, and I would not deceive them; the way was open for them to go if they desired to do so.

They replied that they would not go until I went.

Our three revolvers were hanging over my head. It was desirable to have them as well in hand as possible. I took hold of them, at the same time saying to our Piute interpreter, "These are in my way; what shall I do with them?"

As I spoke, I passed them behind me to the Smiths, not wishing to give any cause for suspicion that I had any fears, or expected to use the weapons. I told the Smiths not to make any move until we were obliged to.

The Navajos continued to talk for some time, when I was given to understand that my turn had come.

I told them of my long acquaintance with their people, and of my labors to maintain peace. I hoped they would not think of killing me for a wrong with which neither myself nor my people had anything to do; and that strangers had done the deed.

I discovered that what I had said the day before had some influence with the gray haired men. None but gray haired men belonged to the council, but others were allowed to speak.

The young men evidently feared that the council would oppose their desire for revenge. They evinced great intensity of feeling. The wounded man was brought in, his wounds exposed to the council, and a stirring appeal was made for retaliation by a young warrior. It stirred up the Indian blood from its very depths. He closed by asserting that they could do no less than put me to death.

For a few minutes I felt that if I was ever permitted to see friends and home again, I should appreciate the privilege. I thought I felt one of the Smiths at my back grip his revolver. I said to him quietly, "Hold still! Do not make the first move, and there will be no move made. They never will get ready to do anything."

This assurance came by the whisperings of the Spirit within me.

When the excitement had died away a little, I spoke to the Piute interpreter. He either could not or would not answer me, neither would he answer the Navajos, but sat trembling, apparently with fear.

The Navajos brought in another Piute, and recommended him as a man of much courage, and said he would not falter; but he was soon in the same dilemma as the other.

After some further conversation they appeared a little modified, and, in lieu of blood revenge, they proposed to take cattle and horses for the injury done them. They required me to give them a writing, obligating me to pay one hundred head of cattle for each of the three Navajos killed, and fifty for the wounded one.

This was a close place for me. I could go home by simply putting my name to the obligation. I reflected: Shall I acknowledge by my act, that my people are guilty of a crime of which I know they are innocent; and neutralize all the good results of our labors among this people for fifteen years? Shall I obligate the Church to pay three hundred and fifty head of cattle for a crime committed by others? It is perhaps more than I should be able to earn the rest of my life.

The sacrifice looked to me more than my life was worth. I replied that I would not sign the obligation.

One of them remarked that he thought I would by the time I had been stretched over that bed of coals awhile, pointing to the fire in the middle of the lodge.

I answered that I had never lied to them, and that I would not pay for the wrong that other people had done. "Let the Americans pay for their own mischief, I will not sign a writing to pay you one hoof."

Here the new Piute interpreter would not say anything more.

A Piute chief standing in the door of the lodge spoke to him in an angry tone, and accused him of having a very small heart and little courage.

The chief then asked if I was not scared.

I asked, "What is there to scare me?"

He replied, "The Navajos."

I told him I was not afraid of my friends.

"Friends!" said he, "You have not a friend in the Navajo nation. Navajo blood has been spilled on your land. You have caused a whole nation to mourn. Your friend Ketch-e-ne, that used to give you meat when you were hungry, and blankets when you were cold, has gone to mourn for his murdered sons. You have caused the bread he eats to be like coals of fire in his mouth, and the water he drinks like hot ashes. Are you not afraid?"

"No," I replied, "my heart never knew fear."

The Navajos wished to know what the Piute chief and myself were talking about. The Piute repeated the conversation in their language. They then conversed among themselves; at times they manifested considerable warmth. I was asked if I knew Hastele.

Replying in the affirmative, they asked, "What do you know about him?"

I answered, "I know that Barben-ce-ta and others of your leading men said, at the great peace talk, that he was an honest man, and that all important difficulties between you and our people should be settled before him. I knew this affair should be settled before him, and have known it all the time we have been talking. I came here on a peace mission. If you will send Hastele into our country to learn the truth concerning what I have told you, let as many more come along as you like. I wish you would send the best interpreter you have along with him.

"It is no use to ask me about pay. In the meantime your people can trade among the 'Mormons' in safety. They will be glad to see you if you will come in the day time, as our people come into your country—not to prowl around your lodges to steal and kill. I came to do as I agreed to do at the good talk at Fort Defiance."

I felt that the last I said had the desired effect. Their feelings began to soften.

After some further conversation among themselves, the interpreter said, "They are talking good about you now."

I replied, "I am glad; it is time they talked good. What have they said about me?"

"They say you have a good heart. They think they will wait until they see their greater chiefs, and believe that the matter will be settled before Hastele."

It was then agreed that I should come to Mowabby, in twenty-five days, and they would see if it was not advisable to send some one over, and satisfy themselves of the truth of my statement. Twenty-five notches were cut in a stick, and when they were all gone by cutting off one notch each morning, I was to be at Mowabby.

The history of my intercourse with the Indians on the east side of the Colorado, for fifteen years, had all been talked over. In fact, I had been on trial before them for all my sayings and doings that had come within their knowledge. I was able to answer all their questions, and give good reasons for all my acts.

My mind had been taxed to the utmost all this time. I had been in the farther end of a crowded lodge, with no reasonable probability of getting out of it if I wished to, and without the privilege of inhaling a breath of fresh air.

Some roasted mutton was brought in and presented to me to take the first rib.

The sight of the roasted meat, the sudden change of affairs, together with the recollection of the threats of a very different roast to the one I had on hand, turned my stomach. I said to those around me, "I am sick."

I went to the door of the lodge. It was refreshing to breathe in the open air, and look out into the glorious moonlight. I thought it was midnight; if so, the council had lasted about twelve hours.

A woman's heart seems kindlier than man's among all people. A Navajo woman, seeming to comprehend my situation, came to me and asked me if she could not get me something I would like to eat.

She mentioned several varieties of food she had on hand, none of which I desired. She said she had been at my house in Kanab, and she saw I liked milk, and she would get me some. With a dish in her hand she went about among the goats, stripping them by moonlight.

She brought me about a pint of milk, which I drank, went into the lodge, and lay down and slept until some of the party said it was light enough to see to get our horses.

I asked the Navajos to bring up our horses. I felt it was safer for me to remain in the lodge, than to be out hunting horses, and liable to meet some angry spirits who had been about the council.

The horses were brought, and the Smiths and I were soon in our saddles, and leaving behind us the locality of the trying scenes of the past night.

Again was the promise verified, which was given me by the Spirit many years before, that if I would not thirst for the blood of the Lamanites, I should never die by their hands.

CHAPTER XXI

I HERE give place to a letter from Mr. Smith to the Pioche *Record,* which was also re-published in the *Deseret News*:

"MOWABBY, MOHAVE CO., ARIZONA,
February 5, 1875.
... "On the third day, a Piute Indian, sent by the Navajos arrived. After a long talk, we gathered that the young men of the tribe were at first determined on war, but that the chiefs were opposed to it, for the present, at least; and that they desired to await the arrival of Jacob Hamblin, who had acted as representative of Brigham Young, in all negotiations of importance with the Indians for the past twenty years, and learn what settlement of the affair he was willing to make.

"We communicated to Mr. Hamblin the message from the Navajo chiefs, and, merely pausing to take some refreshments, he started at once for the nearest Moqui village, to send a messenger to them to notify them of his arrival, and request their presence, my brother and I accompanying him.

"We reached there about sundown, and found, to our extreme disappointment, that all the Indians had gone to a big dance at the Oriba villages, sixty miles distant, with the exception of one lame Piute.

"We remained there that night, and the next morning started for the Oriba villages, taking Huck-a-bur, the lame Indian, who is a good interpreter, along with us.

"We had not ridden over fifteen miles, when we met the Piute who had acted as the Navajo envoy on the former occasion. He said he was going to see if Hamblin had arrived, and expressed great delight at seeing him, saying that the Indians were extremely anxious to see him, and urging him to go back with him to the camp of the nearest Navajo chief, which he said was not more than fifteen miles distant, and talk the matter over there.

"After consultation, being anxious to lose no time, we consented, and after riding some twenty-five miles, instead of fifteen, we reached the Navajo camp, which consisted of only two lodges. A tall, powerful Indian, on whose head the snows of many winters had rested, welcomed us with impressiveness and an embrace like the hug of a grizzly bear, and invited us to enter.

"The lodge (wick-e-up), which was substantially built of heavy cedar logs about fifteen feet long, was circular in form, like the skin lodges of the Indians of the plains, with an opening near the top to give vent to the smoke, and, being covered with bark and dirt, was very warm and comfortable, which was none the less agreeable to our party, as it had been snowing hard all the afternoon. There were three Navajos and three squaws, one of the latter a very pretty girl, and two Piutes.

"After a friendly smoke, they furnished us a good and substantial supper of broiled and boiled goat's flesh and corn meal mush, the squaws grinding the meal in the old-fashioned way, between two stones.

"Then the talk commenced. Hamblin, be it remembered, though perfectly familiar with the Piute tongue, knows nothing or very little of the Navajo language, so the services of our Huck-a-bur were called into requisition. The chief we came to see, I forgot to mention, was not there, but was only, so they said, distant a few miles. As we were anxious to get back, we got the Navajo to despatch the Piute to him that night, so that he might be there early in the morning, and the business be closed that day.

"After his departure the talk went on. The Navajos present expressed themselves anxious that the affair should be settled without further bloodshed, and said that was the wish of the principal men of the tribe. They said the Navajos had long known Hamblin, and they believed he would do what was right.

"Everything looked promising, and we retired to rest on a pile of buffalo skins and Navajo blankets worth a horse apiece, and slept soundly and well.

"The next morning the Indians gave us an excellent breakfast and we passed the morning sauntering about examining such articles of Indian manufacture as were new to us, and endeavoring to while away the time till the arrival of the chief.

"A little before noon twelve Navajo braves, armed with bows and arrows and rifles, rode up on a gallop, and dismounting, entered the lodge without shaking hands, and called in an insolent tone of voice for tobacco. We gave them some, and after smoking awhile, they threw everything out of the lodge, saying there were more Navajos coming, enough to fill the lodge. Sure enough, there soon rode up some more Navajos, making nineteen in all, but still no chief.

"To our inquiry as to his whereabouts, they replied he was gone to Fort Defiance. We took our seats, completely filling the lodge, and all hands smoked in silence for some time. Then the Indian whose lodge we occupied commenced talking, and spoke with only an occasional momentary interruption from the others for about an hour.

"After him five or six others talked in rapid succession

and from their earnest tones and impassioned gestures, so different from the usual manner of Indians, we could see they were much excited.

"We could not, of course, understand much of what they said, but could gather enough to know that the temper they were in boded no good to us. One old scoundrel, of brawny frame and hair as white as snow, talked in a stentorian voice, and his frequent use of the gestures of drawing his hand across his throat looked particularly ominous.

"In about an hour more they ceased speaking, and, after a pause, told their interpreter to talk. He arose slowly and walking across the lodge, seated himself by Hamblin. He was a Piute, a slave of the Navajos, and as they have the unpleasant habit of sometimes killing their interpreters when they don't interpret to suit them, and as what he was about to reveal was not calculated to render us very amiable, I could excuse the tremor that shook him in every limb.

"He finally commenced, in a low tone, to speak to the following effect: The Navajos believed that all Hamblin had said the night before was a lie, that they thought he was one of the parties to the killing, and with the exception of three, our host and two others of the old Indians, all had given their voice for death.

"Most of them were of the opinion that it was best not to kill my brother and myself, as we were 'Americans,' but to make us witness the torture of Hamblin, and then send us back on foot. As we were not likely to desert a comrade at such a time, this was but small comfort.

"Hamblin behaved with admirable coolness, not a muscle in his face quivered, not a feature changed, as he communicated to us, in his usual tone of voice, what we then fully believed to be the death warrant of us all.

"When the interpreter ceased, he, in the same even tone and collected manner, commenced his reply. He reminded the Indians of his long acquaintance with their tribe, of the many negotiations he had conducted between his people and theirs, and his many dealings with them in the years gone by, and challenged them to prove that he had ever deceived them—ever spoken with a forked tongue. He drew a map of the country on the ground, and showed them the impossibility of his having been a participant in the affray.

"To their insolent query, 'Imme-cotch na-vaggi?' (Ain't you afraid?), he replied with admirable presence of mind, 'Why should we be afraid of our friends? Are not the Navajos our friends, and we theirs? Else why did we place ourselves in your power?'

"He spoke for a long time, and though frequently and rudely interrupted, his patience and nerve never gave way, and when he ceased, it was apparent that his reasoning had not been without effect in their stubborn bosoms. But the good influence was of short duration.

"A young Indian, whom we afterwards learned was a son of the chief, and brother of two of the slain Indians, addressed the assembled warriors, and we could see that the tide was turning fearfully against us. He wound up his impassioned harrangue by springing to his feet, and, pointing to an Indian who had not yet spoken, called to him to come forward. The Indian came and kneeled before him, when with one hand he took back his buckskin hunting shirt, revealing the mark of a recent bullet wound, and with the other pointed to the fire, uttering, or rather his-sing, a few emphatic words, which we afterwards learned were a demand for instant death by fire.

"The effect was electrical. The sight of the wounded brave roused their passions to the utmost fury, and as we glanced around the savage circle, our hands involuntarily tightened their grasp on our six-shooters, for it seemed that our hour had come.

"Had we shown a symptom of fear, we were lost; but we sat perfectly quiet, and kept a wary eye on the foe. It was a thrilling scene. The erect, proud, athletic form of the young chief, as he stood pointing his finger to the wound in the kneeling figure before him; the circle of crouching forms; their dusky and painted faces animated by every passion that hatred and ferocity could inspire, and their glittering eyes fixed with one malignant impulse upon us; the whole partially illuminated by the fitful gleam of the firelight (for by this time it was dark), formed a picture not easy to be forgotten.

"The suspense was broken by a Navajo, our host, who once again raised his voice in our behalf, and after a stormy discussion, Hamblin finally compelled him to acknowledge that he had been their friend; that he had never lied to them, and that he was worthy of belief now.

"The strain was over, and we breathed freely once more. We smoked the pipe of peace, and a roasted goat being shortly produced, we fell to with a will, and gnawed ribs together as amicably as if it had not been just previously their benevolent intention to roast us instead of the goat.

"By this time it was past midnight, the discussion having been prolonged for eleven hours. I never was so tired in my life. Eleven hours in a partially recumbent position, cramped for room, with every nerve strained to its utmost tension, and momentarily expecting a conflict which must be to the death, is tolerably hard work.

"After supper, it was arranged by Hamblin that we should go home in the morning, and await the arrival of the chief, for whom they promised to dispatch a trusty messenger. We slept by turns till morning broke, when we bid our amiable friends good-by, and started for Mowabby, where we arrived about eight o'clock in the evening, to the great joy of Boyd and Pattie, who had given us up as lost.

"This was five days ago, and today the Navajo chief arrived, and, after a long discussion, agreed to settle the matter for a certain number of cattle and horses; but their demands were so exorbitant that I am sure they will never be complied with.

"Mr. Hamblin leaves tomorrow morning for St. George, to lay the matter before Brigham Young, and he is to meet the chiefs here again, with the answer to their demands, in twenty-five days from today.

* * * * *

"We shall, probably, in the course of the trip, visit the village of the Oribas, a people who build three-story houses of stone, and whose greatest term of reproach to one another is he is a *lazy* man.

* * * * *

"In conclusion, I wish to give my testimony to the bearing of Mr. Hamblin during the trying scene I have endeavored to depict. No braver man ever lived.

J. E. S."

The writer of the foregoing letter and his brother acted a different part from what I did, and acted it well.

[*333*]

He describes some things better than I can. As I have before remarked, ever since I began to have a correct insight into Indian character, I have felt anxious to do all the good in my power, and have endeavored to settle difficulties with them without bloodshed.

Much good, I trust, has been done by going into their midst and reasoning with them, when their minds were made up to avenge some wrong. I reason with an Indian as an Indian.

CHAPTER XXII

I STARTED home with my jaded horse, and got along by alternately riding and walking. I met some families on their way to settle at Moancoppy.

I told the brethren that I thought the place could be safely settled, if they would leave their women and children on the west side of the river until matters were arranged. I camped with them over night, and gave them an insight into our affairs with the Navajos, and particularly requested that they would not converse with them about their difficulty with us.

Soon after arriving at Kanab, I went to St. George and visited Presidents Brigham Young and George A. Smith. I then returned to Kanab, and worked about home until it was time to go over the river to meet the Navajos as I had agreed to.

Through hardship and exposure my health was somewhat impaired. I endeavored to get a light wagon, that I might travel more comfortably than on horseback, but without success. I set out with a horse and three blankets. Soon after a blowing, chilling storm of rain and sleet commenced, and I became thoroughly wet.

I rode twelve miles to Johnson, when I was scarcely able to sit on my horse. I could proceed no farther, and stopped with Brother Watson, who was living in his wagons and a temporary camp prepared for winter. Sister Watson cared for me as well as circumstances would permit.

The storm continued the next day until afternoon, when the weather appeared a little more favorable. I was scarcely able to mount my horse, but I did, and started on my way.

The storm soon came on again, and again I was thoroughly wet. I traveled until after dark, and stopped at a vacated house at the Navajo Wells, ten miles from Johnson. In dismounting I fell to the ground.

It was in a place where travellers on that road usually camped, and the wood had been gathered for a considerable distance around; and had there been fuel I would not have been able to go after it.

It was a dark, dismal time, and it appeared to me that I could not live until morning. I prayed to the Lord to have pity on me and save my life. I succeeded in getting myself and horse into the house out of the storm.

I felt my way to the fireplace, and was much surprised to find some good, dry wood. I soon had a fire, and, leaning against one side of the fireplace, with my blankets drawn closely around me, and with a small blaze of fire, I was soon warm, and slept until morning.

When I awoke I felt well, and quite able to pursue my journey. I went by the Pahreah settlement, and from there Brothers Thos. Adair and Lehi Smithson accompanied me to Mowabby. There I found Ketch-e-ne and a deputation from the Moqui towns.

Ketch-e-ne renewed the former demand for three hundred and fifty head of cattle for the injury done himself and his people. I told him that when I went home I might talk with the chiefs of my people about it, but would make no promises.

Hastele, whom I wished to see, did not put in an appearance.

I went on and visited all the Moqui towns, and told the people the object of my visit. I requested them to tell all the Navajos they had an opportunity of seeing that I had come there according to agreement, and as they had failed to meet me as I had expected, if they would come over the river, I would be on hand to show them that I had told the truth. Feeling satisfied that things would work all right, I returned home.

Some of the brethren who went to Moancoppy visited the Navajos, and talked unwisely about affairs. They in turn, talked and threatened in a way that frightened our people, because they found they could do it, and the mission was broken up.

I had passed through many perils to establish a mission among the Indians on the east side of the Colorado, but on account of the sayings and doings of unwise brethren, the time came for it to be broken up. The Moancoppy was ordered to be vacated, and I went to assist in bringing the people away. They brought away the feeling with them that there would be another Navajo war.

I attended the quarterly conference at St. George, in May. The war question and the necessity of putting a guard at the crossing of the Colorado were agitated.

In speaking in the tabernacle on Sunday, I told the congregation there would be no trouble with the Navajos, and as soon as the summer rains commenced, there would be a party of them over. I felt an assurance of this from what I knew of circumstances, and the whisperings of the Spirit within me.

It was decided to establish a trading post at one of the crossings of the Colorado, east of St. George. For this purpose a party was sent out under the direction of Bishop Daniel D. McArthur.

As I was acquainted with both crossings, I was called upon to go with them. The ferry was selected. In traveling with Brother McArthur to the Ute crossing, thirty miles above the ferry, and back, I gave him a detailed account of our affairs with the Navajos.

I told him that I considered the breaking up of the Moancoppy mission as unnecessary; there would be no trouble with the Navajos, and some of those among them who had authority to settle their difficulties with us would be over as soon as the first rain fell.

That night there was a heavy shower. The following day I started for home by way of the Pahreah settlement, and Brother McArthur went on to the ferry.

Before separating, I told the brethren they would meet the Navajo peace party that night at the ferry, and they would travel to Kanab together.

They asked me how I knew. I told them I knew they would be over, for they would just have time to get to the ferry since the rain.

Arriving at Kanab I found Hastele and his party, including two good interpreters.

I had been away so much, that my family seemed badly in need of my help at home, and I, at the time, thought I was justified in remaining with them. I requested Brother Ammon M. Tenney to go with Hastele over on to

the Sevier River, and satisfy him of the facts concerning
the murder of the young Navajos.

After the party had gone I began to work in the garden, but everything went wrong, and I felt that I had
done wrong in remaining behind.

I continued to try to accomplish some necessary work,
until I was seized with such a violent pain in one of my
knees, that I had to be assisted into the house. I sent for
my horse, was assisted into the saddle, and was soon on
my way to overtake Hastele. The pain left my knee and
I was soon all right.

I overtook the Navajos sixty miles from Kanab. Everything worked well for showing up the facts connected
with the murder. The brethren we fell in with rendered all
the assistance in their power.

I had talked with the Navajos and explained to them
the locations of the "Mormons" and the Gentiles, and
what took place at McCarty's ranch. I had telegraphed to
Bishop Thurber, of Richfield, and Brother Helaman
Pratt to meet us at the lower end of Circle Valley. We arrived there before them and waited. I told Hastele there
would be two "Mormons" there that evening, who knew
more about the affair than I did, and they were men of
truth.

We were camped near the road, where men were passing both ways, on horseback and in wagons. When the
two brethren were approaching, and still a considerable
distance off, Hastele arose to his feet, saying, "There come
the two men we are waiting for."

As they drew near, he remarked, "Yes, they are good
men, men of God."

As the brethren dismounted, Hastele embraced them
in true Navajo style.

I mention this as one of the many circumstances that have come under my notice, which prove to me that many of the Indians, and especially the honest-hearted, are blessed with much of the spirit of revelation and discernment.

The following morning, when arranging to visit the spot where the Navajos were killed, Hastele spoke as follows: "I am satisfied; I have gone far enough; I know our friends, the 'Mormons', are our true friends. No other people we ever knew would have taken the trouble they have to show us the truth. I believe they have good hearts. Here is Jacob; he has been traveling about to do good all winter and spring, and is going yet. When I get home I do not intend my tongue to lay idle until the Navajos learn the particulars of this affair."

Hastele started for Kanab; Brothers Thurber and Pratt, a Mr. Boyd, who was sent by the agent at Fort Defiance to accompany the Navajo delegation, the two Navajo interpreters and I went to Grass Valley, to see the place where the Navajos were killed. Having satisfied the interpreters, we returned by way of Richfield.

CHAPTER XXIII

RETURNING to Kanab, we found Hastele and his companion waiting for us. It was thought advisable for me, with Brother A. M. Tenney as Spanish interpreter, to visit the Indians on the east side of the Colorado River, and go to Fort Defiance and have matters properly understood there. We visited the Moqui towns, and had much interesting talk with the people.

Arriving at the Navajo agency, we found there a Mr. Daniels, who had been sent out by the government to inspect the Indian agencies. He had called on the agent at Fort Defiance to report the condition of his agency. Learning of the Utah difficulty with the Navajos, he made an effort to throw the blame on the "Mormons."

The Indian who escaped wounded from the massacre in Grass Valley was there. Mr. Daniels examined him very closely. He also heard the report of Mr. Boyd, who accompanied Hastele, to learn the facts of the case. All the facts elicited gave a favorable showing for our people. Mr. Daniels was disappointed and evidently vexed. He gave me to understand that I did not belong to the council, and was not wanted there.

As I left the room, a Rev. Mr. Trewax, who was there by government appointment to preach to the Indians, invited me to his room, saying that he would very much like to talk with me.

I replied that I had no objection to talking with him if his object was to obtain correct information.

Being seated in his quarters, he asked what our religious faith was, and from what source we had derived it.

I told him "We prove the truth of our religion by that book" (pointing to a Bible that lay on the table). "If you will read what Christ taught, you will learn what our principles are. They are from heaven."

"Is it possible," said he, "that your people believe the Bible?"

I replied, "We are the only people I have met during the last forty years that do believe the Bible. Many profess to believe it, but when I open and read it to them, I find they do not."

Said he, "My dear sir, I believe every word of it."

I replied, "Then we are brethren." I spent nearly half a day with him. He assented to the principles of the gospel as expounded in the New Testament.

When asked to explain what was meant by the stick of Ephraim and the stick of Judah, in the 37th chapter of Ezekiel, he said he thought it meant that both Judah and Ephraim should write. He believed the Bible to be the stick of Judah, but where the stick of Ephraim was he did not know. He had thought much about it, but it was a mystery to him.

I told him to wait a short time, and I would bring him the stick of Ephraim. I went out and came back with a copy of the Book of Mormon, which I had brought from home. He appeared much surprised, and grasped the book with some energy. He examined the testimony of the three witnesses, and said, "Surely this book is the best or worst thing that ever was."

I permitted him to keep it. When I left the place he told me he had read some thirty pages of it, and had not discovered anything in it contrary to the Bible.

Matters were settled between the "Mormons" and Navajos on the basis of our great peace talk at the same place, the 2nd of November, 1871. The truth was brought to light, and those who wished to throw the blame of murdering the young Navajos upon the Saints were confounded.

This business was finally closed at Fort Defiance, on the 21st of August, 1875. The Navajos expressed themselves as fully satisfied that I had told them the truth when I visited them the previous winter. I felt that the Lord had greatly blessed me in filling the mission assigned me, of convincing the Indians that we had not injured them, and thereby maintaining peace.

Doubtless a war had been prevented, and the faith of the Indians on the east side of the Colorado greatly strengthened in our people.

It is evident to me that I was indebted to the special favor of my Heavenly Father, for the preservation of my life to accomplish this work. At the close of these labors I found myself three hundred miles from home, rather jaded and careworn, but full of thanksgiving for the happy termination of my labors.

On our way home we had some very pleasant visits with the Indians.

In the winter of 1874-5, I assisted in carrying on a trade with the Navajos at Lee's Ferry. One of my sons was with me. I introduced the boy to Ketch-e-ne, the father of two of the Indians killed in Grass Valley. He turned away and wept, apparently much dejected. His friends told me that the loss of his sons was killing him. I afterwards learned that he died about two months after I saw him at the river.

The Navajos carried on quite an extensive trade with our people, principally in exchanging blankets for horses.

In 1875, a number of brethren were called to again establish a mission at Moancoppy.

The winter of 1875-6 I had the privilege of remaining at home. My family was destitute of many things. Some mining prospectors came along, and offered me five dollars a day to go with them, as a protection against the Indians. To go with them could not injure the interests of our people. It seemed like a special providence to provide necessaries for my family, and I accepted the offer. I was gone sixty days, for which I received three hundred dollars.

CHAPTER XXIV

IN MAY, 1876, Brothers D. H. Wells, Erastus Snow and other leading men among the Saints, were sent to visit the new settlements in Arizona. I was sent with them as a guide. The Colorado was then high—a raging torrent. The current shifted from side to side, and the surging of the waters against the rocks caused large and dangerous whirlpools.

We put three wagons and some luggage on the ferry boat. We were under the necessity of towing the boat up stream one mile, to give a chance for landing at the proper place on the other side of the river. When taking the boat around a point of rock, the water poured over the bow. Word was given to slacken the tow rope. In doing so, the rope caught in the seam of a rock, and the draft on the boat continuing, the bow was drawn under water.

In a moment the rapid current swept the boat clear of its contents. Men, wagons and luggage went into the surging waters.

When I plunged into the cold snow-water to swim, my right arm cramped, which caused me to almost despair of getting ashore. A large oar was passing me, and I threw my arm over it to save myself from sinking. About the same time Brother L. John Nuttall caught the same oar, so I thought it best to try to swim with one arm. However, I was soon able to use both, and went safely to shore.

I ran down the river bank, got into a skiff with two others, pulled out to the head of the rapids, and saved a wagon and its contents on an island. The other two wagons, with all the valuables they contained, including the most of our supplies, passed over the rapids into the Grand Canyon of the Colorado.

On getting together we found that Brother Lorenzo W. Roundy was missing. He was said to be a good swimmer, and it is probable he was taken with the cramp and sank at once. His body has never been found.

Brother Lorenzo Hatch sank deep into the river, but saved himself from drowning and was picked up by the skiff.

Brother Warren Johnson and another man hung to a wagon until they were taken up with the skiff, just in time to save them from going over the rapids.

This unfortunate affair occurred on the 28th of May. We gathered up what was left of our outfit, and visited the missions at Mowabby and Moancoppy, and the settlements on the Little Colorado.

About the 1st of December, President Young desired me to take a small company, and look out a route for a wagon road from Pierce's Ferry, south of St. George, to Sunset on the Little Colorado; "for," said he, "our people will want all the choice places where there is water and grass."

Brothers Wilford Halliday from Kanab, Joseph Crosby, Calvin Kelsey, Samuel Alger and Hyrum Williams from St. George, accompanied me.

We left St. George the 13th of December, 1876. We took a route to the ferry a little east of our former one, in order to strike the new crossing of the Colorado, five miles above the old one.

We remained at the river two days, and assisted Brother Harrison Pierce to construct a skiff, with which we conveyed our luggage across; but we forded our animals. After crossing the river, we still took a course east of our former one and the first day arrived in Wallipie Valley, an unknown country to me.

We camped on the north side of the valley under a bluff, where we found a seep of water, or wet ground. We dug a little and found sufficient water for our use.

The finding of this water was entirely providential, as none of us were acquainted with the country, and we had no guide. It fulfilled a promise made to us by President Young when we left St. George, that when thirsty we should find water where we did not expect it.

In the morning we took with us what water we could. We traveled a south-easternly direction, and, as fast as was practicable. At night we made a dry camp, and guarded our animals. The next day we pursued the same course as the day before.

During the long, weary day's travel, the brethren asked when I thought we would get water again. I told them they knew as much about the water as I did, on the course we were going, but we were going the course President Young had told me to take, and I felt impressed that we would get water that night.

We slowly wore away the miles, until, nearing the foothills of a mountain peak, our hopes ran high on discovering signs of stock. Two or three miles farther, as we turned around the point of a hill, we came to a house and corral. We found the place occupied by a Mr. Stevenson. He told us to turn our animals into his yard, and that there was a pump and good water.

It was a mining camp, and water had been obtained by digging. From Mr. Stevenson I obtained information of the watering places between there and the part of the country I had before traveled over. This relieved us from any anxiety about water.

The day we left Mr. Stevenson's we came to an old road which had not been used for some time, but it could be followed. This led us to our settlements on the Little Colorado.

Arriving there, we found the Saints feeling well. I was much pleased to see my daughter Louise. One is likely to appreciate friends and relatives when found by traveling in the desert.

After a short visit we started home, intending to return the same way we had come. The third night out it commenced snowing and blowing. In the morning we concluded that it would not do to continue our journey, as we could see only a short distance on account of the storm.

The best available shelter we could find was a log cabin without a roof, and the spaces between the logs unchinked. We had a wagon sheet which we stretched over our heads, and we were partially sheltered from the driving storm. There we remained two days and nights, during which time it snowed incessantly.

The storm abated the third morning, but the snow lay very deep. Hunger and cold had so used up our horses that we concluded to make the best of our way south, out of the mountains. The third day we got out of the snow, and to the sunny side of a hill, where there was plenty of green, luxuriant grass for our animals. They had plenty, but there was little food for ourselves.

Going out, we had cached supplies for our return trip, but being under the necessity of taking a different route, it was not available.

We went to a military post called Camp Apache, and asked for supplies. We were refused, as it would break orders from the government to let us have them. We applied to a Mr. Head, who kept a sutler's store, and made known our situation. He thought we ought to know better than to travel without money.

I prayed to the Lord to soften the heart of some one, that we might obtain food. I again went to Mr. Head, and told him that we were from Utah; that when we left home we did not expect to see any one to spend money with; that instead of money we took plenty of supplies, which we left in the mountains to use on our return trip, but we could not go the same way home on account of the snow, and if he would let us have enough food to last us home we would send him the pay.

"Oh," said he, "you are Mormons, are you! What do you want to last you home?"

He then let us have what we asked for.

Arriving at the crossing of the Colorado, south of St. George, we found that the flour and meat we had left there had been used, but we obtained some wheat which we boiled and lived on for five days, or until our arrival in St. George.

I gave President Young an account of my trip. I had considerable additional conversation with him, in which he said to me:

"I know your history. You have always kept the Church and Kingdom of God first and foremost in your mind. That is right. There is no greater gift than that. If there are any men who have cleared their skirts of the blood of this generation, I believe you are one of them, and you can have all the blessings there are for any men in the temple."

It was the last time I talked with President Young. He died the following August. The assurance that the Lord and His servant accepted my labors up to that time, has been a great comfort to me.

In the spring of 1877 I thought I would try to raise a crop. I found that the land had been so divided in the

Kanab field, that what was considered my share was nearly worthless. I sowed some wheat, but it proved a failure.

Some time in August I gathered up a little grain, and started for the mill, about one mile and a half above Kanab, in the canyon. On the way I met an expressman, who had directions for me to start forthwith to the Navajo country, with Deputy-sheriff Fouts, of Richfield. A criminal had broken from jail, and it was believed that we could prevent his escape.

I took my horses from the wagon, agreed with another man to do my milling, and in a very short time was on my way for the crossing of the Colorado.

Here we first learned of the death of President Brigham Young.

We learned that the man we were in pursuit of had not crossed there. It was thought advisable to visit the Moqui agency, and make arrangements to secure his arrest should he appear in that part of the country. We traveled one hundred and fifty miles east, in the hot days of August.

In passing through the Moqui towns, we found the people making much ado to bring rain to save their crops. They scattered corn meal in the paths leading to their fields; the women dressed in white, and sat on the tops of their houses, looking to the ground through an opening in a blanket wrapped around their heads.

Others of the people went about with solemn countenances to induce the great Father of us all, as they express it, to send rain. By doing as they did, they believed He would be more ready to pity them and grant their request.

Several came to me and requested that I would pray for rain, asserting that I used to help the Piutes to bring rain, and they thought they were as much entitled to my prayers as the Piutes.

I felt to exercise all the faith I could for them, that they might not suffer from famine. In all their towns there fell, the following night, an abundance of rain.

Returning from the Moqui agency, we found the people of the towns feeling well. They said enough rain had fallen to insure them a crop of corn, squash and beans. We noticed that in and around their towns and fields it had rained very heavily, but on either side the ground was dry and dusty.

On my return home, I found that the fall crop I had planted was too far gone with drouth to make anything, but through the blessings of the Lord I was able to provide necessaries for my family.

This seems a fitting place to close this little narrative of incidents in my life.

In my simple way I have furnished the facts for the pen of Brother Little, with the hope that their publication may be a testimony to many of the truth of the gospel, and of the power of revelation to all who will seek for the whisperings of the Holy Spirit.

I desire this narrative to be a testimony to all who may read it, that the Lord is not slack concerning any of His promises to His children. My whole life, since I embraced the gospel, proves this fact.

If this little book shall leave a testimony of this to the coming generation, I shall be satisfied.